Call Me Debbie

Call Me Debbie

TRUE CONFESSIONS OF A DOWN-TO-EARTH DIVA

Deborah Voigt

WITH NATASHA STOYNOFF

HARPER

An Imprint of HarperCollins*Publishers*

This is a work of nonfiction. Some names and identifying details have been changed in order to protect the privacy and/or anonymity of the individuals involved.

HarperCollins books may be purchased for educational, business, or sales promotional use. For information, please e-mail the Special Markets Department at SPsales@harpercollins.com.

FIRST EDITION

Library of Congress Cataloging-in-Publication Data has been applied for.

ISBN: 978-0-06-211827-1

15 16 17 18 19   OV/RRD   10 9 8 7 6 5 4 3 2

For Mom, Dad, Rob, and Kevin.

I love you all very much.

Acknowledgments

THANK YOU TO my wonderful, funny, loving family: Dad and Lynn, Mom and Don, Rob and Angie, Kevin and Tara, and Marianne.

And to my nieces and nephews that warm this aunt's heart: Maddie, Kailee, Abby, Nicholas, Graham, Olivia, and Morgan.

And thanks to my cousins Martha, Amy, Peggy, Tony, Brian, and Todd—with whom I've shared a lifetime of memories.

A big thank you to Jesslyn Cleary, my assistant through thick and thin and the mistress of "Camp Cleary for Yorkies and Cats."

Jaime Aita, this book wouldn't have come together without you. Thank you!

My gratitude to Jane Paul, my mentor and friend—and to Nancy Estes, Ruth Falcon, David Jones, Levering Rothfuss, and Brian Zeger.

To Paul Côte, my first manager, for believing in me all those years ago.

At Columbia Artists Management, many thanks to Ronald Wilford, Elizabeth Crittenden, Alec Treuhaft, Damon Bristo, Tim Fox . . . and to Andrea Anson, for your unconditional support and encouragement. I love you.

To Albert Imperato at 21C Media Group ("Alberto!"), a heartfelt thanks for your vision and boundless enthusiasm! Same goes to Sean Michael Gross and Michael Lutz.

Natasha Stoynoff, my co-writer; I've never bared my soul to anyone as much as I have with you. Thank you for that, and for all those sleepless, marathon, eating-writing sessions.

To Jonathan Burnham at HarperCollins, I'm so grateful for your endless support and patience. Many thanks to Laura Brown and Bob Levine for their valuable contribution to the book.

Thank you to Kim Witherspoon at Inkwell Management.

And to Herbert Breslin, who always loved "a good scandal."

To my first opera family at the San Francisco Opera—Andrew Meltzer, Christine Bullin, and Sarah Billinghurst.

Thank you to my dear friends: my buddy Jack Doulin, for our morning chats to solve the problems of the world; Victoria Gluth, for endless hours of laughter and amateur psychiatry; Julia Hanish, because I love you, Tyson, Tyce, and Lyles; and Sue Burhop Muszczynski—my secret-voiced, ice-cream caper pal forever.

John Leitch—because you never quite get over your first love.

And finally, thank you to Peter Gelb, Jimmy Levine, Joe Volpe, and the rest of my Metropolitan Opera Family.

Contents

Call Me Debbie

Overture:
Heavenly Voices

WHEN I WAS fourteen years old, God spoke to me.

I know it will sound unbelievable to most—and if it hadn't happened to me and someone told me the same thing, I might accuse him or her of hallucinating. But it happened, and I remember it as vividly today, forty years later, as if He'd spoken to me yesterday.

There was no burning bush, no blinding flash of light—but it was a miracle to me nevertheless, even if it was low-key and over in a matter of seconds. Those few mystical moments when I was a teenager forever changed the course of my life.

It happened just a little past dawn on a fall morning in 1974 that began like any other in our suburban home. The rest of my family—my parents, Bob and Joy, and two younger brothers, Rob and Kevin—were asleep, and the usually noisy household was quiet and still. I'd woken up early and was treasuring the silence as if it were a piece of rare and beautiful music. The light was peeking through my bedroom curtains and I snuggled under the blankets, sleepily watching the sun's first rays slip across the room's lemon walls.

That's when I heard Him, a voice that came from everywhere, and out of nowhere. The voice was as clear as day; it was both as loud as a lion and as soft as a whisper. He said five simple words, but they were powerful enough to put me onto the path I would follow from that moment onward:

You are here to sing.

I know, writing this now, what it must sound like. But I promise you: I sat up in bed and searched the room, wide-eyed. There was no one else there, and for a second I wondered, did I just dream that? No, I was definitely awake. And there was no doubt in my mind who that voice belonged to, I just *knew*. It was otherworldly but so very *real*. I have never been able to describe the timbre, cadence, accent, or inflection of that voice, but if I heard it again I'd know it like I know my own.

I held my breath, waiting to hear if there would be more . . . some additional message, instruction, or revelation . . . anything. But there wasn't. Five words was it, that's what I got. I wasn't given an earth-shaking command to lead my people out of bondage, or to plow up my Illinois cornfield, or to stand on a box in New York's Times Square and warn the wicked to repent because the end was nigh.

Nope, my message was simple and intensely personal, and, in a way, it was more of an affirmation than a directive.

You are here to sing.

God told me to do what I had always innately sensed I was born to do. And not just demurely, but proudly—with every ounce of passion in my soul and every fiber of my being. It was a dream of mine, even when I couldn't articulate it.

I never imagined myself becoming a world-famous dramatic soprano who'd share the stages of the biggest opera houses in the world with the most celebrated vocalists of our time. I didn't yearn to meet presidents, princes, Pavarottis, and Plácidos.

As a child, I only knew I loved to sing.

Had I not heard the voice of God in my bedroom that day, my unarticulated dream may have gotten lost. Because even though I'd always felt that music was my destiny, the first several years of my life I struggled to hold on to it, to not let that calling be denied.

But as I said, God's voice that day would firmly plant my feet and my voice on the path that would lead me to fulfill it.

And that dramatic journey begins, appropriately, as all great operas do . . . with music, and a story that stirs the soul.

ACT I
PICCOLA

My Fair Little Lady

MY FATHER SAYS I was singing before I was even talking.

His mother, Grandma Voigt, owned a vinyl copy of the *My Fair Lady* movie soundtrack when I was a toddler. And, as family folklore has it, I'd tug at Grandma's dress and beg her to play the record for me whenever we all visited her in Mount Prospect, a forty-minute drive from our home in Wheeling, Illinois.

Mom and Dad were strict Southern Baptists and, with a few exceptions, any form of non-Christian "secular" music was forbidden in our own ultraconservative home. But my three-year-old mind didn't comprehend censorship, and to my young ears *My Fair Lady* was as sweet, fun, and innocent as candy, and it made me want to run to the center of the room and sing the songs out loud.

Grandma Voigt was a heavy-set woman—I take after her physically—with a slightly dour disposition. She wasn't particularly musical and was definitely not the whimsical, gamine, Audrey Hepburn type, so how she ended up with *My Fair Lady* in her record collection, I can't say. But it was there, and it caught my eye. Every Sunday when we'd visit her, I'd run in the door and rush to Grandma in the kitchen.

"Grandma . . . please, please. *My Lady?*" I'd manage to get out as I tugged at her apron.

"Oh, Debbie. Again?"

She'd wipe her hands and make her way to the long, teak stereo console in the living room, with me following close behind. After she put the record on, she'd give me her apron to use as my costume—which I accessorized with a netted pillbox hat from the front closet and one of Grandma's shiny brooches, and took my position center stage on the living room floor.

"I'm going to sing now!" I'd announce loudly.

Everyone would stop what they were doing and come in. With the hat falling over my eyes, and with a Cockney accent that would impress the likes of Michael Caine, I belted out at the top of my lungs one of the great refrains in English musical theater:

"Jusst you 'ait, Enry Iggins, jusst you 'ait!"

I think you get the picture.

I was a pint-sized, self-assured, living room diva who performed for the sheer joy of it—not to mention the thrill of having a captive audience.

It took only a few Sunday visits before I had the entire album—all the music and all the lyrics—memorized, an ability I wish stayed with me decades later when my opera career depended on memorizing thick librettos in a variety of languages. But I could do it then with ease, and once I'd conquered *My Fair Lady*, I moved on to a new repertoire, *The Sound of Music*, which came out the following year, and which my mother bought for me (it was one of those secular exceptions—after all, Maria *had* wanted to be a nun). By age four, it had become about more than singing for me—I loved the drama of it all. I'd sashay across the living room in my apron and truly *feel* Maria's desire to banish all her doubts and fears and find courage and strength inside of her:

"They'll have to agree, I have confidence in MEEEEEEE!"

My family played along as best they could and clapped, commenting to each other, "Oh, isn't she cute!" and then, probably, "Don't worry, she'll grow out of it." Because what was most likely at the forefront of my parents' baffled minds at the time was: "Who *does* this kid think she is? Where did she come from?"

No one in my family, not my parents or their siblings or cousins or even any of my four grandparents had ever shown an out-of-the-ordinary gift for music or a burning desire to perform. And suddenly here I was, this little kid parading around the house, belting out Broadway melodies at the top of her lungs and overemoting like a silent-film star. I'm sure it was shocking to them, even frightening.

My mother liked to sing and play piano, but she mostly expressed her love of music in church, where she played hymns and sang in the choir.

At their religious core my parents believed that any great talent, be it an athletic ability or a beautiful voice, was a gift from God, and that the proper use of that gift was to glorify God. So hymns sung in the house of our Lord were good; most other music sung elsewhere was sinful.

Performers who boldly strutted their secular stuff across any other stage were condemned as *prideful*, which my father ranked as the number-one Deadly Sin—keeping one's pride in check was a big, big deal, both at church and in our home. If we had a family crest, our motto would be: Pride Goeth Before a Fall. Or, as our pastor at Prospect Heights Baptist Church never tired of quoting from Proverbs during Sunday sermons, "Pride goeth before destruction, and a haughty spirit before a fall!" My parents were also influenced by their own parents' old-fashioned, puritanical disdain for performers—especially female performers, who were considered "loose" women, tramps.

So for them to see their little girl prancing about coquettishly with one eye on the footlights, it would have been nothing less than alarming.

WHEN I WAS born, in Wheeling, Illinois, on August 4, 1960, my mother was seventeen and my father a year older. They were high school sweethearts who had, I romantically imagined later, succumbed to adolescent passion in the backseat of a mint-green Buick Skylark. Unromantically—nine months later—after a hastily arranged wedding, Debbie Joy Voigt made her debut into the world.

My mother, Joy, was a pretty and voluptuous midwestern girl with a bright smile, kind heart, and a shy, trusting nature (aren't they always the ones who "get in trouble"?). Even as a kid, I felt protective of her and didn't want to leave her alone to go to school. She, in turn, showered me with affection. In my packed school lunches I'd find little "I love you" notes decorated with hearts atop my tuna sandwiches.

My father, Bob, was her opposite—a salesman with a type-A personality: outgoing, driven, ambitious, and a natural-born charmer (aren't they always the ones who get the nice girls in trouble?) with penetrating hazel eyes.

In many ways my parents were amazingly mismatched, and I picked up on the tension from a very young age. Both were, no doubt, unprepared and ill-equipped to deal with the demanding realities and messiness of being teenage parents. They liked clean lines and control—when we had company coming over and Mom vacuumed, we weren't allowed to walk onto the carpet and mess up the vacuum lines.

MY FATHER ALSO had a temper, and an odd sense of humor, and the combination of the two frightened and confused us kids. Often at dinner, in a quiet moment, he'd suddenly bang his elbows onto the table as hard as he could for no reason at all—sending the dishes clattering across the table and scaring me and my brothers. He had no trouble displaying anger or disapproval, but he did have difficulty expressing tenderness. Even though I see us together in old photos, me smiling in his arms, I don't have any memory of him hugging me or telling me that he loved me. As affectionate as my mother was, he was that cool and distant—unreachable.

My theatrical self-expression as a child may have been my way of reaching across that divide, or acting out the drama I saw around me. All the elements of a Puccini tragedy were played out in front of me during my formative years—lust, betrayal, jealousy, rage, heartbreak.

My earliest memory is from age three, a few months before my Cockney-flower-girl turn. It's a hazy memory: I was in my brother Rob's room with my mother and it was night—this I remember, because I kept staring at the glow of Rob's night-light, trying not to look at my mother's face. The scene began with my little brother in his crib, and my mother, tearfully and furiously packing a suitcase that lay open atop a chest of drawers.

"Debbie, we're going to visit Grandma Helen and Grandpa Henry," she said to me as she tossed our clothes into the suitcase. "Go get your teddy bear." My brother was crying, and I shifted my gaze to my father, who had wandered into the scene stage left and was leaning against the door frame, shoulders slumped, head hanging low. All we needed to complete the tableau was the appearance of Puccini's betrayed geisha, Butterfly, to sing the heartrending "Un bel dì vedremo." That is, if opera music was permitted under house rules.

Something was terribly wrong. I stood in the middle as my parents talked in strained voices—as if they were screaming at each other in whispers. They kept mentioning another woman at our church. Mom kept opening and shutting drawers loudly as Dad looked at her pleadingly, sorrowfully—a look you rarely saw on his face—and I wanted to cry, but I held it in. Days later, like all their arguments, the tragedy ended with a reunion and a lyrical love scene. From my bedroom, late at night, I could see their shadowy figures in the living room meet in a kiss, their silhouettes highlighted against the flickering light of our black-and-white TV. I was relieved to see them happy again, but hopelessly confused about the interactions between grown-up men and women.

AT AGE FIVE, after a successful two-year engagement belting out show tunes at Grandma's, my passion for singing was rerouted by my parents and channeled toward the children's choir at church. Somewhere along the way, they let me know, with nonverbal cues, that there was something not good about how and what I was singing. The connection dawned on me slowly, but once it did, I experienced a feeling I never had before and could not name at the time—shame.

My brief, happy gig as a song-and-dance girl came to an abrupt end and I was relocated to the church altar beside the other kids, where my voice could be used for a higher, nobler purpose—to celebrate the glory of God.

It was now 1965, going on '66, and the rest of the world, especially young adults my parents' age, were listening to the Rolling Stones, to the Mamas and the Papas, to the Beatles' radically new, electric-guitar-pumped *Revolver* album. But my parents were having none of it. They may have come of age in the sixties, but their cultural feet were planted back in the conservative, clean-cut fifties, and they were more Pat Boone and Debbie Reynolds—pretty square. But they still appreciated music. Money was tight, but Dad bought us a piano, and we all took lessons. Mom would teach herself songs from *The Fifty Top Romantic Songs of the Era*—sweet, melancholy ballads like "Red Roses for a Blue Lady"—as I sat next to her on the piano bench with my eyes closed, listening to her pretty voice.

At church, I had traded in my pillbox hat for a navy pinafore and a repertoire of gospel hymns. I happily discovered that the hymns were beautiful love songs about God, like "His Eye Is on the Sparrow," and that I could sing them with all my heart, too.

I sing because I'm happy, I sing because I'm free.
His eye is on the sparrow and I know He watches me.

I adored their spiritual sweetness. But if my parents thought they could exorcise their little girl's inner diva by choosing what and where I sang, they were mistaken.

My very first public performance in church, at age five, was to be a duet, "Fairest Lord Jesus," with another girl from the choir. The church was filled with at least a hundred congregants, and all eyes were on us. I wasn't nervous or self-conscious—after all, I had years of experience under my belt. I was excited—this was to be my first "real," nonfamily, audience! But my little singing partner was petrified, and when we reached the second stanza she flubbed a line.

"No, no!" I corrected her loudly, bringing the performance to a halt. Everyone was silent as the pianist tried to get us back on track, playing the same bars over and over as the choirmaster motioned from the sidelines to keep going. But my public scolding completely paralyzed my singing partner, who stood frozen at the altar. My parents, front row center pew, were horrified at what I'd done, I'm sure.

As a consummate professional, I knew the show had to go on; I continued the duet as a solo. And even though they could not clap in church, I could see my audience was pleased.

Soon, I was also able to transplant my budding acting skills into a role that served God and was therefore approved by my parents. The Sunday school teacher had noted my can-do spirit in that duet fiasco and began assigning me roles in the Sunday school pageants. My debut role was as a lead angel, but, being every bit as driven and ambitious as my father, by Christmastime I had petitioned for, and won, the coveted role of the Virgin Mary in the Nativity play.

I committed to it with all the fervor and passion in my young heart, knowing that, in the Greatest Story Ever Told, this would be my greatest part of all time. Never mind Eliza Doolittle and Maria von Trapp—I now had the responsibility of playing the Mother of God, for heaven's sake! I had arrived! I practiced casting my gaze downward modestly in front of the bathroom mirror, and our show a few weeks later was a huge success. The pastor himself took me aside afterward and told me that, even with my slight Cockney accent, he had never seen a more convincing Mary.

EVERYTHING WAS GOING well for me, and that's why what happened next was so disturbing. My parents had gone out on a rare "date" one Friday night and left Rob and me in the care of Paige, the babysitter, a bookish teenager from our church. She arrived just as we finished dinner, so she knew I'd been fed. But as soon as Mom and Dad were out the door I made a beeline for the kitchen. Paige was playing with Rob in the other room as I opened the fridge door and stood in the light's harsh glare. There it was, on the top shelf, like a siren singing an irresistible song—a jar of green olives stuffed with red pimientos. I wasn't hungry; I'd just eaten a big dinner and my tummy was as stuffed as those olives. But for some reason, as soon as Mom and Dad left the house, I had an uncontrollable urge to eat as many of them as I could.

I'd been a good girl and done what everyone wanted, hadn't I? I deserved it. I stood in the open doorway and ate the entire jar with my fingers, then tipped the glass to my lips to drink the juice.

"Debbie!" Paige was at the kitchen door, in a panic. "Do your parents let you drink olive juice like that?"

"Yup!"

It wasn't really a lie. My parents had never told me *not* to drink olive juice like that. I didn't think I was doing anything bad. But by the time my parents got home I was already in big trouble. Like Violet in *Charlie and the Chocolate Factory*, who turns blue from the blueberry pie gum, I was as green as the olives.

When Dad drove Paige home she ratted me out, describing my

spectacular act of gluttony to him. Meanwhile, back in my bedroom, Mom had shoved the family's silver barf bowl in front of me. By the time Dad returned, I was heaving olives and pimentos into the polished dish. Eating and drinking a jar of olives clearly wasn't the smartest thing to do, and I was learning this lesson the hard way. Unfortunately, Dad didn't think it was hard enough. He burst into the house fuming and came into the bedroom as I was mid-hurl.

"Did you tell Paige we allow you to drink olive juice?"

"Yeah," I said, weakly, vomit dripping from my mouth.

"You *lied*."

"Yeah," I repeated, gagging.

"You lied to someone . . . *from our church*!" Dad continued, stepping closer to me. For the first time in my life I was afraid of what he might do to me.

"I'm sorry," I squeaked.

"Never mind sorry. You are going to get a spanking, because we don't lie in this family."

I had never been spanked before; I'd never needed one. Perhaps I should have quoted my alter ego, Eliza: "I'm a good girl, I am." My father took another step toward me, and my mother put her hand on his arm.

"Bob, she's sick, she's learned her lesson and she said she's sorry. That's enough. Let it go." My father hesitated.

"This won't happen again, right, Debbie?" Mom asked.

I nodded, and Mom ushered Dad out of the room. He didn't say another word to me. Mom stayed up with me for the next few hours—emptying the silver barf bowl, bringing me water, and putting cool compresses on my forehead.

Eating the olives and lying about it to Paige was a bad thing, I got that. But what had really set my father off was that his good little church daughter had lied to someone from church. I had embarrassed and disgraced him, and, along with being prideful, that was the worst thing you could do.

"Debbie," my mother asked again, trying to soothe the both of us, "do you promise not to lie like that again? We don't want your father to be angry."

I nodded.

But there was something else going on with me, something much more troubling than lying, something my parents were completely missing.

I had just experienced my very first out-of-control food binge with no idea where it came from or what it meant. And I had a horrible sense of dread that I had opened a dangerous door somewhere deep inside of me that could not be shut.

(2)

Jesus Loves Me

FOR MY ENTIRE childhood, my mother was on a diet.

Some days she ate hard-boiled eggs and tomatoes. Other days it was cottage cheese and grapefruit with Melba toast. At least once a month she'd go on a water-only fast for a day or two, or spend a week whipping up odd-looking pink shakes. One time the lid flew off the blender and the pink stuff spewed out like it was projectile-vomiting Pepto-Bismol.

When she wasn't weighing, measuring, or blending her food, she was "sweating off" the calories. This was the sixties, and women weren't flocking to the local Pilates studios in their lululemon yoga pants yet. Housewives stretched and crunched using broomsticks while watching Jack LaLanne on TV, or they devised their own homemade methods. My mother was a firm believer that fat drained from the body out of the pores via sweat, so she took every opportunity she could to work one up.

In the summer she'd put on her bathing suit and mow the lawn, then get down on all fours and pull weeds until she was dripping and aching. Then she'd come inside, turn off the fans (no air-conditioning for us back then), and clean the house in the stifling humidity while the rest of us nearly passed out.

"Oh, Debbie, I've got to get this weight off me," she'd say, catching a glimpse of her bathing-beauty figure in the hall mirror as she went up and down the stairs.

My mother was by no means overweight. True, she wasn't the skinny-minny type like the supermodel Twiggy, who was all the rage at the time. Mom had a voluptuous and curvy figure that, a decade earlier, when the blonde in style was Marilyn, most women would've killed for. I'm sure my father appreciated it back then, but apparently she'd put on a few pounds after having kids, and so she was in a constant battle to take them off to please him. My dad was on her case about it from the moment they got married. We didn't want her to get as big as Grandma Voigt, did we?

Grandma Voigt was a stout size 18 for most of her life, but Dad didn't inherit her fleshy genes, and neither did my two lanky brothers. All three of them could wolf down two helpings of Mom's meatloaf and potatoes and never gain an ounce.

For Mom, though (and, later, for me), Dad was on constant diet patrol. I had a nickname for him by the time I got to my teens: the Food Marshal. He'd limit the junk food that entered the house, and if he ever caught Mom sneaking a bite of her favorite peanut-caramel candy bar, PayDay, which she kept hidden in her purse, he'd say with much concern in his voice, "Joy, honey. Do you *really* think you need that?"

Mom would shake her head no, then wrap it up and put it back in her purse, smacking her lips.

AS FOR ME, with the exception of my inexplicable and shocking olive-juice bender—which would come back to haunt me as an adult in the form of too many dirty martinis—I was a normal kid who ate normal portions of regular kid food—toast with melted cheese for breakfast, a tuna sandwich for lunch (with Mom's love notes tucked in). I didn't place any special importance on food. I could be a picky eater, so sometimes I was even ordered to finish my dinner, especially on Friday fish nights.

"Debbie, eat your fish sticks. Show me you're a member of the Clean Plate Club," Dad would say, when he saw me toying with my food.

"But I'm not hungry."

"It doesn't matter. Eat it all up anyway."

The cues I got about food confused me. My mother starved herself, but I was told to eat when I wasn't hungry. But I shouldn't eat too much, and it shouldn't be the wrong, "bad" food—just the food that was sanctified by my parents. And still, not too much of it. It felt like my music rules: don't be too exuberant or showy, and definitely not about the "wrong" type of music. If you crossed that blurry line, with either music or food, you were greedy, selfish, and undisciplined. Both were passions, appetites, I had to control.

I was somewhat clear on the music rules—I should sing songs about God, for God, in front of God, and because of God. But I wasn't so sure whom I ate for, or how to do it right: I ate too many olives, but not enough fish sticks. I got love notes with my tuna sandwiches, but a disapproving look when I reached for a third cookie. I wasn't chubby, but neither was my mother. And yet she and Dad were continually worried about what she put into her mouth and how it ended up on her pretty, young body.

I did my best to navigate my way around the powerful and dangerous world of food. The last thing I wanted was for my father to be angry at me, or to say to me the chastising words he said to my mother.

THE FIRST TIME my weight became an issue was after I got home from a two-week vacation with Grandma Helen and Grandpa Henry Gruthusen, when I was about six years old. We'd spent two weeks by a lake in Ely, Minnesota, and, apparently, I'd returned home rounder than usual. I remember hopping onto my mother's piano bench while my shocked parents led my grandparents into the kitchen for a private conversation. I could hear them, though.

"What did you feed Debbie?" my mother asked. My father said something, too, and it sounded angry. Being of good German stock, my grandparents fed me the same food they loved to eat—bacon, sausages, and pancakes, which I happily wolfed down without the Food Marshal around. After dinner, Grandpa Gruthusen took my brother and me to the public sauna, and I was sure whatever "bad" food I had eaten was draining from my pores, just like it did for Mom. Apparently, it didn't do the trick, and from that point on, my parents took even more interest in what I ate.

I wanted to be good, but it wasn't easy. I had diverted my interest in music to the church, and that had worked. Perhaps I needed supernatural distraction from food, too?

My timing was perfect, because this was right around the time Dad introduced "devotional time" at home. Mom was expecting my baby brother Kevin, and it was time, Dad said, we all learned more about our faith as a family. I was glad for the extra reinforcement to keep me on the disciplined path and help me suppress any lurking food benders threatening to surface.

Every night, after dinner, Dad would gather us all in the living room and read from the Bible. He'd tell us about David and Goliath and Noah and the Ark, and my brother and I were in awe and full of questions.

"Dad, how did Noah find the kangaroos?" I asked. "And did the penguins walk all the way from the North Pole?"

I was a precocious child, and Dad didn't have all the answers. But I had faith in him that whatever he was telling me was the God's honest truth.

I WAS INSPIRED by my father's religious example, and further motivated by a missionary who visited our church to talk about her work spreading the word of God in Kenya. After one Sunday sermon, she showed us slides of the village where she'd been stationed and pictures of the little African children she taught to love

Jesus. I was amazed at this stranger's boldness—that she'd choose to be single and venture out to preach God's word by herself, so far from home; how unconventional, how melodramatic, how self-less, how . . . *adventurous*.

She was the first grown-up woman I'd met who was different from my mother, except for my first-grade teacher, Mrs. Bieber, who was statuesque, divorced, and wore tight sweaters and colorful scarves wrapped around her hair. Both these women lived on their own terms, but this missionary used her teaching skills for God, just as I did my music. I was hooked. The next day at school I hatched a plan.

"Meet me by the fence during recess," I whispered to my class-mates within earshot of my desk. "We're gonna have Bible study."

I had no idea what religion my classmates were, if any at all—it was a public school, so for all I knew I was gathering a bunch of Jewish kids to convert to Christ. The bell rang and we met under the big oak tree; my followers sat cross-legged in a circle as I began my ministry.

"I have to tell you all," I said, holding up my children's Bible in one hand, "you are all going to the devil if you don't become Chris-tians right now."

"What?" asked one terrified pal.

"You have to be born again!"

"How do you do that?" asked another.

"Well, Jesus died on the cross for our sins."

"What's a sin?"

Sigh. Didn't they know anything?

"It's when you lie to your mommy, or . . . taking a cookie from the cookie jar when you're not supposed to, or . . . drinking all the olive juice."

"The *what?*"

"You'll burn up in fire for all of eternity."

I'd heard the minister say words like this, and they seemed ef-fective in church. My audience was rapt, and I emoted the scene beautifully. I even wore the perfect costume: my homespun, patriotic sundress with the red, white, and blue flowers on it that Mom made. I was so into my role, I'm surprised I didn't think to take an offering—missed that opportunity.

But try as I might, my passion didn't sway my friends. They were not as committed as I. When Good Friday and Easter came around, I'd cry, thinking about what Jesus had done to save me. Such a sacrifice appealed to me on a dramatic, soul-searching level. So much so, that one day I took the leap.

I had seen people become "born again" on Sundays when the minister called people forward as we all sang "Just As I Am."

"Is the Lord speaking to you?" he'd call out to the crowd, "do you feel a moving in your heart for something else? If so, come up!"

Going up to the front and formally accepting Jesus as your savior was the first step to becoming a Christian in our faith. If I was serious about God, I had to do it.

In Sunday school, soon after, as the class colored pictures of Mary and Joseph, I looked up at the portrait of Jesus on the wall. He was handsome, with long, blondish hair and electric-blue eyes. I couldn't wait for the sermon call; the time was now. I sprung from my seat and strode down the aisle toward my teacher.

"Mrs. Heggland, I want to accept Jesus as my savior!" I blurted out, breathless.

She looked up at me over her bifocals—surprised at first, as if she wasn't prepared for such a responsibility, and then very, very serious.

"Debbie, are you saying you'd like the Holy Spirit to live in your heart?"

I nodded. Yup.

"Do you understand that Jesus died for your sins?"

I thought of my olive binge; what a thing to die for—but I was grateful. The other kids in class were now watching from their seats, transfixed at the scene being played out in their very own classroom.

Some in the back strained to hear the dialogue, so I pumped up my volume. I clasped my hands together, as if in a prayer. And in a clear voice, from deep within my diaphragm, I projected:

"Yes, I do. I understand that, Mrs. Heggland. Jesus died for my sins."

"Well, then, Debbie," she said, looking very pleased, "sit down with me and let's pray."

After class, she went to my parents in church and let them know of my Big Moment. Yes, I had done it all by myself, she bragged to them. Yes, yes, in front of the entire class! No, I wasn't nervous at all, she added. I was a natural.

In keeping with Dad's and my new zeal, our family started attending sermons twice on Sundays. After the first sermon, we'd come home, lay our nice clothes on the bed so they wouldn't get wrinkled, then hop in the station wagon to pick up a bucket of Brown's Chicken in nearby Chicago. This was the big family treat of the week, and even Mom was permitted to splurge. Then it was back home, have a nap, put on our Sunday best again, and back to church for the five p.m. show.

Now that I was getting older, I listened to the pastor's words more intently.

"You are all born sinners!" he'd yell, pointing to us from the pulpit. "You must repent!"

He urged us to examine our actions and consciences and ask the Lord for forgiveness and strength to correct the wrongs we'd done. If we didn't, we'd suffer those fires in hell forever. I was scared, and wondered: Was I a sinner? Did I deserve to be punished?

Around the time Dad instituted devotional time, he also introduced spanking into my childhood curriculum. I was basically a good kid, but I got spanked anyway. I never knew when I was going to get it, because I was never sure when I'd done something bad. At any time he could approach me in my room and let me know I deserved a spanking.

He'd sit down on my bed and put me over his knee and whack hard on my bare behind using his hand. The spanking came with a running commentary.

"You're getting a . . . WHACK . . . spanking . . . WHACK . . . Do you know why . . . WHACK . . . you're being . . . WHACK . . . punished? I want you . . . WHACK . . . to tell me . . . WHACK . . . what you did . . . WHACK, WHACK, WHACK . . . wrong . . ."

Hell was being unleashed onto my bare bottom; that I was sure of. What I had done wrong—I had no clue. Maybe I wasn't good enough, or smart enough, or pretty enough, or slim enough. If I didn't answer him the spanking went on longer, so I soon learned to mumble something incoherent, anything, just to end it.

At night, I began to start my bedtime prayers like this: "Jesus, forgive me of my sins . . ."

THE FOLLOWING YEAR, I started to feel sick in the mornings. I had a stomachache, my head hurt, any number of symptoms a kid could think of to stay in bed. Sometimes I really was sick, sometimes I was pretending. I wanted to stay home with my mother, I was afraid to leave her. I wasn't sure if it was for my own sake or for hers. I felt an impending doom, a fear that I couldn't pinpoint.

"Mom, what will you do without me if I leave the house?" I asked her one morning, lying in a fetal position in bed and clutching my stomach.

"Honey, what are you talking about? Now c'mon, don't you feel well enough to go to school today? You've already missed two days this week."

She took me to the doctor and I had a battery of tests and X-rays that showed nothing wrong with me. Not physically, anyway. My mother was worried about me, and I was consumed with worry for both of us.

I'd always felt protective of her, ever since that time she was packing our bags when I was three and Dad loomed in the doorway. I felt her fragility, as if I should be mothering her, instead of the other way around. I felt as though she was too young to struggle in this harsh, adult world, and I didn't want anyone to hurt her, be it my father or a stranger.

Another incident from around that time compounded my concern. We didn't have a washer-dryer at home then, and Mom recently had baby number three, my brother Kevin. She and Dad were struggling to make ends meet; and she was extra-stressed because my father was away a lot for his job, leaving her on her own with the three of us. That day, with our last few hundred dollars in the bank, Mom had bought some much-needed clothes for my brothers and me, and after our shopping expedition, she'd taken us to the Laundromat to wash the new clothes. We watched them spin in the wash, then went grocery shopping while they dried. When we returned, the dryer was empty—someone had stolen our stuff.

With Kevin in her arms, Mom collapsed atop a beat-up foldout chair next to the dryers and sobbed. "They didn't even wait for our clothes to *dry* . . ."

THE DAY I proclaimed to Mrs. Heggland that I'd accepted Jesus as my savior I had hoped everything in my life would improve. But I guess God, in His infinite wisdom, wasn't ready to save me just yet. I had more to learn about being a sinner first.

In fourth grade, my new best friend was the boisterous Sandy Baker, known to all on the block for her raven, untamed hair, and a personality to match. Sandy had been one of my potential converts back in the school playground, but my preaching didn't take.

Now, two years later, Sandy introduced me to *her* world. If my home was a house of God and worship, Sandy's was a veritable Sodom and Gomorrah. After school, we'd go to her place and all hell would break loose.

It began in the kitchen, where we opened the pantry door to re-veal boxes and boxes of—oh, joy of joys—brown-sugar-cinnamon Pop-Tarts with vanilla icing. To my eyes? Forbidden fruit! We'd pilfer a box and pour glasses of cherry Kool-Aid, then take it all up-stairs on a psychedelic plastic tray (this *was* 1969, after all) to her bedroom.

Both of Sandy's parents worked and didn't get home until din-nertime; she was part of that new generational boom of "latchkey kids." To be so unsupervised was unusual for me. But even if her parents had been home, they wouldn't have minded our snack. They were as free-spirited and liberal as mine were strict, which I fur-ther discovered when I used the upstairs bathroom for the first time. Across from the toilet on a magazine rack I spied a pair of bunny ears and pulled out the magazine—*Playboy*.

I nearly fell off the toilet. The closest we came to any photos of a sexual nature in our house was a record in my parents' collection by Herb Albert's Tijuana Brass: *Whipped Cream & Other Delights*. On the front of the album cover was a photo of a nude woman slathered with whipping cream, licking some off her finger. You couldn't see any of her lady parts, though—they were covered.

I sat on the toilet longer than I needed to, flipping through the *Playboy* with my mouth open. Here the women were com-pletely naked and unashamed, confident. They were proud of their nakedness—boldly so.

Back in Sandy's bedroom, our Barbie games took on a playful, X-rated nature. High on sugar and inspired by the bathroom nudies, we married Ken and Barbie and sent them on a honeymoon where they'd rip each other's clothes off and roll around on each other. Sandy and I would give each other playful pecks on the cheek and hug on the bed, pretending to be boyfriend and girlfriend. It was all very innocent, we were curious, as most kids are, and testing the boundaries. Especially for me, it was about being free to follow a natural impulse and express myself—something I couldn't do at home. We wrote imaginary "love notes" to each other, until my mother found one in my pocket as she got the laundry together one morning. I saw her pull it out and read it:

Dear pretty girl Debbie!

I want to hug and kiss you! You are so pretty! Next time we meet, we'll do that again!

"Debbie?" Mom turned toward me, still looking at the note in her hand. "What's this?"

I froze.

"Oh. I don't know, Mom."

I didn't think Sandy and I were doing anything wrong, but I knew my parents might think so. At the ripe age of nine, going on ten, I had already committed three deadly sins—gluttony, pride, and lust—and now I was an experienced liar. That night I asked Jesus to forgive me with extra sincerity.

THE NEXT DAY I woke up inspired. I had accepted Jesus as my savior, but I hadn't been formally cleansed of my sins and saved. *This* is what I needed. At the front of the church, we had a big tub of water—the baptismal. It was where you made your commitment to Jesus publicly. The whole baptismal scene appealed to my theatrical nature, I loved watching people get dunked below the water's surface. When I told my parents and the pastor that I was ready for this step they were very happy, and a date was set. I chose my outfit carefully: plaid culottes and a short-sleeved white shirt—solemn but with a girlish innocence. When the big day arrived, I walked up to the tub of water with a group of others, and when it was my turn, I carefully stepped in. The minister was already waist deep.

He pinched my nose with one hand and with the other dunked me under the surface, then pulled me back up. As I rose in a *whoosh*,

I could hear angels singing from heaven (but really it was the church choir in the balcony). I rubbed my eyes and someone helped me out of the tub. I looked over at Mom and Dad, my brothers, and my grandparents, all smiling and waving from the front pew. They looked proud, and I was proud of myself, too.

As I changed into dry clothes in the back room, I was on a post-performance high. I had been cleansed of my sins, I had saved myself from my bad behaviors. I smiled as I laced up my sneakers. My family was waiting for me outside so we could go home and celebrate with a special chocolate cake in my honor. I quickened my pace; I was really looking forward to a piece or two of that cake. Maybe a little too much.

Oh, if only I knew that my struggles then—food, lust, self-control, self-esteem, pride—would be my same struggles for the next forty years. And that it would take more than a dunk in cold water to wash them away.

Sweet and Innocent

WHATEVER CLEANSING I got from my baptismal dunking didn't last long.

By age ten, the soulful, hippie poster of Jesus on the wall at Sunday school had competition—not from a false idol, exactly, but a teen idol or two. And new music was about to enter my world.

It was the summer of 1970 and the posters Scotch-taped on my bedroom wall were of a toothy-grinned Donny Osmond and his equally harmless peer, Bobby Sherman, he of the groovy chokers and striped hip-huggers.

But my new idols didn't pose a problem for my religious life. Their music was as wholesome as their clean-cut, puppy-dog images—especially Donny, whom I loved the best because he was devoutly religious. He may have been Mormon, a denomination I knew nothing about, but he sang for God, and that was good enough for me. I was still singing for God myself. My mother and I had become regular performers at the annual mother-daughter church banquet on Mother's Day, and we'd harmonize on duets: she was alto and I was soprano. It was great fun, and Mom made us matching empire-waisted maxidresses with puffy sleeves and green felt daisies sprouting from the hemline.

The concern my parents might have had at this point was another new passion of mine—wanting to become a Catholic nun.

With my father out of town a lot for his new sales job, family devotional time had fallen by the wayside and I had begun to look elsewhere to fill the spiritual gap. Through a family friend, I began volunteering after school at a nearby Catholic nursing home run by nuns. I followed the nuns down the urine-scented hallways and handed out glasses of juice and fluffed pillows for the old people. In the process, I became enthralled with a new kind of heroine—the pious nun in her distinctive habit.

Up to then, everything I knew about nuns had come from Julie Andrews in *The Sound of Music*, Sally Field in *The Flying Nun*, and Audrey Hepburn in *A Nun's Story*. I held my breathe when Audrey walked down the church aisle in a white dress and bridal veil, knelt to the floor, and had her gorgeous mane of hair chopped off. I was in awe of her sacrifice.

EVEN THOUGH MY parents had no need to worry about Donny or Bobby and my *Tiger Beat* pix, they still took precautions. They knew what dangers secular music could lead to. That year, under the Christmas tree, I tore the wrapping paper off my "big" present— and my parents' weapon of warfare—a brand-new Philips portable record player.

"And this goes with the gift," my father said, handing me Glen Campbell's gospel album, *Oh Happy Day*. I ran my hand along the smooth album cover, speechless. Which was good, because my father had more to say.

"We expect you to play appropriate music. Your mother and I will be the judge of what that is. No rock and roll."

They didn't name names on the Do Not Play list, like the Rolling Stones or KISS or Led Zeppelin—they wouldn't have known those bands, and neither would I. As far as I knew, Glen Campbell *was* rock and roll. And, again, they needn't have worried about outside musical forces having a negative influence on me. Forces right at home were already doing that.

I never was a good sleeper as a kid. I'd lie awake for hours, thinking about everything; and I was all ears—too much so for my own good. One night, at around age ten, I was staring at the ceiling and heard what sounded like a loud slap coming from my parents' room. They had been arguing a lot lately and I was worried my father was hitting my mother.

"*Daddy!*" I cried out from my room, in tears. "*Stop hurting Mommy!*"

The noise stopped, and I could hear my parents whispering.

"Debbie," my father called out. "Mom's okay, go back to sleep!"

When I got up the next morning, Dad had already gone to work and had left a note for me on the kitchen table. Mom stood by the sink, casually drinking a cup of coffee as I read it.

Dear Debbie . . . the noise you heard last night was not what you thought it was. I love your mother very much and I would never hurt her. Sometimes when mommies and daddies hug at night, they can be loud. . . .

They were loud when they argued as well, especially one night when they were talking about a man we knew from church. This argument had the same recriminating tone as the one when I was three years old and Mom was packing her suitcase. The day after this particular argument, I went skating at a nearby pond with the daughter of the church member Mom and Dad had been arguing about. We raced and twirled on the ice, the pom-poms on our laces bouncing in the air. As we twirled, my friend told me her parents had also been arguing the night before.

"What did *your* parents argue about?" I asked.

"Your mother. What did *your* parents argue about?"

"Your father," I said.

There was nothing more to say. We'd both stopped skating now and were silent, listening to the cutting sounds of other blades scraping and slicing the ice. With just those few words, we understood the gravity of the information we'd just exchanged, and at the same time we knew it was beyond our comprehension. So we skated some more and went home and never spoke about it again to each other.

It was a shock to discover that, like me with my immoral *Playboy* transgressions, my parents, too, had their secrets—especially since they were so vigilant to present a fastidious, devout image on the surface.

By sixth grade, I uncovered yet another family secret. That year in school we were learning the basics of how babies are made in health class. I was telling my mother about it one day as we drove home from the grocery store.

"Mom, we talked about how long it takes to grow a baby," I said. "You and Daddy were married in January, and I was born in August . . ."

Over at the steering wheel Mom was looking nervous.

I tapped my fingers on my lap, doing the math: "January, February, March, April, May, June, July . . . and my birthday is August fourth . . ."

I looked up at my mother. "Mom, that's only seven months!"

You'd think she might have prepared herself ahead of time for when this day arrived, so she could easily assure me, "Oh, honey, you were a premature baby." Instead, she got flustered and said the first thought that came to mind—anything, to steer me off topic.

"Debbie," Mom said, as she swerved sharply into our driveway, "don't count on your fingers, honey, it's not polite."

That shut me up, but it didn't stop me from thinking. I may have been too young to be told the truth, but I was also too smart not to understand the math and what it meant. Just like my chat with my friend at the ice rink, nothing more needed to be said here; the silence spoke volumes. I didn't bring it up again for years—I could take a hint—but from that moment on, I knew the deal: Mom and Dad got married when she was sixteen because she got pregnant with *me*.

MEANWHILE, MY OWN sexual curiosity was stirring.

I'd started babysitting for the O'Hearns, whom Mom and Dad knew from the neighborhood, on Saturday nights. They had two adorable, easy kids, a kitchen cupboard full of junk food, and a bedroom drawer packed with erotic photographs and literature. You might say they were a babysitter's trifecta jackpot. After entertaining the kids for an hour or two, then putting them to bed, I'd head for the master bedroom—a.k.a., the Den of Lust.

My first Saturday there, I was shocked to find, during a preliminary exploration upstairs, that Mr. and Mrs. O'Hearn had a round bed—something I'd never seen before. That in itself was titillating. *What do these people do on a round one that you can't do on a regular square one?*

By Saturday number three, I'd found their stash. I was a natural-born snoop, always wanting to see what people had hidden away in their cubbyholes. Maybe I just wanted to know if other people were like my parents and me—showing one proper face to the world but having another, interior, world that was vastly different. Or maybe I was just looking for an outlet for my budding sexuality outside my strict Baptist confines.

Going on twelve, I had already begun to develop, and was wearing what we used to call a "training bra." Grandma Voigt saw it as a containment device. On nights when we kids would go for sleepovers at her house, the message I got from her was clear: *Cover those things up.* As bedtime approached, we'd finish watching TV, and Grandma would say, "Okay, everyone get into your pj's. Debbie, don't forget to keep your brassiere on underneath."

At the O'Hearns, on the other hand, it was all about exposure, not covering up. In the bottom drawer of a bedside table I hit gold—

piles of *Penthouse* magazines and erotic paperbacks. By Saturday number four I'd spread them out on the round bed—with one eye on the bedroom window for approaching headlights and, alternately, on the bedroom door for stirring children—and gobbled them up.

I knew it was wrong to be snooping around other people's houses, and, worse, looking at and reading pornography. I'm sure even my parents, with their own extracurricular activities, would have been shocked to know their twelve-year-old daughter was doing this. But I couldn't stop, and I didn't want to.

Punishment came soon enough. My mother and father had no idea what I was up to, but there was always a feeling in our house that we kids must be doing *something* wrong, or were about to. I was always on edge—*don't say the wrong thing, don't do the wrong thing, shut up, be a good girl.*

My new mode of punishment that year was to get my mouth washed out with soap when I was "sassy" to my mother—which was anytime I tried to express myself or voice an opinion. That kind of self-confidence was not tolerated in our house.

"Debbie," Mom might say, "I told you to clean up your room three times."

"And I heard you all three times."

(pause)

"Wait until your father gets home."

My mother was never the one to dole out punishment, that was Dad's domain. Once he got home, Mom would turn me in and I'd be marched to the bathroom. There, Dad would roll up the sleeves of his crisp, white shirt.

"To the sink, Debbie."

I'd watch as he methodically rubbed the soap and washrag together under the hot water until the rag was good and soapy. Then he'd wind the rag around the bar to get a good grip and shove it into my mouth.

"You will *not* speak to your mother that way. Do. You. Under. Stand?"

He'd get that soap in good and deep, until it hit the molars. And then he'd twist it around in my mouth to make sure he didn't miss a spot.

Even my spankings took on a new dimension. We didn't have a Ping-Pong table in our house, but Grandma Voigt did. How else would Dad have gotten hold of a paddle? Forty-odd years later, I still don't remember doing anything so terrible (that they knew about) that would warrant a spanking on my bare ass with a piece of sporting equipment.

"You will never do that again!" WHACK! "That was a bad thing to do!" WHACK!

I remember limping away from one spanking with blistering welts on my behind.

THE YEAR I entered seventh grade, at Holmes Junior High School, I was more than ready to rebel.

I met my new friend, Sue, at choir practice, and she would become my new *agent provocateur* and partner in crime. We had a secret voice, a high, squeaky trill based on our nerdy teacher Mr. Weller, that we used constantly throughout the day—in class, in the halls, after school, on the phone—I'm surprised my voice didn't get stuck there. (The Voice was so high, it may have contributed to my vocal development. We talked how I imagine John Irving's character, Owen Meany, sounded like.)

For one month we were put in charge of the ice cream wagon in the cafeteria at lunchtime. (Upon hearing the news, Sue and I looked at each other: *They've got to be kidding!*) We were told to sell the ice cream and put the money in a little tin cash box. Except, that's not exactly how it turned out. Each shift, my waistline and thighs netted at least three ice cream sandwiches for free—and Sue scarfed down at least three Eskimo Pies. We were eating half the profits, and we gave away the rest, dispensing free ice cream to our ever-grateful friends.

I had now broken the "Thou shall not steal" commandment, but I wasn't too bothered by this. Instead, I was high on the feeling of being wild and naughty and getting away with it.

All a teacher had to do was take one look at me and they'd have known I was guilty of ice cream theft. I was always a bit bigger than other kids, tall and stockier in build; but a few months into junior high I started to round up quite a bit. In addition to our illicit ice cream, Sue and I had a feasting ritual in which we'd stroll the length of our local strip mall, from one end to the other, hitting each food counter along the way—McDonald's, the glazed-doughnut place, Butterfingers and chocolate-covered pretzels at the candy counter—we were equal-opportunity bingers. It never occurred to me to ask myself why I had begun to overeat like this.

At home, Mom had become my binge buddy, too. My father was out of town at least one overnight a week, and when he was gone, the fear and control atmosphere in the house lifted. We all felt it. Free from his ever-watchful, scrutinizing gaze on what we ate and did, we let loose—it was party time.

"What should we have for dinner, Debbie? Pizza? Hamburgers and fries? A bucket of chicken?"

"Let's go to Dogs n' Suds!" I'd say, excited.

The boys would pile into the backseat and I'd sit up front with Mom and we'd drive to the local carhop chain and order hot dogs, fries, and root beer floats delivered right to our car. On the way home we'd stop at Dairy Queen for sundaes. Later that night, after my brothers were in bed, it would be special Mom-Debbie bonding time (read: eating time). Mom would make a huge bowl of popcorn and drench it with a stick of melted butter and tons of salt and we'd stay up and watch Johnny Carson.

Dad didn't know about our free-for-all eating nights, but he noticed the aftereffects. One day toward the end of junior high,

Mom and I were walking ahead of him on the sidewalk on a warm summer afternoon, wearing shorts, when we heard him sigh behind us.

"Like mother, like daughter," he said from the rear, noticing our similar figures. I think his intent was to tease, but I didn't hear that I was pretty like Mom, or curvaceous like Mom. I heard: *Debbie's headed for trouble. I see I'm going to have to be relentless with her, too.*

THE ONLY CONSTANT for me, through all this, was music.

I first spotted my music teacher, Miss Cronin, the year before, when she'd brought the junior high choir to my grammar school to perform in our gymnasium. She was a former nun, I soon found out, who had the voice of an angel. After the choir finished, she sat down on a chair with her guitar and sang folk songs like "The Water Is Wide," and I was mesmerized. Miss Cronin had the bearing of the nuns back at the nursing home, but she was young and enthusiastic, with musical talent. She was my real-life answer to Maria von Trapp! She was also a bit of a renegade herself.

In class, we studied the rock opera *Tommy*, by the Who (a group definitely *not* on my parents' "safe list." Had they known I was listening to "The Acid Queen" they would have gone into conniptions.) When my virgin ears first heard it, I felt an explosion shatter my formerly overprotected senses.

In addition to introducing me to rock music, Miss Cronin was the first person to tell me my voice was special. She urged me to sign up as a soloist in a vocal competition sponsored by the Illinois State Music Teacher's Association, in which our school choir was to take part that year. I hesitated, fearing I didn't have the chops for it.

"Debbie, you have a special voice and a special talent. You should do this."

The competition was being held at a local high school, and I brought Sue along for moral support, which she gave. In the hallway, before I went into the room to sing, Sue went into our Weller

Voice, and we exploded in hysterics until Miss Cronin shushed us. Thanks to Sue, I wasn't nervous.

I stood in the middle of the dusty classroom in front of two female judges. One wore inch-thick glasses perched at the tip of her skinny nose, the other had a beehive hairdo teased so high I was queasy from the hairspray fumes. Behind them was a chalkboard with smudged algebra equations. I had prepared "Oh, What a Beautiful Mornin' " from *Oklahoma!* Mom and I had seen it a few months earlier, my first live stage musical, and I'd been swept away—the lights, the costumes, the dancing, the acting, the songs—everything.

I cleared my throat and began. The sight of the judges and math equations fell away. The stuffy schoolroom became a field of grass and haystacks. . . .

There's a bright, golden haze on the meadow . . .

I took home a first-place pin in the shape of the state of Illinois—my first win!

My success, and Miss Cronin's encouragement, planted the hint of a dream deep within me—that maybe one day I could have some sort of career in music. That desire was further stoked the day I first heard, on the radio, the most beautiful sound ever—Karen Carpenter. Her voice was so creamy, her phrasing so beautiful, that I fell in love with her and wanted to sing like her. I rushed out and bought my first LP, the Carpenters' *A Song for You*, and lay on my bed, playing it over and over on my Philips turntable.

One day I sat down at the piano in the living room—I was thirteen now—thinking I was alone in the house. I began to play and sing a lilting show tune—I can't remember which one it was. But I thought no one else was home, so I let loose with my voice and my feelings. My fingers flew across the keys and I sang out to the last rows of imagined Broadway balconies with abandon. I hadn't sung at home like this since my *My Fair Lady* days, before I had been taught to be self-conscious about it.

Just like when I was three years old, this felt right. It felt happy. It felt . . . *transcendent*.

I heard my father's heavy footsteps coming up the stairs and around the corner.

I froze, my fingers stiff above the keys. My parents' mantra repeated in my ear: "Don't be showy, don't be prideful . . . pride goeth before a—"

Dad walked over to me at the piano. He might have laughed a little; I don't know if it was out of nervousness or if he was making fun of me or if he was angry or uncomfortable or afraid or what. And I don't remember his exact wording, either, but I'll never forget the feeling it gave me.

"*Who*," he asked, "*do you think you are?*"

I felt humiliated and ashamed. Whether it was his intent or not, I thought he was telling me that I was doing something bad, something wrong—that the way I loved to sing was immoral and ungodly.

For months after that day, I felt sick inside. As if the delicate dream I dared to hope for had been murdered.

Until the morning God spoke to me and brought it back to life.

4

High School Musical

YOU ARE HERE TO SING.

Forty years later, I can still hear that authoritative, ethereal voice and feel the impact of those five words; the experience changed my life. They were more than mere words; they were my destiny. And as my bedroom filled with morning light that day and I lay in bed, silenced and humbled by the enormity of what had just happened, I was also determined about my newly defined mission. Without a doubt, no matter what anyone else said or did, I now had to find a way to sing in whatever way I was meant to do so. I assumed the details would reveal themselves along the way.

I sat up in bed and reached for my guitar, which was leaning against the wall—my parents had given it to me as a Christmas present at the encouragement of Miss Cronin—and I softly strummed a few chords. For the rest of the day I moved through my regular routine in an otherworldly daze and didn't tell a soul of my chat with God. Who would have believed me? I wanted to keep the experience untainted and private, so I didn't say a word—and wouldn't for at least another decade.

Around the same time I heard God's voice, my life changed drastically in another way, too.

Weeks before I started high school, in '74, Dad was promoted and transferred to a new job, and we were uprooted southwestward across the country, from Illinois to Orange County, California. His office had given him two choices for his new position, California or New York. So we took a road trip—Dad, Mom, and me—to look at neighborhoods in Ossining, New York, the home of Sing Sing Correctional Facility, before he made his decision. As we wandered through one beautiful colonial house in Ossining, we heard the sound of beautiful voices raised in song, which I at first took as a heavenly sign that this was the right place for us. (After all, if I could hear God speak, why not angels singing?)

"Oh, those are the prisoners singing," explained the real estate agent who was showing us the house. "On some summer nights, if the wind is blowing the right way, their voices rise above the prison walls."

Funny that the prison was called "Sing Sing," I thought to myself. And even funnier that I could relate to their need to sing beyond their physical and emotional prisons. I crossed my fingers, hoping that Dad would pick the East Coast job, but he chose California, and I was distraught.

The Beach Boys' *Endless Summer* album was all over the radio as we packed up the house, but I had no interest in being a surfer chick or a "California Girl" spending Christmases in seventy-five-degree heat, which we did that first December. I imagined a world of skinny girls going to school in bikinis, and after my father's "like mother, like daughter" remark, I was not comfortable showing my body— especially not in shorts or a bathing suit, the year-round uniform of Southern Californians.

My nightmare scenario was realized when we arrived in Placentia, thirty miles southeast of Los Angeles, and I attended my first church youth group event. Our new church, the Yorba Linda Evangelical Free Church, was more hippie-dippy than we were used to, and, as I suspected, the teenagers were more invested in pool parties than Bible verses. I was invited to attend one that first week, and my parents urged me to go and make friends, so I put on my conservative one-piece and a big cover-up and stayed that way. In California, I discovered, even the devout Christian girls looked like Twiggy. I was miserable.

It's not as if I was terribly overweight. I was fourteen and size 14, and voluptuous—a curvaceous girl growing into womanhood.

But I *felt* obese. The messages I'd been given while growing up with a constant dieter and a food marshal convinced me I was bigger than I was, and certainly bigger than I should be. I had boobs and an ass and hips and thighs, and while that was normal for my sturdy body type, it was considered fat in my house. Perhaps my womanly curves worried my father. Maybe seeing his daughter developing into a sexual being was too much for him to handle and subconsciously he wanted to stop it.

At that time, I had a classic, hearty, country girl's steak-and-potatoes appetite and I liked my cookies. But I still wasn't too much of an overeater, nothing beyond the sort of teenaged girl's frenzied, emotional, hormonal overindulging that I had done with Sue and with Mom. It was the kind of eating that, given a few more years of maturing, I probably would have gotten a handle on. But if you tell me repeatedly that I've got a weight problem and to stop eating, well, dammit, I'm going to eat everything in sight.

"Debbie, get your hand out of that cookie jar!" I'd hear from somewhere in the house every time I lifted the jar's heavy ceramic lid. So I'd sneak back later, when no one was in earshot, to grab twice as many. It was a power struggle, I suppose. (Later on, this dynamic would play out with my parents and me around the men I was dating: "Debbie, we don't want you to be with that man." It only made me want to be with him more, of course.)

My former binge buddy, Mom, became my new diet buddy as I joined her on various weight-loss diets. We had a little Weight Watchers scale that we used to weigh our three ounces of skinless chicken breast as we forced ourselves to drink eight glasses of water per day. When we got home after going out shopping together, we both had to pee so badly it was a race out of the car to see who could get into the house and to the closest bathroom first. The loser sometimes ended up peeing in her pants.

Sweets became a precious, rare, and sought-after commodity in our household—even more than before. So much so, that Dad began to hide his own goodies. One day as I was setting the dinner table, I opened up a hutch drawer and found a dozen packages of my beloved Hostess Suzy Q's—chocolate cake squares with cream slathered in the middle— lined up like diamonds in a jewelry display.

"*Mom!*" I yelled out to her, "*what are these doing here?*"

"They're your father's," she said, standing in the doorway, hands on her hips. "Don't touch them."

Was she kidding? I was desperate and hungry, but not crazy. I was now, thankfully, past the spankings and soap-in-mouth punishments. They had ended once I started junior high school; but, in any case, I wouldn't have eaten my father's stash. I had too much respect for another person's personal binge needs.

I TRIED NOT to focus too much on my relationship with food, which was growing more complicated, and instead threw my energies into my new life purpose. That, to me, was clear and all mine.

You are here to sing.

I JOINED THE choir at El Dorado High School, where my vocal teacher, Mr. Fichtner, would soon become another key player to help me get onto my music path. He put me in his madrigal group, a dozen handpicked singers from the choir who sang Renaissance and Baroque music a capella. Outside of school, I threw myself into performing with a new fervor. I sang solos in the church choir and helped run the music program there; I performed in local shopping malls and entered competitions; any opportunity I saw to get out in front of people and perform, I took.

To this day, my parents still talk about the time I decided to play all of Beethoven's melancholic Moonlight Sonata at an evening church service during the offertory. It was always a small crowd at night, so the offertory passing was finished within a minute or two. Beethoven, not so much. When I glanced up halfway through the sonata, I could see the ushers standing in the back, politely but impatiently tapping their feet, and the pastor trying subtly to gesture to me from the pulpit, with an expression that said: *We're going to go into overtime because of this, kid. Wrap it up, wrap it up!*

With my love of drama, I signed up for a theater class and auditioned for the musical *L'il Abner*, winning a part as one of the Dogpatch girls. My skimpy costume consisted of Daisy Duke cutoff short-shorts and a checkered midriff-revealing blouse that tied above the waist. For this body-conscious, suburban, midwestern Southern Baptist girl, it was a racy outfit. But I discovered something freeing on that high school stage the first night I sang and hoofed my way across, pretending to be someone else. If I was playing a part, I could do, say, and wear anything, and it was allowed. There were no rules when you were acting, *because it wasn't you.*

My parents attended opening night, and I'm sure they were shocked when they saw me onstage in my sexy outfit, but they didn't say anything about it. I think by now they had decided that acting in a school play wasn't going to send anyone to hell. Grandma Voigt didn't say anything about my outfit either, bless her soul. But from onstage, I could imagine what she was thinking: *Cover those things up!*

The following year, I played the plum role of secretary Agnes Gooch in *Mame* and found I had a flair for comedy. At the school's

thespian banquet I won several awards, including the Best Supporting Actress award for my Gooch turn, and returned home that night
buoyant with an armful of certificates and trophies. One by one, I
took them into my parents' room and showed them—"You were
wonderful in that part, honey," Mom said; and they were both genuinely happy for me. I was trying to be proud, but not prideful, and I
wanted them to take my singing seriously.

It worked. Soon after, my parents asked around about voice
teachers and heard about Seth Riggs. He was the preeminent voice
teacher in Los Angeles, with a specialty in pop music, and he'd
worked with vocalists like Michael Jackson, Stevie Wonder, Ray
Charles, and Barbra Streisand. My parents, to their great credit, may
not have understood exactly what I was doing, or where my talents
might lead me, but once they saw how hard I was working—and
that I did, indeed, have talent—they were supportive of my goal financially and in other ways. They drove me for the audition with
Mr. Riggs, who wanted to take me on; but the hourlong commute
seemed too much.

That's when my music teacher, Mr. Fichtner, suggested his
wife, Pat, as a singing coach. She was a former opera singer and
taught classical vocal technique. It was "an operatic approach," he
explained—not like the pop music I was fond of, but it would be
good for me.

Opera? Never heard it. Wasn't that old people's music? But Mrs.
Fichtner taught within walking distance of my high school and
charged only a quarter of Seth's fee, so I signed up.

During our first warm-up, I discovered my vocal range was two
and a half octaves, which was quite good. (Mariah Carey claims to
have three or three and a half). Mrs. Fichtner started me off with the
beginner's "bible" of classic Italian art songs, *Twenty-Four Italian
Songs and Arias of the Seventeenth and Eighteenth Centuries for Me-
dium High Voice.*

Soon enough I saw my first opera, with Grandma Voigt as my date. She knew I'd been studying classical music—"Much more dignified than Broadway show tunes," she said—and thought it was high time we heard some. At the San Diego Opera we saw Prokofiev's *The Love of Three Oranges*, a very random choice for one's first opera and one that is rarely staged. The cast didn't have any famous singers, and I don't remember being moved by the story or acting. Grandma, too, was a bit confused and didn't know what to make of it. But the beautiful stage in front of us, the majestic way the curtain rose, and the power and passion of the singing overwhelmed me.

AT FIFTEEN, I wasn't officially allowed to date yet.

"You can date when you're sixteen and not one day before that," my parents informed me. As if something magical and miraculous would happen to me the night before my sixteenth birthday that would make me mature and wise enough to venture into the dating world. I'd go to bed and wake up with the ability to tell the good boys from the bad ones.

That, I already knew how to do. The trick was convincing oneself to *want* to date the good boys, and not the bad ones—I still haven't mastered that one. A few months later, my parents chucked their rule when the preacher's son, Randy, came to call. Naturally, they adored and trusted him and their trust was well placed. He was a good and respectful kid—too good and respectful for my taste, it turned out. Randy was one year older than me, but even less experienced. On the advice of his church buddies, we drove up into the hills on Skyline Drive where all the teenagers parked. The trick, his friends instructed, was to tear down the road when you saw a patrolling cop car approach, which they did on the hour, and then return ten minutes later.

Randy had a car with a flat console between the two front seats and once parked, I hopped over the console to try some French kissing and nearly scared poor Randy to death.

"If I wanted to kiss your tongue"—he pulled away, in disgust—"I would have kissed your tongue!"

If Randy was too slow, my next beau was too fast. I still wasn't officially dating age, and Richard was two years older than me, but he was on the football team and told me he'd noticed me in the halls wearing my silky blue dress with the elastic top—how could I say no to a man with such an eye for detail? Apparently, I could. If my parents were worried I was going to be taken advantage of, I wish they'd seen how I handled Richard. He was the kind of guy who knew exactly where to park and always kissed with his tongue. Making out one night on Skyline Drive, he kept slipping his hands under my T-shirt and inside my bra. Believe it or not, I still considered myself a good Christian girl and I had my boundaries.

"No, Richard—no! I don't want to do that. I told you, I'm not ready!" I pushed him away. "Why do you keep insisting?"

"After the games, all the guys in the locker room talk about what they did with their girlfriends the night before," he said, "and I never have anything to say!"

I made him drive me home and I dumped him along the way.

THEN CAME JOHN. I'd noticed him at the public library, where he worked in the audiovisual department with a friend of mine and I had a major crush on him. He was tall with long, dark hair, and handsome. He loved to sing, like me, and was into jazz, another genre I knew nothing about. He was also twenty-one and had no idea how young I was. A few weeks before my sixteenth birthday, we were both at my friend's house for a swim (by now, I'd succumbed to the bathing suit pressures of my new environment. I couldn't get away with wearing a cover-up for the rest of my life while living in California).

John sat at the edge of the pool, watching me as I lingered in the shallow end, still shy and keeping submerged. He gave me an intense look from the pool's edge like no guy had ever given me before, so I paddled closer.

"So, when can we go out on a date?" he asked.

"Well . . . my parents won't let me date until I'm sixteen."

He looked momentarily surprised, but that didn't stop him.

"Well, when are you going to be sixteen?"

"In two weeks."

"Okay, then. Two weeks it is."

On the morning of my sixteenth birthday, when my mother asked me if I'd like anything special for my birthday dinner that night, I nonchalantly broke the news.

"Ma, I can't. I have a date!"

I lied and told my parents John was twenty, thinking he'd sound safer if he was under legal drinking age. I'm sure they were still freaked out. What would a twenty-year-old want with their barely sixteen-year-old daughter? Well, they knew exactly what—but what could they say? They hadn't given me a ruling on the age of my date. John picked me up that night with a wrapped birthday present tucked under his arm and took me out to dinner.

We spent the next few months making out in his blue, two-door secondhand Monte Carlo, and I was crazy about him. With John, I broke from the confines of my strict childhood for good.

He'd take me into bars and order me colorful, frothy girl drinks that tasted like fruit punch but were loaded with gin. And after my years of being held under lock and key by the Food Marshal, John offered this starving girl a banquet, and I devoured it all. We were regulars at Shakey's Pizza, where we'd have seconds and thirds at their all-you-can-eat buffet and wash it down with cheap, warm beer. Ours was a young love of appetites. After years of pent-up desire and denial, John was my portal to all the pleasures of the senses.

Almost all. After months of making out, I still insisted on saving myself for marriage. It drove John so crazy that one rare night when my parents and brothers were all out of the house, he drove over, parked his car on the street behind ours, and climbed over our neighbor's fence to get to me. It was very *Romeo and Juliet*. We always had an incredibly hot time together, but still I refused to "do it."

Until the day came when I changed my mind.

I'd kept in touch with my junior high buddy Sue since I left Illinois, and we updated each other about our various shenanigans with constant letters. She was the first person I consulted about my monumental decision:

Dear Sue,

I'm pretty sure I've made the decision to DO IT with John. . . .

WITH ALL THIS drama going on in my life, I didn't notice what was going on with my mother.

First, there was the sudden departure of our poodle, Fluffy. We'd brought her with us from Illinois, and she was more mine than anyone's—she often slept in my bed with me. But she was a mean dog, the kind who'd growl if you nudged her with your foot. And she also was epileptic, and she'd have seizures on occasion. I loved her, but I was never home, and my mother was having a tough time taking care of her.

One day I came home from school and Fluffy was nowhere to be found. I checked inside my closet, where we kept her bed, but it was gone. I found my mother in the backyard, watering the flowers.

"Mom, where's Fluffy? I can't find her!"

"Well, honey," she said, as she kept watch on the water, "I decided Fluffy needed a new home. You kids don't pay any attention to her, so I found a home for her with a woman and her young daughter out in the country where she can run and have fun. She's gone to live with this lady."

I was stunned. I couldn't believe she'd gotten rid of the dog without talking to any of us first. I burst into tears, and when my brothers got home from school, I dropped the bomb: "Mommy gave Fluffy away!" Soon we were all crying, and my mother felt terrible.

Two weeks later, we got a postcard from Fluffy in the mail, in my mother's handwriting:

Dear Debbie, Rob, and Kevin—

I wanted to let you know that I love my new home. The little girl here is so nice to me. We play all the time and I love running free in the country.

Love,
Fluffy

At some point, my brothers and I came to believe that our mother did Fluffy in (*"done her in!"* as Eliza Doolittle would say). I mean, who'd take in an old, sick, mean dog?

It was all very strange. Something was going on in our house that I couldn't put my finger on, but it felt like an unhinging. One morning soon after, as Dad left for work he told Mom to have the backyard brush area cut before he returned home. Our yard backed up to a ravine, and beyond our property line a thick row of brush grew wild and messed up the neat edge of our lawn. Dad hated that.

I was too busy sunbathing on the upper deck to help my mother, who was slaving away (burning a lot of calories!), using shovels, pruners, and other implements of garden torture to uproot that stubborn brush. Rob was trying to help her, but they were getting nowhere fast, and time was ticking away.

She never explained her thought process to me later, but I can imagine how it must have played out in her mind. She looked at her watch, saw how late it was, and panicked.

We don't want him to be angry, she would have thought. She would have looked around desperately, trying to come up with a solution for the tight spot she was in, and saw the cans of gasoline in the garage. Suddenly, Mom was inspired with a brilliant idea.

I'll burn it off!

Rob described later how she methodically sprinkled gas along the edge of our boundary line, told him to stand back against the house, and then dramatically tossed a match to it.

A few minutes later, from the deck, I smelled smoke. A minute after that, I heard the shrill sound of sirens getting louder, and closer. I jumped up and looked down to the yard and saw Rob running in and out of the house, carrying buckets.

And there was Mom, standing in the middle of the backyard in her bathing suit, holding her hose up high like a graceful statue in an ornate fountain, trying to douse the flames.

In front of her, our yard was ablaze.

5

Wild Things

SOON AFTER THE grass-burning incident, I was worried my mother would hurt herself.

I woke up after midnight to the sound of sobbing coming from her room and rushed in. She was lying in bed, under the blankets, crying to my father over the phone and threatening to take pills. On the bedside table next to her was a bottle of sleeping medication.

After years of fighting and making up, Mom and Dad had finally decided to separate a few weeks earlier. Dad had moved to Newport Beach and Mom was distraught—and, from the looks of it, suicidal. I didn't know all the details of why they split, and I didn't want to. I assumed there were dalliances on Dad's end and that everything had finally combusted, like Mom's backyard inferno.

I'd never seen my mother so broken. I immediately dove into "caretaker" mode—something I was by now used to with Mom. I stayed calm, to the point of numbness, and carefully took the white princess phone from her hand.

"Dad, Mom is hysterical and there's a bottle of sleeping pills on the nightstand."

"Debbie, put your mother back on this phone."

"No."

I sat on the bed next to my mother and got it out of her, through tears, that she hadn't taken any pills, thank God. I slipped the bottle into my nightgown pocket and got back on the phone.

"I'm hanging up now, Dad. Mom's had enough talking with you for tonight."

He mumbled something about how he was not the only guilty party and that I should ask her about a few things, but I didn't care to hear any more. I put the pretty phone back on the receiver to tend to Mom. She'd quieted down a bit, and I sat with her a while, until she fell asleep. As I watched her, I vowed to myself that I would never, ever, *ever*, be so crazy about a man that I'd be driven to this.

IRONICALLY, THOUGH, MOM and Dad's little drama made me cling to John even more. And their behavior inspired a sense of lawlessness in me.

With Dad out of the house, and clearly not following church rules, I let a wildness take over me and finally took the plunge with John. I didn't want what Mom and Dad had in a relationship, but at the same time, with all that was going on, I held on to John like he was a life preserver in a raging storm at sea.

Our first time together was on the living room floor at John's parents' house. It wasn't exactly the fulfillment of all my youthful fantasies, and afterwards I felt guilty. It was the same tug of war I'd felt since childhood, between what I was taught was the right, good-girl thing to do and what I actually wanted to do. I knew sex before marriage was "wrong" according to church teaching. John was Christian, too—he had even started singing in the church choir with me. But he obviously didn't think it was wrong. And neither of us intended to stop. In my teenage heart, I was in love with John and I wanted to explore it further. Those guilty feelings, I found, would quiet down with a handful of cookies or a burger and fries.

And, as I had been learning and observing throughout my entire childhood, relationships between men and women were complicated and changeable. Six months after they split, Mom and Dad called a family meeting to tell us they were getting back together.

"Your mother and I have made amends," my father explained to me, Rob, and Kevin as we sat like a row of ducks on the living room couch, "and we're all going to try to be a family again." This new trying included going to church together every Sunday as a family again.

As Dad spoke, I looked over at Mom, sitting a few feet away on the love seat. She was looking up at Dad adoringly, then turned and gave me a reassuring nod and smile. *Why is she putting up with this?* I asked myself. *How many times is she going to go through this?*

After Dad returned home, he and Mom began noticing the steamed-up windows of John's car parked in our driveway and they jumped into high alert, DEFCON 1 mode.

First, they tried to find out if we were actually having sex— they did everything except ask me directly. One weekend when my parents went out of town with my brothers for a family gathering, I invited John over. We pulled out the hide-a-bed downstairs in the family room and had ourselves a romantic weekend for two. Come Sunday night, it was time to shoo John away and wash the sheets before the sex marshals returned. As I was putting the sheets into the washing machine, I noticed something in one corner of the bottom sheet: a tiny, seemingly random, but very specific, black pen mark.

Ugh!!!!! Mother!!!

She knew that if John and I were having sex, we'd sleep there and that I'd wash the sheets afterward. The disappearing pen mark would be her proof! And now that I'd already stripped the bed, I had no idea which corner of the bed she had positioned the dot on. I was so ticked off, I was determined to outsmart her at her own game. I washed and dried the sheets, and put a pen mark on all four corners of the sheet so that whichever one she looked at, she'd see her dot and think, "Oh, I guess she's not doing anything wrong."

Of course, if she saw all four dots I'd be found out, but I took my chances. After they returned home, Mom never mentioned a thing so . . . chalk one up for the daughter.

Until . . . I woke up in the middle of the night a few weeks later to the shocking brightness of my bedroom light and Mom standing over my bed. In her hand she held a packet of birth-control pills she'd found in my drawers. I had no intention of ending up in the same situation my mother had found herself in at sixteen. I'd been taking them for a few months by the time Mom shoved the evidence in my face.

"What's this, Debbie?"

Gulp.

"Oh, ummm . . . what, what? Oh, *that*," I said, stalling, till I could think up a story. "Mom, it's not mine. They belong to a girlfriend."

"You swear?"

"Yes, Mom, I swear. I'm holding on to them for her so that her mother won't find it."

"But Debbie, I see a week of pills missing."

"Yeah, well . . . that's because . . . I've been taking a pill to her every day at school."

I don't know how I thought that up half asleep, but it was good enough that she accepted it—for the time being.

A few weeks later, she finally tried to talk to me about it. We were in the car, as usual, but this time I was driving. Mom and I had never talked about her getting pregnant before marrying my father after that day she scolded me for counting on my fingers. Now I could see she was trying to warn me, but without saying too much. I could see she was afraid that history might repeat itself with me, and it scared her. She wanted to caution me, but at the same time she didn't want me to think of myself as an "accident." It was quite the balancing act.

"You know, Debbie," she began, "your father and I always

wanted you. From the moment we knew I was pregnant, there wasn't a second we ever thought anything else but that we would have you and be married . . ."

"Mom," I said, shaking my head. I was tired of secrets. "Nobody is pregnant and unmarried at sixteen in 1960 and *happy* about it. I'm sorry. I know that you and Dad love me, and that you did the absolute best that you could. But let's be honest, you had to be scared shitless."

Mom flinched at my language. I didn't curse much, so she was surprised. And she knew I was right. She was scared shitless then, and she was scared shitless now—this time, for me.

My father wasn't as subtle as my mother.

One night a few weeks later, I was late for my ten p.m. curfew. I was at John's, of course; we were fooling around in his car in the driveway. My father knew where he lived, and at midnight we heard a loud knock on John's car—on the steamed-up passenger side, where I was sitting—and there stood my dad. I rolled down the fogged window.

"Get in," he said to me, motioning for me to get into the family car and come home with him.

The next morning, he had a serious meeting with John at a nearby restaurant.

"Are you aware that you are committing statutory rape?" he said to John. "Are you aware you are committing a crime with my daughter? Do you have real feelings for her? Does she mean more to you than just sex? You are not going to steal my daughter's future away from her, do you understand?"

My poor father; he was just as afraid as my mother. They took away my driver's license for a few months and grounded me and threatened me and pleaded with me, but there was no use. I was a crazy teenager who thought she was in love, and the more they tried to pull me away from him, the more I was desperate to see him. Until finally one morning, they gave in . . . or gave up.

Mom was driving me to school and, with a sigh, she said something to me I never thought I'd hear.

"Debbie, I think maybe it's time for you to go on birth control—if you are not already."

Clearly, my parents, at their wits' end, must have decided that if they couldn't stop me from sinning and save me from the fires of eternal, damning hell . . . they could stop me from making the same mistake they did.

I WAS SO consumed with the drama of John that my schoolwork was suffering. I was even failing phys ed. How do you fail phys ed? You don't show up. It was my last class of the day, and I hated it; I was uncomfortable moving around and showering in front of all the skinny girls. And John got off work right about that time. He'd gotten a new job driving tour groups around, and at some point he'd moved out of his parents' house and gotten an apartment. He'd come pick me up with the bus before my last period and we'd take off.

I went to speak to the gym teacher and beg for leniency. We made a deal that in exchange for a passing grade, I would come in early every day for a semester and clean the locker rooms. Which is how I got my (thankfully temporary) nickname from her and the other kids in school—"Cinderella."

But the problem was bigger than that, of course. One morning I was pulled out of class and told to report to the counselor's office.

"You're skipping classes, your grades are dropping, and . . . you're gaining weight," she said, looking at me from across her desk, truly worried. "What's going on with you? Are you okay?"

I hadn't expected her to be so compassionate and I choked on my answer. What was I supposed to tell her, the truth? That I felt myself getting obsessed and out of control, that my parents were having problems and I was worried about my mother, that I felt guilty about everything I did and I was destined for hell for all of eternity?

"Nothing's going on," I told her. "Nothing . . . nothing."

She was right; I was packing on pounds like a snowball speeding downhill, gaining momentum and size as it barreled down.

In the year since John and I started dating, my weight had jumped from 155 to 175. Part of it was because I had turned sixteen and could now drive and had the freedom to get junk food on a whim, and eat as much as I wanted without anyone wagging a finger. It was easy to stop off at Burger King on the way home, scarf down a Whopper, fries, and shake as I zigzagged through the streets, then dispose of the crumpled wrapping-paper evidence. My part-time job at Del Taco that year didn't help, either. I probably consumed a burrito for every five I rang up at the cash register.

My bad habits kept escalating—like a speeding car, I was a wreck waiting to happen—until one early evening I crashed in one grand, dramatic, symbolic collision.

My parents had sent me to pick up Rob at the movie theater and on the way I stopped in at Burger King for my usual driving meal. I was driving and eating, heading westward, with the setting sun in my eyes. I remember looking in the rearview mirror and seeing a motorcyclist behind me as I leaned over to take a sip of my chocolate shake, and then . . .

The rest was in slow motion. The cyclist flipped over the roof of the car and was knocked out cold. Then, a flash of images: people saying, "We've called for help" and someone getting me out of the car and sitting me down on the curb . . . fire trucks, ambulances, and then . . . the sight of my father standing above me.

Dad whisked me out of there and got me home, then went to the hospital to check on the cyclist. He had regained consciousness, but when the doctors gave him a drug for shock he had a horrifying allergic reaction that left him paralyzed from the waist down for days. Needless to say, I was a basket case; we all were. My parents even let John come over to console me so I wouldn't sink into depressed oblivion.

Thankfully, once the drug wore off, the man's paralysis disappeared. Soon after he was released from the hospital, the man drove past our pretty, upper-middle-class home and decided to sue us for hundreds of thousands of dollars, even though he had completely recovered and was fine. The lawsuit hung over my father for two years, until it was dismissed.

I was too scared and ashamed to admit to anyone that I'd been paying attention to the food I was gobbling up instead of the road when I mowed that man down.

BUT I KEPT eating, and gaining weight. At least I had my singing and music to sustain me. It was the one thing God told me to do that I obeyed.

In my final year of high school, our drama teacher chose *The Music Man* as that year's musical. I had begged and pleaded with her to choose *My Fair Lady* so that I could sing Eliza and realize my childhood fantasy onstage, but she stood firm with *Music Man*. I auditioned for the lead role of Marian the Librarian, played by Shirley Jones in the 1962 film. My only real competition for the part was a slim, pretty, and talented classmate named Yvonne, who was a year younger than me. We both auditioned and I got the part and was elated.

As I was leaving school that day, after auditions, I passed Yvonne's boyfriend in the hall.

"Hey, Voigt," he said, "congratulations on getting the part."

"Oh, thank you!"

"You must have got it because of your *figure*," he said, with a sneer.

I was speechless. I kept walking and held in the tears, pushed them down. How could he say something so cruel? It was the first time someone outside my home had made me feel really bad about how I looked. It was the first time I really, truly understood I was fat. Not chubby, not big-boned, not voluptuous—*fat*. But music wasn't about how a person looked, it was about talent and ordained gifts and ability. It was the one place that wasn't touched by my crazy life, my crazy eating. Or so I had hoped.

The following year, that same drama teacher put on *My Fair Lady*, with lithe and pretty Yvonne in the romantic lead. I had pleaded for that part, but I guess I was too big to play Eliza. I wasn't a romantic lead, I didn't fit the dress.

By graduation, I was tipping the scales at 190 pounds.

I stood on the bathroom scale, wondering how, at my size, I was ever going to sing and perform like my idol, Karen Carpenter, who was getting skinnier and skinnier as I got fatter and fatter. And how was I going to sing the Broadway show tunes and play the parts I loved if I was expected to be slim like Yvonne? God had told me I was meant to sing, and I trusted He was going to lead me in the right direction and onto the right road, but lately my own navigating skills were not so good.

I had to think up a new path to get me wherever it was I was supposed to go. I had to find a place in music where my career would not depend on my weight and my looks. After a bit of research, I registered at Chapman College (now Chapman University) to study choral conducting at their music conservatory. The school was highly regarded and was just a twenty-minute drive from home, though I had every intention of living on campus.

It was time for me to be on my own and sort myself out. It was time for me to separate from my parents and make concrete decisions and move on. Apparently, my father was in the same frame of mind.

One day before I left for school, I was watching TV in the family room with Mom when Dad called her to come upstairs. When she returned, a few minutes later, she crumpled into a chair next to me—crying and defeated, like that day in the Laundromat, but worse.

"What's wrong, Mom?"

Before she answered, I already knew, just by looking at her. After all the years of arguments, separations, reunions, and recriminations, my parents' marriage was finally broken beyond repair.

"Your father asked me for a divorce," she said.

She buried her face in her hands and cried and cried.

ACT II

ACCELERANDO

6

When the Student Is Ready

CONVENIENTLY, THE LITTLE convenience store was only a five-minute walk from my dorm.

Every day, instead of going to class, I'd sleep until noon, then walk over and stock up: Ruffles potato chips, onion dip, and my new discovery, Pepperidge Farm's three-layer coconut cake with vanilla frosting. And diet soda—always diet soda. Had to save on calories somewhere. Back in my room, I'd attack the cake with a fork and eat the whole damn thing, then I'd start on the chips and dip, and binge until I passed out.

I'd wake up later surrounded by the smashed cardboard cake boxes and torn-open Ruffles bags, icing and onion dip smeared across my mouth, like a vampire after a violent feeding frenzy.

I was now about six months into my first year at Chapman, and it was not going well. I hated my classes and started skipping them around month two, then finally dropped out halfway into my second semester, I was so miserable. I had a nightmare roommate for the first three months, an exchange student from China who cooked up strange and unknown concoctions in her wok in the room and walked in on me and John even if I'd looped a tie on the doorknob, as per our prearranged signal.

"On the door! The tie! Didn't you see it?" I'd explode, as John dove for cover under the sheets.

WHEN I'D STARTED school, John and I sort of broke up, but not really. He was going to be out of town a lot for his bus-driving job, and I had to concentrate on my studies, so we decided we'd go with the flow, maybe see other people. I wasn't going with the flow so well. John would visit me at my dorm, but when he wasn't with me, I'd go into stalking mode. I'd heard he was dating a friend's sister, so I'd drive by her apartment to see if his car was there. If it was, I'd park and prowl through the alleyway behind the girl's apartment and peek into her kitchen window through a crack in the drapes, trying to catch them together.

The pressure of being alone at school, coupled with my parents' split and John's being away, threw my usual clingy nature—and my eating—into high gear.

It's not as though my parents' split came as a surprise. I knew from age five that they shouldn't be together. Still, I was having a hard time handling it, handling everything. On top of all this, I had a voice teacher at school intent on torturing me. In class, we studied operatic history and had vocal workshops, and once a week I separately met with this vocal coach for one-on-one sessions in her studio.

She had an ugly, squeaky voice and instructed me to watch myself in a giant, full-length mirror as I sang. Every time I looked in that mirror and opened my mouth, I felt like I was looking in one of those distorting funhouse mirrors that make you look blown-up and grotesque. I tried to sing but instead I'd burst into tears.

"Debbie, what's the matter?" she'd ask, impatiently, in her grating voice.

"I can't do it. Why must I do this? I'm not going to have a mirror in front of me when I'm performing. What's the point?"

"You need to see what you are doing with your facial muscles and mouth and jaw as you sing. Why is this so hard for you? All my other students do it."

Why was it not obvious to her why it was so hard for me? In my first two months at school, I had packed on a whopping thirty pounds (how was that even physically possible?), and to look at my reflection was to confront how unhappy I was. I wasn't inspecting how my larynx and diaphragm worked in tandem, or how the roof of my mouth vibrated. All I saw was my sadness and pain.

After a dozen lessons and crying jags, I stopped going to her and went instead to the convenience store for more coconut cake to shove down my larynx.

I HAD BOLDLY struck out on my own to start a new life, but I wasn't emotionally equipped for any of it. I didn't know how to deal with my feelings about my parents, about John, about my difficulties in school . . . so I stuffed them down with cake, a sweet tranquilizer. Whenever my parents telephoned, I'd tell them, "Everything's great! Classes are great!"

After I officially dropped my classes, I isolated myself in my dorm room and was a complete mess—overwhelmed with emptiness and despair. I got a stern notice from the school to vacate. Without my parents knowing, I took the reimbursed tuition money Dad had paid and moved into an apartment with some girlfriends. I would have gotten away with it, too, if the school hadn't mailed my father a receipt that summer, itemizing the monies returned to him due to my incomplete course work.

My parents were livid, and I couldn't blame them. I spent the next two years drifting in and out of meaningless office jobs with no direction, and no faith in anything. Since my parents' separation I'd attended Sunday church services less and less. Church became more of a job for me than a place of worship: I was hired by churches of various denominations that had a lot of money and could afford to bring in a soloist—like the big Presbyterian church at Leisure

World nearby—to beef up the sound of their choirs. During the sermons, I'd zone out. It was a way to keep singing somehow, to keep
me near God somehow.

I still had my faith in God; it was people (myself included) I
wasn't so sure about.

And I still had faith in the music itself.

Even depressed and aimless, I kept up with my private voice lessons. I still wanted to be a musician, and I still believed God wanted
me to sing, but maybe I was meant to do it differently. My new half-
hearted plan was to marry John and get a job as a high school choir
teacher in a small town where John could get a job as a local DJ—he
had by now left his driving job and signed up as a communications
major at Cal State Fullerton. I would live a simple, quiet life . . . perform a concert once in a while maybe. I would still sing.

But, oh, God and His mysterious ways. Once again, having lost
my way, I was plucked from my inertia and set on a new path.

The nearby Garden Grove Community Church (it would later
become the famous Crystal Cathedral) was holding auditions for
their production of *The Sound of Music* and I couldn't resist. I would
have died and gone to heaven to sing the role of Maria, but I didn't
dare audition for her—I knew my size would make it impossible to
be considered for the part. Instead, I auditioned for and won the role
of the Mother Abbess. During rehearsals I discovered that pastor
Robert Schuller's wife, Arvella, was a die-hard opera fan and had
created a scholarship at the church for young singers who wanted
to train in opera. Again, opera had never been my favorite music
genre, but I could sing it. And another plus about opera was that
I didn't have to be a waif—opera singers were big girls, like me.
I applied for the scholarship and auditioned at the Cathedral a few
weeks later, and got it; it was that simple. The money I won afforded
me to study with a new voice teacher, Nancy Estes, at the church—
but not for long.

One day as I performed "Sebben, crudele" ("Tho, not deserving") from the Caldara opera *La costanza in amor vince l'inganno* (it means: faithfulness in love conquers treachery), my voice rose up to the vaulted ceiling. Nancy stared at me silently when I was finished.

"Debbie, you've got to do something with your voice. You've got to sing."

"What do you mean? I *am* singing. I've got my church jobs and—"

"That's not enough." She shook her head. "You really, really have talent," she said and walked over to me and put her hands on my shoulders. She shook me a little, as if she was trying to wake me up.

"Listen to me. Please. You *really* have talent. Your voice is a gift and you've got to do something about it."

You are meant to sing.

A MONTH LATER, I was enrolled on a full scholarship as a voice major at California State University, Fullerton, studying with the head of the vocal department, Jane Paul. Nancy had pressed her number into my hand and urged me to call her. After I sang a few arias for Jane in her living room, she nodded. "The timbre, the warmth of your voice . . . yes, I'd like to work with you."

Jane would be the most influential voice teacher in my life. Not only would she become my coach on and off over the next fifteen years, but she'd also become my dearest friend and biggest supporter and encourager.

The program at Cal State focused on classical training and opera, a genre I was still warming up to. The conductor at one of my church jobs gave me a record of Puccini's *Tosca* sung by Spanish soprano Montserrat Caballé as a gift and I listened to it, but I didn't *love* it. I was encouraged, though, by the photo of Caballé on the album cover; she was a large woman like me.

Soon after that I attended my first live operatic concert. Beverly Sills passed through town on her "farewell" tour and I was moved to tears when she spoke about the "joy and passion" she felt for her career, and that she hoped to help other young singers realize their dream to sing opera. So while I wasn't one to listen to or attend operas as a fan, I was drawn to the passion of it, to the pure *doing* of it.

When I sang in the safety of Jane's studio in Placentia, I could feel myself connect with the music. There was something basic, something primal, something timeless that happened when I opened my mouth and became one with the melody. Everything else fell away—every problem vanished, nothing else existed or even mattered: it was simply my beating heart connecting with the beating heart of the composer and the beating heart of whoever might be listening.

It was love. It was God. And it moved me.

Jane watched all this happen as I sang in front of her, and she understood. She'd been a dramatic soprano herself and had sung the same repertoire I was working on. She was in her mid-fifties and saucy, smart, played in a rock-and-roll band, and loved all arts with a passion. Her studio was decorated with prints of her favorite painter, Gustav Klimt, and I stared at the vibrant posters of lovers kissing and nude bodies intertwined as we went through her big books of Brahms and Strauss for thirty minutes, twice a week.

Unlike that squeaky voice teacher at Chapman, Jane and I clicked right away, and she immediately understood my strengths and vulnerabilities as a vocalist and performer.

"You don't want to sing in front of the mirror?" she asked me, "then don't! Debbie, you're not going to sing in front of a mirror for the rest of your career, you are going to sing from *sensation*." Jane made a fist and put her hand on my heart and gave my rib cage a soft *thump*. "It's not about how the singing looks from the outside, it's about what you feel here—inside."

We got to work. She told me I had a very "naturally placed" voice, that I was very much "in the mask," as we call it in the opera world, which means my voice was coming from a solid place at the front of my face. Many girls in the teen years go through a very breathy stage, but I never did; I always had a very focused, large sound, which was good, said Jane, and a good middle range. "But you have no top," she noted. "You have a strong low voice, but your top needs work."

Because she got me so well, Jane could employ unique little tricks that helped me connect my emotions to the music in a way that I could understand.

"Much of singing is imaginary," she told me. "It's not enough to have a beautiful voice. You have to have the imagination to know how to use it."

During one session, when I was trying to breathe from deep in my diaphragm, she said to me, "Debbie, you must imagine that you have a straw running up through your body and that the air is rushing up and pouring out." And it worked.

At that time there was a commercial on TV for the cereal Rice Krispies, and the advertisement showed an everyday American family sitting around the breakfast table, singing "Vesti la giubba," the heartbreaking aria from Leoncavallo's *Pagliacci*. Because the cereal box was empty, the family sang with intense dramatic suffering, *"Noooo mooooore Rice Krisssssspiessssss!"* It was funny, and Jane was fond of referring to it. Whenever I was singing and I wasn't giving enough passion from the *inside*, Jane would tap her hand on the piano.

"More Rice Krispies, Debbie! More Rice Krispies!"

And I knew exactly what she meant and wanted—more emotion, more connection with the beating heart of the music. Because that is what touches people, she taught me. Yes, a technically beautiful voice touches people on its own, there's no question about that. But there had to be something behind it, something under it—something giving it meaning. And that something, said Jane, is what separates the opera singers from the opera stars. It is what makes an audience feel. And you can't teach that or buy that, says Jane—you must be born with it.

Jane was a diligent musician, a whiz at the piano—and a real taskmaster, which I needed because of my history of skipping classes and sinking into a state of self-doubt and coconut cake. But Jane was also very kind and loving—perhaps what I needed most in a teacher, and in a friend. She provided a safe environment for me to expose my vulnerabilities as a young woman and as a singer. Singing is such a personal, intimate activity, you cannot separate yourself from it.

So much so, that I often cried during my lessons when there was something I couldn't get right.

"I'll never get it, I'll never get it!" I'd moan.

"Shut up and let me teach you!" She knew how to handle the likes of me. Jane understood my tears; she was a musician-whisperer.

"Music is a journey, for the singer as well as the audience," she'd say, consoling me. "To get to what happens beyond *here*," she pointed to her lips, "we have to get to what happens *here*," she pointed to her heart. "It is not like an instrument, where you make a mistake and you adjust your fingers. With singing, you are exposing yourself.

"Now, for heaven's sakes," she'd say, getting back to business, "let me teach you voice instead of being your psychiatrist!"

Because we were both dramatic sopranos, we found we shared a similar emotional depth and intensity—something one needs when singing the repertoire of grand characters with big, emotional arcs. The range of emotional growth and feelings experienced by Wagner's shieldmaiden, Brünnhilde, during the course of the epic Ring Cycle, for example, can't be compared to that of Mozart's young chambermaid, Susanna, in *The Marriage of Figaro*. Jane and I were made of the same stuff in that way, and that also added to our kinship. I felt so comfortable with her that I could talk to her and cry to her about anything—even my weight.

While at Cal State, the numbers on the scale kept rising. I was living at home and had resumed my fast-food-in-the-front-seat habit. By my early twenties I had reached size 22—my biggest yet. But opera singers were allowed to be big, right? I had my *Tosca* photo of Caballé, and I knew Beverly Sills was hefty in her earlier years before she lost seventy-five pounds.

A friend of Jane's who was also active in the opera world, set me straight on that delusion.

I had recently endured a costume fitting at school for an upcoming performance, but now nothing was fitting, of course, and I was telling Jane about it when in walked the chain-smoking friend—he always had a cigarette in his mouth and a vodka in his hand. He called me "Doobie"—I'm not sure if it was because he was always tipsy and he wasn't enunciating, or because he had a predilection for mind-altering substances. Either way, he had heard our chat and gave me the hard dope on my size.

"You will have this problem in every costume fitting you go to, my dear," he said, sloshing the ice around in his glass, "if you don't do something about your weight."

Jane started to give him a look, like, *Don't go there.* But he was determined to give me sage advice.

"Doobie, the best way to lose the weight is with cocaine. You should try it."

Jane and I were both startled, and in my mind I thought: *Like I really need another addiction.*

EVERY SEMESTER AT Cal State, the voice majors had to perform in front of a "jury" and it was nerve-wracking. It was like a vocal exam, and I had to present ten songs I was working on and have them memorized. Memory work was a challenge for me. I had no problem as a little girl memorizing pop ballads, or entire Broadway albums at age three. But learning these operas in other languages was difficult for me and I never felt completely ready. Even today, I experience that same feeling of terror and unpreparedness whether I'm about to perform at Teatro alla Scala in Milan, or in front of a table of college professors in Southern California. I always procrastinated and began preparing too late, never felt ready, and would show up at Jane's studio before each jury in tears.

"The jury is tomorrow and I can't remember a word," I cried. "I can't do this."

Jane would sit me down and hand me a tissue and talk me through my nervousness.

"What other songs do you know? Let's put together a list, you can change the lineup, they won't care. All they want is to see progress in your singing technique."

Jane saved my sanity too many times to count over the two and a half years I was at Cal State, and many times during the years and decades after that. I think maybe she was the very first person I truly, truly trusted in my life. That's probably why she was the very first person I told my secret to.

We were in her studio and I was, once again, in tears—this time it was about something to do with John, I can't remember what. Jane kept trying to talk to me about getting out and auditioning, but I was sulking over John in that insecure, clingy way I had.

"Debbie, how dedicated are you to your career as an opera singer?"

"What do you mean? I'm very dedicated!" I told her. I had been entering competitions and winning money at that point. I remember winning $1,000 as a prize, and that was a lot of money for me at that age. I felt a certain amount of authentication that I'd actually won and earned that money, it was big. But that was just the beginning, in Jane's eyes. And she didn't want anything to get in the way of what lay ahead.

She was concerned about my relationship with John, she went on to say, and how it would impact my career choices. Will I be willing to travel, to uproot myself, to live out of a suitcase if I stay with John?

"He lacks ambition," she said. "I'm worried you won't push forward if you stay with him. And you have so much talent."

I looked up above her piano and stared at her poster of Klimt's *Kiss* for a moment. I wasn't sure how to explain to Jane that my seriousness and dedication to my career wasn't a random choice, it was divinely inspired. It had been nearly ten years since that early dawn light streamed into my bedroom and I'd heard the voice of God. I had never spoken about that experience with anyone—not my parents, not anyone at church, and not even my close friend Sue. I wasn't sure how to word it, how to start.

"Jane," I said, quietly, "something happened to me when I was a teenager that I've never told anyone about. It was surreal . . ."

I told her every detail—the light, the voice, and what He said— and Jane's eyes welled up with tears. I started to cry, too. I was both embarrassed and overwhelmed at finally saying the words out loud to someone, the moment had been locked up in my heart and imagination for so long.

"You don't doubt what happened for a minute, do you?" she asked. For Jane, what I described did not take a leap of faith to believe. She and I had talked about God before and she knew how I felt about my faith.

"I don't believe that was a dream for one second," she said, standing up as if for emphasis. "The first time I heard you sing, I knew you had a voice that could do anything and that you were meant to use it."

We hugged, cried some more, and then got to work on the next piece. Now more than ever, Jane was determined to make sure I fulfilled my God-given instructions.

At her urging, I auditioned for two major opera companies even though I still had another year to go at Cal State.

The first was for the Metropolitan Opera National Council Auditions (every year the Met sponsored a competition to help develop new young singers). I went to New York, and among my listeners that day were: the famous pianist and conductor James Levine; the Met's longtime general manager, Joseph Volpe; and Matthew Epstein, who was both the guru of the opera world at the time and an impresario at Columbia Artists Management. (Joe Volpe began his career as a carpenter at the Met and moved up the ranks until he was running the place—a lot of people respected him greatly for that.)

But the illustrious company didn't make me terribly nervous. That's the irony of the early auditions and performances: you are so new and nobody knows you, and you don't know them, so you don't feel a heavy weight of pressure. You go out there and open your mouth and there's this young, big, beautiful Voice with a capital "V" that no one's heard before and they get all excited and say things like, "We haven't heard a voice like that since Jessye Norman!"

So I belted it out on the Met stage, singing the arias Jane and I worked on, and I was one of a handful of winners. Everybody was buzzing as I got off the stage. I passed by Matthew Epstein, who was known to be very opinionated and blunt. He congratulated me.

"Your career's about to start," he said. I smiled, and probably blushed a bit.

"Now all you gotta do," he added, "is sustain it for the next twenty-five years."

I laughed at what he said, not knowing that years later his words would prove to be absolutely right. I was soon to enter the honeymoon phase of my career where I couldn't get a bad review, couldn't take a wrong step, couldn't lose a competition. I would soon become a new, glittery toy that everyone would be excited to play with. But that's the easy part—then you've got to sustain it. What are you going to do ten years, twenty years down the road to keep an audience, and yourself, interested?

I never forgot his words. And looking back, I realized that most of the joy I experienced in my career indeed came during that early phase. There were no expectations, and you're the new kid—you're *fantastic*. You open your mouth, you're dumb, you're naïve, but the voice just comes out. You love it. They love you. You don't really know if you're bad or good, but . . . *look what I can do*. It isn't until the audience and the press and the administration at the opera houses start to know you that the bar gets raised.

Actually, right after I'd won the Met audition, you might say my "fantastic" quality had already begun to diminish. At least in the Met's eyes. But it had nothing to do with my voice. As one of the winners, I was served my first dose of weight discrimination. I was invited to have a one-on-one meeting with the executive director of the Metropolitan Opera National Council Auditions, Larry Stayer, who was looking for candidates for the Met's Young Artist Development Program. He ran the program with Risë Stevens, the wonderful, retired mezzo-soprano from the Bronx, who was also famous for being very beautiful and very thin. I was clearly one of the best singers they'd seen that year, but they didn't invite me to join the Young Artist's Program.

"We're not sure we want to take you right now," Ms. Stevens told me, "but . . . don't accept any offers from any other programs until you talk to me first, okay?"

Then she added some off-the-record advice: "I think you have a glorious voice, but if you don't do something about your weight, you won't have a career."

I was hurt by the comment, of course. I figured if they really wanted me, my weight wouldn't matter. So I didn't call them before accepting another offer.

My other audition that year was for the apprentice program at the San Francisco Opera company. Every year they held rigorous auditions for up to a thousand hopefuls and winnowed the number down to twenty-three singers who would then enter the company's prestigious Merola Opera Program, a summer of intense voice, body, and acting training. From there, one could advance to their

Western Opera Theater tour that lasted five months, and finally to the program's third tier, the two-year Adler Fellowship program in residence, where you take master classes, do small roles at the opera, and understudy leads.

Jane and I worked hard for months preparing five arias that would be my go-to audition arias in the future: "Leise leise, fromme Weise" (from Weber's *Der Freischütz*); "Come scoglio" (from Mozart's *Così fan tutte*); "Il est doux, il est bon" (from Massenet's *Hérodiade*); "Ernani, Ernani, involami" (from Verdi's *Ernani*); and "Nun eilt herbei, Witz, heit're Laune" (from Nicolai's *Die lustigen Weiber von Windsor*). When I got onstage for my audition, I had that coming-together feeling of preparation meeting opportunity: I won a place in the Merola Program for that summer.

I had done well at these two auditions, but in general, auditions would never be my strong suit. I never felt good about them because I was sensitive about being judged in general, and my weight added to my self-consciousness.

It's not that I'm not competitive—in fact, when I was in a competition I usually sang the piss out of whatever I was singing—and won. That's because in a competition it was all about "the voice"— and that voice could come in any package (or at least, in those days it could. Maybe not so much anymore).

But when I was auditioning, I walked into the room knowing that the person I was singing for had a preconceived idea of what they wanted the character to *look* like. Singers deal with that all the time, losing jobs sometimes even if they have the wrong eye color. After all, even Tosca is supposed to have brown eyes, telling the painter Cavaradossi to paint the Madonna's eyes brown to match her own. I was a blue-eyed, 300-pound Tosca and managed to pull that off. Had I auditioned for that role, I would have known from the outset that I didn't have the right look, and knowing that would have affected my performance.

I could never get to the same level of performance in an audition as I could in a competition, because how I looked was being scrutinized so closely. I can't recall a time when I ever got a job from an audition. In the early days, I often got roles by winning contests that had a performance attached to them—like the Tchaikovsky competition in 1990. The prize was a performance at the Ravenna Festival in Italy. From that, Italian conductor Riccardo Chailly heard me and invited me to sing in Bologna. I won a lot of roles when I paired "Leise leise" and "Sola, perduta, abbandonata" from Puccini's *Manon Lescaut* together in a competition, because the two arias are so dissimilar they showed my versatility. American conductor James Conlon, the current music director of the Los Angeles Opera, heard me sing those two arias at a competition very early in my career and it led to many future roles with him, starting with my debut and only official performance at La Scala in Weber's *Oberon* (though I must admit I cringe when I remember it: I squeezed all 290 pounds of me into a lime-green harem-pants-and-turban costume—not a great look for me).

The only audition I ever remember feeling sure I aced was for the Grand Opera of Geneva. I sang a Mozart, a Weber, and a Verdi—and sang them so well I was certain I'd get the job. Nope! I found out later from my manager that I didn't get it because I was so heavy—and that they'd made their decision about me the moment I walked out onstage. Still, they let me sing three very difficult arias. It's no wonder I was so sensitive about the audition process.

THE DECISION TO leave school early was one of the easiest decisions I ever made. I was twenty-four years old in the summer of '85, and my bags were packed and in the car, and so was John. We decided he'd leave his classes at Cal State, too, and come to San Francisco with me and we'd live together in sin. My parents weren't delighted about that, but they knew they couldn't tell me what to do anymore.

I didn't leave town without a little farewell performance, however. Two, to be exact.

I said goodbye to my parents and my childhood the best way I knew how—in song. Just before John and I took off, I sang at two weddings in the space of one week—strangely enough, for both of my parents. Mom had met Tim, a warehouse worker, at our church, and Dad had proposed to his secretary, Lynn. Dad got married on a Friday night in Newport Beach and had a reception at one of those eighteenth-century-themed restaurants with waitresses dressed as wenches; Mom got married at her new home in East Anaheim the following Saturday. I couldn't help but feel it was a race between them—*I'll show you, I'll get married, too!*

For Dad and his new wife, I sang Karen Carpenter's "We've Only Just Begun"; for Mom and her new husband, I sang "The Lord's Prayer." It was strange for me to be singing at my parents' weddings to other people. At the time, I didn't feel so ready to embrace these newcomers into the family. (Later, Lynn and I would become very close.) But I knew it was a time for changes and moving on, for me and for my parents, and that we all needed fresh starts with new people and new surroundings.

This time, leaving home was easy. I was stronger and had a definite path, and I wasn't doing it alone. After the weddings, I didn't stay around long for any encores—I was eager to get on my new road.

Leaving Jane, on the other hand, was emotional for both of us. Even though I planned to come back every few months to see her and continue our sessions when we could, we hugged goodbye in the driveway outside her house as John waited for me in the car, and we had one of our little cries. And just for old time's sake, I gave Jane a farewell dose of my classic low self-esteem rant, lest she miss it while I was gone.

"Jane, I don't know if I can do this . . . if I'll ever amount to anything."

"Be patient, Debbie. Have faith. Even if you don't know it, I've known it all along—you have it in you to do it."

Jane believed in me. The big question was, did I believe in me? John and I took off and drove north on Interstate 5, toward my future, whatever it might be.

(7)

Covering Butts

ONCE I ARRIVED in San Francisco, there was no turning back—my road was clear and I was moving forward with a single purpose: I was going to be an opera singer.

The next few years would consist of intense coaching in movement, acting, breath work, musical style, and role preparation . . . followed by four months touring the country on a Greyhound bus with my fellow apprentices . . . then two years studying small roles and understudying seven major operatic roles, including Donna Anna in Mozart's *Don Giovanni*, Fiordiligi in *Così fan tutte*, Lisa in Tchaikovsky's *Pique Dame*, Amelia in Verdi's *Un ballo in maschera*, and Leonora in Verdi's *Il trovatore*.

For the first time in my life, I was supporting myself fully with music. The company gave me a yearly salary of $35,000 and John found a job at a local Good Guys, selling electronics. We rented a little one-bedroom apartment on Franklin Street, two blocks from the opera house and in the heart of downtown San Francisco, sandwiched between City Hall and the Courthouse. It didn't occur to us to go to that Courthouse next door and get married—we planned to live in sin for a while and see where it took us.

SOME OF THE most invaluable roles for a young opera-singer-in-training are the ones that you understudy. In opera, we call understudies "covers"—I'm not sure why. I liked to call them the "cover your butts," and I covered many a well-sized butt in my early days (and later on, had my own butt covered).

I understudied for top sopranos like Leontyne Price, Kiri Te Kanawa, and Jessye Norman—the great divas of the era, because I sang in the same "fach" as they did. *Fach* is a German word meaning "compartment," and in the opera world we use it as a way to categorize voices. A singer's fach is his or her comfort zone, the place where one naturally belongs on the spectrum from bass baritone to coloratura soprano, the vocal range where one's voice is most natural, expressive, and powerful without strain.

Starting out in San Francisco, I was a "spinto" soprano, which meant I could push my voice ("spinto" means "pushed" in Italian) to reach large, dramatic climaxes. Jane Paul and I did a lot of work on strengthening my upper register when I was her student.

From there, the natural progression of my voice over time would grow and mature to being a "jugendlich-dramatischer" (a young dramatic soprano), and then, finally, a dramatic soprano, which is my category today, where I sing over big orchestras and perform roles of soaring gravitas.

Covering a lead role is both exhilarating and frustrating. To an opera singer trying to break into the scene, performing a coveted role in a major opera house could ignite one's career; all it takes is a sniffle coming from the leading lady's dressing room. But more often than not it's frustrating. You can sit in "the house" for hours and hours every day for the entire run of an opera, watching the person you are understudying rehearse and perform, and never get onstage to sing those arias yourself. It's tedious and exasperating because, as a singer, you have to have a certain amount of ego to start with (to my parents' dismay) and believe you can do the role. Sometimes, you even believe you can do it better than the person who's up there (and in some cases that may be true).

Sometimes you get so close to going on—you're wearing the

big gown, the big wig, the big makeup—that you can taste it. But then . . .

One of my first big "cover" assignments was to understudy Welsh soprano Dame Margaret Price, who was then very famous and poised to star as Amelia in *Un ballo in maschera* at the San Francisco Opera House.

It was several weeks before my cover assignment was to begin. I was on a bus at the time, traveling somewhere from Biloxi, Mississippi, to Wichita, Kansas: two dozen of us were on tour going from town to town with our production of *Don Giovanni*.

Twice a week, four singers in the group also performed "An Hour for the Opera" and did early-morning opera "variety" shows for schoolchildren before their classes began. Those were tough, because we had to get up at six a.m., often after being up late the night before with a show, and sleepwalk our way through costume and makeup while trying to find something to eat that the guys in the bus hadn't already gotten to. We all bitched and groaned because we were tired and not getting paid extra for it, but once we got onstage we loved it! The children, ranging in age from five to ten, would rush up and lean on the edge of the stage with their elbows, looking up at us with their little faces and eyes as big as saucers.

They were the best audiences ever, laughing out loud and clapping and shrieking when my character, Carmen, had a spat with Madame Butterfly. We really hammed it up for them, and sometimes it was hard for us to maintain our composure, especially when a little kid would be up front picking his nose when we'd barely digested our morning cereal. We were in small, small towns, in run-down little schools—I remember one was a paper-mill town with a population of 2,000—and these kids had never, ever seen anything remotely like these opera characters clowning around like crazy for them.

Life on the road was a kind of opera bootcamp. Some nights I sang the lead of Donna Anna, and on other nights I sang in the chorus. It was rigorous work, and we were a young, talented, driven-for-success, rowdy bunch. We learned how to get along with our colleagues on a day-to-day basis, we learned how to stay healthy on a bus where if one person got sick we all did (especially when there were late-night romances going on). Hours on the bus every day gave us "bus butt" and "bus hair" and "bus cramps," and we complained about it and laughed about it and endured it. But back to Ms. Price.

We had already been on the bus for several weeks when I got a panicked message from the opera house. Rehearsals hadn't even begun yet, but she was ill and had canceled. They were looking to replace her for the entire run. As her official cover, I was in the running.

"Get off the bus right away," the message said, "and get to the nearest airport and fly back to San Francisco. We want you to audition for the head of the theater and the conductor. We need to see if you are ready to take over this role on the main stage."

Ready? I was twenty-five, which was pretty young to be put onstage in such a big part. And not for one or two nights, for the entire run!

I flew back and went straight to the opera house from the airport for the audition, a chance-of-a-lifetime role for a green ingénue. I had already begun learning the role of Amelia, but because rehearsals hadn't started yet I wasn't scheduled to be back in San Francisco for quite a while so I wasn't "off book" yet—I didn't have it memorized. I did the audition with the music stand in front of me—which is the first clue that someone probably isn't so ready to take on a major opera lead!

I sang the aria from Act II, "Ecco l'orrido campo," and then approached the moment in the aria called an "unaccompanied cadenza," which is basically a florid without any instruments, it's just you singing notes a capella. I had to pluck the notes out of the air and sing them. Just as I was about to do that, the tenor in the show that evening began warming up in his dressing room, which was just offstage. As soon as I heard him, I lost all sense of pitch and could not figure out what note I was on. The theater manager and the conductor had no idea what was happening, since they couldn't hear the tenor from where they were sitting. All they knew was, I was not good. I blew it. I heard a quiet, disembodied voice from the dark:

"Thank you, Debbie."

The artistic manager met me in the wings as I came offstage to tell me I wasn't ready to do the entire run, but that they wanted me to continue being the cover. I thanked them, and got my own well-sized butt back on the Greyhound bus with the other hopefuls until it was time to return and begin my covering-butt duties. Of course, in retrospect, they were absolutely right. Even if I hadn't had the mishap with the rehearsing tenor, I was no more ready to do that part onstage than I was to fly to the moon.

They chose soprano Carol Neblett to take Ms. Price's place, and I got back onto solid ground for rehearsals at the company, falling more and more in love with the role as I rehearsed it, and wanting so much to play it onstage.

Then, another chance for my "big break" came. One morning I got a phone call:

"Ms. Neblett isn't feeling well, so you're on call this evening if she needs to cancel. Be at the theater by five p.m. for hair and makeup."

I called up my mom with the news, and she and my newest stepdad, Don, jumped into the car and sped the six hours from Placentia to San Francisco. (Don was Mom's third husband. For their wedding, I sang a recycled, encore version of "The Lord's Prayer." I'm happy to say, the third time was the charm for her. Don was a kind teddy bear of a guy and proved to be Mom's Prince Charming. The whole family fell in love with him.) A half an hour before the curtain was to go up, they were in their seats as I sat in front of the mirror in a tiny dressing room with wig and face done, ready to go on.

Waiting to hear. Tick-tock, tick-tock. I hear a knock on my dressing room door.

"Debbie, Ms. Neblett would like to speak with you."

Fuck. What does that mean?

I go down the hall to her dressing room and tap on her door. It opens to reveal three cool, menthol vaporizers blowing at full speed, plus a row of medicines—antihistamines, decongestants, aspirin—lined up in front of her makeup mirror. She turns around and stares at me.

"Why are you in costume and makeup?"

"Well, Ms. Neblett, I'm on call. They told me that you were ill. I'm just here to cover for you and protect you in the eventuality that you feel you can't go on."

She smiled a very polite smile, but her eyes were not smiling. In a very calm voice, she said, "Oh, that's very nice."

I was excused from the room ten minutes before the curtain went up, and you've never seen such a miraculous healing take place. It was like all the vapors in the room suddenly evaporated and the medicines disappeared and she went out on that stage and sang like a goddess—you would've never known that she was ill. No, I never got onstage in that production. And since that day I've always maintained that if you want to get your diva out onstage, send in her cover. Or make sure the diva can hear her cover warming up somewhere backstage.

I had a lot of experiences like that, where I'm either understudying or singing opposite divas who say, "I'm sick, I'm sick, I'm sick," and then they don't cancel. I think that's why I'm particularly sensitive to that situation. If I have my cover called in, it's because I'm *really* sick.

When I was starting out, the cover wouldn't be in the regular rehearsal room with the star. You didn't see your cover until you were onstage and she was in the audience—because a cover always has to be within twenty minutes of the opera house during a performance, in case they are needed. Today, the cover is sitting in the room while you are staging—and it drives me crazy. Sometimes these women have understudied roles several times that I'm just learning, and they are not subtle about showing that they know the words when I don't yet, mouthing them during rehearsal as I sing.

When I was doing Puccini's *La fanciulla del West* in San Francisco in 2011, I was learning the role of Minnie for the first time, and I was struggling with the text, as usual. So I kept looking over at my cover across the room because she was mouthing the words; little did she know it, but she was acting as my live prompter! When she realized that's what I was doing, she shut her mouth pretty darn fast.

ANOTHER TIME, I was called in to take the place of a Canadian soprano who was singing Leonora in *Il trovatore*, which I was understudying for the San Francisco Opera. The soprano, whose name I can't recall, had a sudden throat problem and they needed me that same night in Victoria, British Columbia. I knew I could get there, but I also knew there was no way her costumes would fit me—I had seen a photo of their soprano and she was tall and lean. I called up friends in the costume shop in San Francisco and arranged to borrow a bunch of costumes that already fit me, packed them in several suitcases, and made it across the country to the customs counter at the airport in Victoria where Canadian officials stopped me. They opened up my suitcase and pulled out what were obviously not street clothes.

"What are these for?" asked a very stern customs official. I had made the mistake of saying on my declaration card that I was coming over the border for work, not thinking it would be a problem. I was delayed for hours. By the time I left the airport it was 7:15 p.m., and I was zooming toward the opera house for the eight-o'clock curtain. When I pulled up, at 7:45 p.m., the house manager was pacing up and down in front of the theater.

"We don't have time to get you changed and put you onstage," he said, rushing me backstage, running, "so you're going to sing from the pit and (the other soprano) will lip-sync from the stage."

I was wearing the worst thing possible for the pit—a billowy white dress with puffy sleeves and bright geometric shapes all over it, completely distracting for the audience. But the show had to go on. I sang through it and we got rousing applause; the next morning I was on a plane back to California.

WHEN I DID get onstage, or when we rehearsed, I immersed myself in my role and loved the acting part of the profession. Some singers only love the singing, but I love the whole package—as was evident from when I was a little girl playing dress-up and playing pretend before I could barely talk. When I sit in a dressing room and see myself become a character in the mirror, as the hair is done up and the makeup applied and the costume put on, I love it. During my years in San Francisco, I could see my abilities as an actress stretch and strengthen.

I was gratified to know that even though I was big, what they valued in me in San Francisco was my talent and my presence on-stage. They saw that I could walk onto a stage and make immediate emotional contact with an audience—as Jane Paul said, that came naturally to me, I was born with it.

The head of the Young Artist Program in San Francisco at the time, Christine Bullin, was a great supporter and encourager of young talent, and I was scared to death of her, but I held on to something she once said to me. She told me why she and conductor Andrew Meltzer took a chance on me for their program when the New York Met did not.

"You have the pipes," she said. "You have a voice that has quality and tone. You have an *identifiable sound*."

Because of the nature of the genre, opera singers tend to sound similar to each other. What lifts you a notch above the others is if your voice is identifiable—unique—among the chorus of others. When they heard me singing at my audition, I had "a Deborah Voigt sound" that was my own, and that's what they latched on to.

STILL, I WORRIED that the more weight I gained, the less evident my acting would be to an audience or a director. When you look at someone whose face is buried in fat, which mine was because I tend to carry weight in my face, and it was getting bigger and bigger, expressions don't read as clearly—especially on a big stage. That's why in my heavier days the makeup artists used to try to "paint on" features for me by shading and contouring the sides and underneath my face.

Another obstacle for an audience when watching a very, very big (read: obese) person onstage is the stereotypes they must confront, whether they are conscious of it or not. I think when people see a big, fat person, they automatically assume the person can't move well and, even worse, that nobody could possibly love them in a romantic way. In other words, how can a three-hundred-pound woman play the romantic role of Aida if the audience doesn't believe the tenor onstage would find her attractive?

Near the end of my first year in San Francisco, my father came to visit, and, per family tradition, we had a snippet of intense conversation while driving in the car. I had just started some new diet and was explaining the measuring and caloric specifics to him as he drove. His eyes were on the road when out of the blue he said:

"Debbie, I feel so bad and guilty that I contributed to your gaining weight. And I'm sorry for anything that I did that might be the reason for it. I want you to lose this weight. Please, lose this weight."

I was in shock. I'd never heard my father apologize before, at least not to me. And he sounded like he was near tears, a sound I'd never, ever heard from him. Was the Food Marshal taking some responsibility for my food issues? Or was he saying that my size was a disappointment to him? Like that time at the piano, when I was thirteen, and he asked me, *"Who do you think you are?!"* I couldn't decipher his intent or meaning. I appreciated what he was trying to say, but neither of us understood yet just how deep and far-reaching the damage my childhood would have on me. I wished it was so simple that an apology could fix everything.

I didn't know what to say, so I said nothing. We rode together in silence for the rest of the drive.

Next Stop,
the Wiener Staatsoper

AS A MIDWESTERN suburban girl transplanted to Southern California, the most exciting worlds I'd seen so far were Disneyland and the local super mall. Europe was a distant dream, a faraway, impossible place where the composers whose words and music I sang drew their breath and inspiration. Near the end of my time in San Francisco, I had my first chance to visit this world . . . and Grandma Voigt was my ticket overseas.

The head of the San Francisco Opera's Artistic Administration at the time, New Zealander Sarah Billinghurst, had offered to shell out two thousand bucks for me to study with the world-famous Madame Régine Crespin in Paris for a few weeks. Madame Crespin had been an internationally famous dramatic soprano since the fifties, and a fixture at the Opéra National de Paris, where she was known for her Wagner and Strauss heroines, the roles I was being groomed to sing.

As her career wound down she was giving voice lessons at the Conservatoire de Paris, and Sarah arranged to give me a grant to pay for the lessons, and also offered to set up auditions for me at all the top opera houses in Europe, including the Vienna State Opera, the National Theater Munich, the Paris Opera, and, perhaps the most famous of them all, La Scala, in Milan.

I wouldn't be auditioning to sing a principal role in these companies; I was still considered a "baby" dramatic soprano and wasn't at that stage. The auditions were more for the opera house managers to meet me, get to know me a bit, and maybe offer me a temporary position where I'd understudy several roles under their tutelage for a few months—much like what I'd been doing in San Francisco. It was an experience any young up-and-coming opera singer would jump at. Except me.

"I've got John, I can't go away for months," I told Sarah. (As I spoke, I could hear Jane's voice haunting me—*You won't push forward if you stay with him.* . . .)

"Debbie, it's really important for you to have this experience," she urged.

It just so happened that around the same time that Sarah wanted to set up my opera-house tour and Paris voice lessons, Jane was getting ready to go to Europe. Every year she took a handful of her Cal State students to Vienna—she had lived there for several years in her youth and spoke fluent *Deutsch*—for them to soak up the musical culture and the composers of some of the most famous Germanic operas. So the timing was perfect. All I needed now was the money. The San Francisco Opera arranged for a six-week whirlwind of auditions, and would pay for my two weeks with Madame Crespin in Paris, but I'd have to come up with the money for hotels, airfare, food, and other expenses. John and I didn't have the cash to cover a trip like this, and I was telling my father this on the phone.

"I have a proposition for you, Debbie," he said. "If you'll take Grandma Voigt with you to Europe, I'll pay for your flight and your hotel."

Grandma, who was now in her early sixties—still young and with a lot of energy—had never seen Europe, either. She'd always been a very independent woman—she was the primary money-earner in their household when Dad was growing up—so even though she hadn't traveled much, I figured she'd be a confident traveling companion. And ever since Grandpa Voigt died, on Christmas

Day a few years before, she and I had grown closer. I visited her every weekend during the year after he'd passed, and sat with her, holding her hand and listening to old family stories. And we'd had our first opera outing together, so the idea seemed inspired and a good fit.

And it was, it really was—for the first five hours. By the time we got to our layover in New York, Grandma was already overworrying about the customs officers we'd meet in Munich the following week.

"What if something happens to us? What if there are Nazis?"

"Grandma, nothing bad is going to happen. We have our passports; we'll be fine. They don't have Nazis anymore." Uh-oh.

WE ARRIVED IN Vienna in what was officially the coldest, cruelest winter they'd had in two decades. It was so cold, the homeless people on the street were urged to take shelter in the subways to sleep. The double-pane window in our one-star hotel filled up with so much snow between the two layers of glass that our room was pitch black and we couldn't see out. We were freezing and in the dark, and, as inexperienced tourists, at a loss as to what to do first. Then in swept Jane with her students the following day, and suddenly our days were filled with museums, concerts, beer halls, and, of course, Belvedere Palace to see Jane's beloved Klimt paintings.

"Art informs the music," she told us, and she was right. To see art that was created at the same time as the music I sang was enriching.

One morning we paid our respects at the most famous cemetery in Vienna, the Zentralfriedhof, with almost 600 acres and over 300,000 graves, including those of composers Brahms, Beethoven, and Schubert. That night, we went to the Musikverein, which is one of the most beautiful and acoustically glorious halls in the world. I don't remember who was singing or what they were singing; I just remember being overwhelmed by the colors and sounds of a country so new to my senses.

Grandma loved it, too, though she was queasy because every-one still smoked like a chimney in Europe. She was also still in hyperparanoid mode ever since her Nazi comment, and scared to even buy a pack of gum for fear she'd be taken advantage of. "Grandma, stop worrying. No one's going to screw us over on a pack of gum or a cup of coffee. If you want to buy a diamond, then we'll worry."

A week into our trip, after we'd seen the magical sites of Vienna, and after Jane had left, I came down with something. But rather than stay cooped up in our cramped hotel room, Grandma and I went out to see Beethoven's *Fidelio* at the Wiener Staatsoper (the Vienna State Opera).

Dame Gwyneth Jones, a very famous Welsh soprano at the time, was singing, and Grandma Voigt and I sat in a tiny box in the bal-cony of the horseshoe-shaped theater. I was running such a high fe-ver, I wanted to lean my blazing head against one of the life-size, gilded, topless female sculptures that surrounded the perimeter of the room. *Gustav Mahler conducted here*, I thought, dizzily, then nearly passed out in my seat. I was scheduled to audition on that very stage the next day. What was I to do? I called John that night in tears—I was making only brief phone calls to him every few days during the trip because the long-distance rates were so high. On this call I was both homesick and sick-sick.

I woke up the next morning in our lightless, freezing hotel room with my head and throat on fire. I could barely make the phone call to tell the opera company I was too sick to come. "I need a doctor," I said. An hour later I was tromping through the snow in search of a taxi; I had an appointment with the doctor to the opera stars. His waiting room walls were plastered with autographed photos of the most famous singers in the world. I slumped down in a chair and a moment later in walks one of them—James King, an Ameri-can heldentenor ("heroic tenor") considered to be one of the finest of the postwar period. He had a dark, powerful, dramatic voice, perfect for the typical Wagnerian protagonist, and he sang mostly German romantic repertoire; my kind of heldentenor. We had met six months earlier in San Francisco when I was covering an opera role and he was singing the lead. He walked into the waiting room and gave me that *I know you* look.

"Mr. King, I'm Deborah Voigt," I said, barely able to stand up. "I met you in San Franscisco. I was understudying Eva in *Die Meistersinger.*" I was burning up. He put his hand out to shake mine.

"No, no, no . . . I'm very ill. I'm running a fever. . . ."

He was there for a regular checkup, and we made a bit of small talk until the nurse came out to fetch "Frau Voigt."

"Deborah, do you mind if I come in with you for your exam?" Mr. King asked. "I'm fascinated by the way vocal cords look in different singers. I'd love to see yours."

The last thing I wanted was James King standing over the doctor's shoulder, looking at my vocal cords. He might as well have been asking to come into my gynecologist's exam with me. (If you've ever seen a vocal cord, it looks very much like that part of the female anatomy.) Plus, I was a gagger. I really didn't need anyone to witness all of this.

"Yeah, sure," I told him.

A minute later, the doctor was holding down my tongue with a wooden depressor and sticking something else down my throat. I looked up wildly from the reclining chair to see the peering bug-eyes of the doctor and James King staring down at me, and I started choking and choking . . .

"Deborah, Deborah"—Mr. King patted me on the shoulder, scoldingly—"you have got to learn to relax so the doctor can do a proper examination!"

After much gagging, the doctor was done. "Yeees, dees looked like de vocal cords of a dramatic soprano," he said. What he meant, I had no idea. This doctor wasn't the sharpest knife in the drawer, and the experience was getting a little too bizarre for me. The doctor gave me some sea-salt treatments and antibiotics, then had the nurse point a microwave-heated device at my chest to warm me up and break up the mucus. For three days, I was stuck convalescing in our puny hotel room with the snow-packed windows and Grandma, who didn't dare venture outside without me. At the end of those three days, I was well enough to audition, and I did a good job. I was on their radar, and Vienna would later become a major house in my career.

NEXT STOP, MUNICH. Once I felt better, we hopped a train for my audition at the Bayerische Staatsoper. Everything went well enough (no problems with customs officials, to Grandma's relief), but what I remember most from that stop was an audition I did for a local agent. There'd been a snowstorm the day before and I was wearing my little black heels instead of boots (no boots for an audition!), which was fine because I had no problem getting a taxi at my hotel. His office was a fifth-floor walk-up above an antique shop in the artsy Schwabing district, off Münchner Freiheit Square. I sang for him and he was impressed.

"Deeebbie," he said, with a thick German accent, "Now . . . I vant you to go to thees city, and then thees city and thees city . . . and here is a B opera house, and here is a C opera house, and you must be there, you must have a position there!"

Opera houses, I had learned recently, were ranked alphabetically according to their importance and prestige. The main opera houses in Vienna, Munich, and Milan, for example, would be considered A houses; and although I was not yet ready for them, he thought I could easily get a full-time company position in a B house. A lot of Americans built their opera careers this way, so it would be a stellar opportunity and experience for a baby soprano like me—he was insistent about it.

"You need to go to Heidelberg!" he declared and stood up. "Get on the train today. There's one that leaves at six o'clock tonight. You will go to Heidelberg and sing for Herr *Iforgetzinamen*! I will call him now and arrange everything and you will sing for him! After that, I vant you to get on a train and get to Düsseldorf and sing for them, too . . . and after that . . ."

He went on and on with a list of cities and names and opera houses, and I was saying, *Okay, okay, yes . . . thank you, yes. I will get on these trains, I will go.*

But in my head, I was thinking, *No! No! No!*

I walked outside into a foot-high snowdrift in my little black heels, couldn't find a taxi, and burst into tears. When I finally got back to the hotel room, to waiting Grandma, my feet were soaking wet, and I was still crying. Part of me wanted to do as the agent said because he and other important people in the business were telling me I had the chops to do it, and the United States didn't have as many opera houses or opportunities like this for a singer on the rise. In America, the experience would be more conservatory style, or in small opera companies singing small roles. In a B opera house in Germany, you'd be singing the leads.

"I don't want to do it, I'm not ready," I cried to Grandma. Part of it was that I wasn't ready to leave home, and part of it was John. I thought of Jane's words again, about letting John hold me back. But I also knew that Jane knew me emotionally and would understand it wasn't right for me.

"Calm down," said Grandma, taking charge for the first time during our trip. "If you don't want to go you don't have to go. Nobody's making you do anything. Why don't you call the lady who set up the auditions and see what she says?" Good thinking, Grandma. I rang up Sarah Billinghurst.

"Sarah, it's Debbie"—and I burst into tears yet again.

"Debbie, what's wrong?"

"I've just sung for that big agent."

"Ah, yes! How did it go?"

"Well . . . he liked me very much . . . *sniffle sniffle* . . . but he wants me to go to all these small opera companies and . . . *sob, sob* . . ." I explained the rest.

"Oh, Debbie! You don't have to do it! You're not even done with your Adler Fellowship yet. Tell him you can't do it. Do you want me to tell him?"

So Sarah made the call and got me off the hook. The next day, Grandma and I boarded a train to Milan and the famous La Scala.

MOST OF THE world's greatest operatic artists have sung in Italy's majestic Teatro alla Scala, which opened in 1778. It is the stage of many an operatic *prima* and was a second home to Verdi, who premiered many of his operas there up to his final composition, *Falstaff*, in 1893. Walking into the house for the first time is a stunning experience. Grandma had skipped the other auditions but came with me to this one, and together we stood in the main auditorium and looked up at the grand proscenium in awe. I was glad Grandma was seeing this. She'd had a frustrating time the day before trying to deal with the pizza in Italy, unable to comprehend why it was different from the one at Pizza Hut in suburban Illinois. We were on Week Three, and it was getting more and more difficult to get along. She'd never experienced so many new tastes, sights, and habits, and, like her son, she wasn't the go-with-the-flow type.

Instead of embracing the newness, she was afraid of it. Looking up at the vaulted ceiling at the Teatro, I wondered about my own fears. Did I hesitate to leap into Europe's welcoming arms just because I was afraid of something so big and new? What, exactly, was I afraid of?

Milan was not a good place for me to start any leaping.

I was auditioning that day for the new principal conductor and musical director, Riccardo Muti, who would continue in that eminent position for another two decades. He had a reputation as being tough and is known as a kind of god of Italian music, whereas I'm primarily a German singer and was so even then. Right away we weren't a great fit, and it ended up being one of the most awkward auditions I ever had. I sang an aria from *Ballo* and something German—"Dich, teure Halle" from Wagner's *Tannhäuser*, as I recall.

The stagehands had been working on the set for their upcoming production of Wagner's *Die Walküre* that day and the stage was scattered with props. They had vacated the stage, but as I was doing my audition, they made so much noise underneath the stage, eating their lunch and moving scenery, that I couldn't hear myself sing except to know that I was off-pitch.

"Stop, stop . . . *basta*!" said Maestro Muti, putting his hand up. He was standing in the tenth row of the house with the artistic director, Cesare Mazzonis. The maestro put his hands on his hips

"Why are you singing like that, is there something wrong with you?"

"No, Maestro, I'm sorry. I'm hearing so much noise from below where the stagehands are working . . ."

"Well, come downstage, then!" He was not happy. I moved downstage, stepping on big, flat rocks that were part of the set. Turns out they were made of foam and rubber, and as I put my entire 280 pounds on them, I slipped and—*boom!*—onto the floor. After I gathered myself up in embarrassment, I sang. But Maestro Muti wasn't giving me the time of day. He knew I had so much grooming to do, all he said to me was, "You need to work on your Italian," and left.

For someone so Italian, I think I was just too *German* for him—my look, my voice, even my name. The man scared the shit out of me but I would have loved to have worked with him at some point and I never have. He's a great musician and my colleagues with whom he's worked speak very highly of him. But I wasn't going to let this experience ruin my first time in Italy. Afterward, I took a walk by myself down a little cobblestoned *strada* and turned the corner into a piazza and there, in front of me, was the beautiful, gothic Duomo. It took six centuries to build and is one of the oldest churches in Europe. I stepped inside and looked up—at 148 feet, the church had one of the highest "naves" (the long ceiling leading up to the altar) in the world. I looked up and up. Somehow, looking so high and seeing all that beauty made my little slip onstage seem small and insignificant.

OUR LAST STOP was Paris, where I was to spend two coveted, and very expensive, weeks studying with Régine Crespin. I was looking forward to meeting this grand, controversial character. She had published her very candid memoir, *La vie et l'amour d'une femme* ("The Life and Love of a Woman"), a few years earlier, and the opera world was buzzing with her descriptions of backstage love affairs with both men and women, among other colorful details.

We got to Paris and I telephoned her—no answer. Grandma and I went out to have some *pain au chocolat* at the pâtisserie near our hotel, came back, and I tried her again—still no answer, and no answering machine. The next day, the same thing, and by Day Three, I was getting very worried, until I got a call from her. She's having dental problems, she explained, and tells me to please wait—*Attends!*—and she will call me again when her teeth feel better.

By Day Five and no Madame, Grandma and I were at each other's throats. By now I've been dipping into John's and my savings account so that we could have our own hotel rooms and give each other some breathing space. But as Days Six and Seven rolled around and still no Madame, I'd had it. I loved Europe but after tripping, crying, freezing, getting sick, and having my larynx ogled at, I was over it and was more than ready to go home. I called the airline, changed our return tickets, and when we touched down at San Francisco International I wanted to kiss the tarmac.

The following year, the elusive Madame Crespin, whom I couldn't get to see in Paris, came directly to me in San Francisco. She began teaching part-time at the Adler Fellowship, and I finally got my voice lessons. She was a great teacher and she loved my voice. So much so, that she tried to get me to go back to Paris with her.

"You must come to the Conservatoire in Paris and study with me. You must!"

"Madame Crespin, I'm not ready to do that."

"Why?"

"Because I have a partner here. . . ."

"Pffff!" she scoffed. "Well, you will never have a career, then. Are you married to this man? No! Why don't you leave him?"

"Because I love him."

Madame had no patience for such talk and sentimentality. After she went back to France, her words stuck in my mind, just as Jane's had.

Well, you'll never have a career, then . . .

I wasn't so sure about that. A few months after I returned home from Europe, I got a letter from Cesare Mazzonis, the artistic director at La Scala in Milan, the site of my awful audition.

He wrote:

Thank you for coming to the audition. When I heard you sing, I heard the sun in your voice . . .

Europe had been a rough trip, but also invaluable. It helped me define for myself what I didn't want to do, and sometimes that's just as helpful as figuring out what you do want. I was so "Miss America," and still am, and I knew that this young American soprano was not going to take the European path, as so many do.

I intended to build my career here at home, with my feet firmly planted on American soil and stage.

(9)

Diets and Divas

SOMETIME AROUND THE end of my apprenticeship in San Francisco, I began getting desperate about my weight. Maybe it was that
father-daughter chat in the car that triggered it, I don't know; but I
embarked on a series of dangerous diets and procedures to get some
flesh off me. I was now tipping the scale near 300 and miserable
about it.

First I tried Optifast. Oprah had recently made a big splash on
TV by pulling a red Radio Flyer wagon laden with sixty-seven
pounds of fat onto her talk-show stage while wearing her new size
10 jeans, so I signed up. For months I guzzled the sugar/corn syrup/
red dye #3 concoction and lost fifty pounds. But that's not the whole
truth. Here's how I really did it: I drank glassfuls of the sugary liq-
uid for four days, until I had to go and do the weigh-in at the Optifast meeting. After my weight was recorded in the little notebook,
I'd drive to the nearest Burger King, load up on burgers, shakes,
and fries, and do my famous high school eating binge in the car as
I drove home. I'd binge for three days, then starve for four, then
weigh in, then drive to Burger King for another sabotaging meal—
that was my system. I'm amazed I lost any weight that way, and
God knows what damage I did to my body. By month number four
I couldn't stand the taste of the vile stuff anymore and every time I

tried to drink it, I threw up—and not on purpose. By month five, I'd gained back that fifty pounds.

Then I tried injections of pregnant women's urine. Yes, that's right, pregnant women's urine. The theory is that it contains the hormone HCG, which is supposed to suppress your appetite and trigger your body's use of fat for fuel, so that you can lose several pounds per day. Of course, they also make you follow a 500-calorie-per-day diet, and who's not going to lose weight on 500 calories? Me, that's who. Because it was going to take more than a few pregnant women to suppress my appetite and the complicated reasons that I was eating. Within a few weeks I was back at the Burger King counter. I didn't even want to contemplate how they went about procuring the urine of pregnant women.

Finally, I had an operation to insert a gastric bubble into my stomach. It was the newest cutting-edge weight-loss technique and was considered safer and more effective than stomach stapling or jaw-wiring—those I could not "stomach" the thought of, worried that they would affect my singing. I went into the hospital and they put me to sleep and stuffed a deflated balloon down my esophagus and into my stomach. Once it was in there, they inflated it, and it was supposed to fill up my stomach so that I wouldn't feel hungry. Apparently I was in good celebrity company, because Zsa Zsa Gabor's daughter (or so I was told) and I were the first two people in Southern California to have this procedure done.

At first, I was very sick because my body recognized the balloon as a foreign object and tried to expel it. Once I stabilized a bit, I did notice my appetite had decreased. But I found ways around that. When I got hungry, I'd eat a Snickers bar instead of the recommended healthy small meal. Still, I lost about ten pounds . . . until my body finally did eject the balloon and it passed right out of me, the foul details of that I'll keep to myself.

I still didn't quite understand *why* I was overeating, what feelings I was smothering or anesthetizing; but I was vaguely aware I was trekking on dangerous terrain, both emotional and physical. Just a few years earlier, my childhood idol Karen Carpenter had died from complications after years of starving herself as she suffered from anorexia nervosa—its roots also linked to emotions. I used to look at photos of her, so skinny and pretty, and wish I could be just like her. I overate and she under-ate—I felt a kinship with her, as if we were two sides to the same coin, the flip sides of the same record album.

BUT IT'S NOT as if I was the only opera singer with a big appetite. Rotund singers have been the norm on the opera stage since the art began. And, as I was to learn later, after I lost a lot of weight, that extra flesh helps to engage the abdominal muscles and support the sound. It certainly did for one of the biggest opera stars in the world—big in both stature and breadth—Luciano Pavarotti, whom I first came within two feet of in 1988.

Near the end of my apprenticeship, I began entering voice competitions around the world to make extra money and to help make a name for myself. For a few years, I was winning every one that I entered—I became known in the opera community as the Queen of the Competitions.

One of my most memorable wins was the gold medal at the Luciano Pavarotti Competition in 1988. It was the third annual vocal competition held by the Opera Company of Philadelphia, under the aegis of the famous tenor. There were fifteen hundred competing applicants and just one category—opera singing, that's it. The competition didn't have separate vocal categories. It culminated in a two-day marathon at the Academy of Music with seventy singers, each performing arias with piano accompaniment. Pavarotti was one of the three judges for the finals; the winners would receive a role in a future production by the Opera Company of Philadelphia in which Pavarotti would star.

On the last day of competition, I had sung my standard party pieces—the same list I had auditioned with at San Francisco—and was standing near the front of the stage with John during a break when in walked Luciano. He stood five feet from me in his baggy white T-shirt and trademark Hermès scarf, chatting with some of the other participants.

"Go talk to him!" John whispered to me, giving me a nudge.

"No, I'm not going to go talk to him! Why would he want to talk to me?" I was never good at networking and always felt uncomfortable—and in this case, completely intimidated—approaching celebrities.

"Debbie, you're in his competition. You've made it through to this round. *Those* people are talking to him."

I couldn't do it. I couldn't get past the feeling of *what would he want with me?*

Even though he stood right next to me, happily talking to a handful of other contestants. I slunk to the back of the auditorium and watched him do his afternoon of judging from there, as one by one a host of Violettas, Mimis, Rodolfos, and Zerlinas emoted onstage.

Luciano sat with his enormous Hermès scarf on the table in front of him, wiping his runny nose and sweaty brow with it. At the end of the day, when he got up onstage to announce who'd made it to the next round, he'd wrapped that scarf around his neck. I couldn't help but think . . . *Hey, can I wash that for you?*

LATER THAT SAME year, I made my European debut in Brussels in Richard Strauss's one-act opera *Elektra*, in the small role of the fifth maid at the beautiful Théâtre Royal de la Monnaie. Now, if you're going to be a maid in *Elektra*, the fifth is the one you want to be—she's got the most fire.

John traveled with me as much as possible, but for this extended stay he couldn't, and I got very homesick. I was starting to hate traveling—and travel is a definite requirement for someone who wants to be an opera singer, as Jane warned me. I had always had a difficult time being on my own and isolating myself too much. Alone in a hotel room late at night in a foreign city, with no one I knew nearby, loneliness and self-doubt visited me like unwanted, unshakable guests. The only thing that eased their hold on me was . . . food. So I kept eating.

The *Elektra* director was, I recall, very, very thin, and she'd had some problems trying to stage me because I wasn't able to move the way she wanted me to. I was feeling bad about that. She never said anything to me, but on opening night she gave each cast member a gift with a card, and on the cover of mine was a picture of an angel trying to fly into the air but being held down by a rope wrapped around her waist and tied to a giant rock on the ground.

I was feeling pretty down one evening when I had dinner with the soprano Catherine Malfitano, who was also in Brussels performing, and her husband, Stephen Holowid. Stephen was a former actor, singer, and musician working as artistic coordinator for the New York City Opera when they met and he later became Catherine's personal adviser. They'd invited me to their apartment for dinner, and after hearing me complain all night about traveling and feeling lonely, Stephen shook his head and said to me, "Well are you a singer or aren't you?"

"What do you mean?" I asked.

"I mean *do you want this or not?*"

It was a humbling moment, reminding me of Jane's question: "How dedicated are you?" Why was I always so hesitant, so reluctant? I'd been given a rare opportunity—to have a career in the high arts and a life that took me around the world, singing the operas of the greatest composers. To touch people's hearts and stir their emotions was a special gift, and something I should not, and did not, take lightly.

This was a lesson I learned from Jane years earlier, when I was still in college.

I had sung in a small concert and didn't think it had gone very well, and neither did Jane. But afterward, people came up to me and said how much they'd loved it.

"Oh, but this was wrong and that was wrong. . . ." I was very busy telling them why they shouldn't have liked my singing that night. Jane pulled me aside.

"Don't ruin it for people. They've had an experience. Whether you or I think it was good or not, we can discuss later."

I never forgot that. To this day, when I know a show was not so great, but people come up and say, "Oh, you were wonderful!" I put a clamp on it and say, "Thank you."

It was difficult for me to take praise—pride goeth before a fall, and all that.

IN MY LATE twenties I was "double cast"—that's when two parallel casts alternate performing the roles each night—while working with an opera company based in Orange County, California, called Opera Pacific. I was in the "B cast," or "silver cast"; and in the "A cast," or "gold cast," singing the lead role, was the American lyric soprano Carol Vaness.

Carol was older than I was and much, much more experienced, of course, but I was moving up and had won all these awards and had gained enough confidence to feel that I might have a better instrument than she did.

Or, if not better, more suited to the particular repertoire we were doing at the time. And then I watched Carol in rehearsal. She knew how to carry herself onstage, she knew how to hold the moment, she knew that a singer's stillness sometimes relayed a greater, deeper moment to an audience than a physical gesture. Her deportment onstage was something you don't learn in a practice room—unless you have a teacher like Jane Paul, who really knows. I learned so much watching Carol that I never again doubted that there might be something to learn from someone when you don't expect it.

*   *   *

THE OTHER SIDE of the "pride goeth" coin was the diva behavior opera stars were known for. It was a stereotype sopranos of the past like Maria Callas fed to the hilt with their big personalities and flamboyant lifestyles.

I'm more the anti-diva. I was ultra-aware not to draw attention to myself. Whenever I acted the diva at home, growing up, it was not tolerated, so it would never occur to me to do it as an adult, in public, at work.

But for some divas, like soprano Jessye Norman, whom I would understudy several times, it was still tolerated when I was entering the profession. Some of it had to do with the era—people were still in awe of that kind of figure and enjoyed the diva character.

The first time I met Jessye, I was understudying her in Chicago for Gluck's *Alceste* in the late eighties. The director was Robert Wilson, who was known for his brilliant, but very difficult, stagings. His reputation was such that the theater indulged him and paid for all his "covers" to come to the theater six weeks before the principals arrived so that he could work out and practice his staging using us. It was highly unusual even then to do this, and today it would be unheard of because it would be too costly.

But I was there to do what he asked of me, and it was six weeks of intense physical work. At one point he had me spread-eagled on the ground, my arms out, face down.

"Debbie, do you think that Jessye would do this?"

"Well . . ." I mumbled, my lips against the dusty floor, "I don't know her, but I'd be surprised if she did."

When Jessye showed up, the theater told me I was not required to do any rehearsals from that point onward unless she was sick. Jessye showed up for the first day of rehearsals dramatically dressed in a flowing, colorful cloak, big jewelry, and her hair wrapped in a turban. She was very grand, very big, and (with that turban) very tall, but with a beautiful, thin face—and when she was introduced to me she barely acknowledged me, which was fine. I tried not to take it personally.

Finally it came time for Robert to stage that spread-eagle scene, and I was watching from the corner. And wouldn't you know it, Jessye turns around to me and says, "Well, do you think the cover can show me what you've been doing?"

In other words, she wanted me to do it for her. I don't know where I got the guts, but I looked at her and asked, "Well, are you ill?"

"No, why?

"I was told I should only do this if you are ill."

Some balls I had! But I just can't stand a diva! She got up and did it. But every single night after that, she complained there was a draft onstage and made noise about canceling.

I never went on, though. I found out later she was known to be a very delicate diva—she could feel every breeze. Apparently the Met had set up a private dressing room for her on the second floor, not with the rest of us mortals on the main floor, because she had a mysterious allergy to the carpeting. Or something. Her lungs were very, very sensitive, I discovered, when I was covering her in the role of Ariadne some time later. There was one performance (finally!) when she was too ill to go on, and at the last minute I got my chance.

When I heard the call "Miss Voigt to the stage"—my cue—and quickly made my way from my dressing room to the stage, bursting through a pair of double doors, I was accosted by two hulking guys on the other side with spray tubes who started misting me with vapor.

Aaaargh! What the . . . ?

"Oh," they said, putting their tubes down. "You're not Jessye Norman."

"No, I'm not!" I sputtered, wiping my face—while trying not to smudge my makeup—and racing to the stage so I wouldn't miss my entrance.

"Who the heck were those guys?" I asked my dresser, who was running next to me.

"Oh, them. They're Jessye's 'misters.' They mist in front of her as she walks to the stage to get the dust out of her air."

SOME DIVA STORIES have become legend around the opera houses.

When I first got to the Met, soprano Aprile Millo was the reigning diva, and I understudied her all the time. She's American, she came up through the Met's Young Artists' Program, and the rumor in the house was that she was born April Mills but changed it to be more exotic. I couldn't fault her for that, I'd done the same thing. My birth certificate has me as "Debbie," and when I went professional I was worried my name sounded too *"And now, live from the Grand Ole Opry!"* and decided "Deborah" sounded more operatic, more sophisticated, more like I wasn't just plain ol' Debbie from suburban Illinois who hadn't been anywhere or done anything.

I WAS A team player, so I usually got along with everyone. In my career, I was only to have big conflicts with two major divas.

I butted heads with one of them when I went to Israel for the first time to sing with the Israel Philharmonic Orchestra. We were doing Mahler's Eighth Symphony, also known as the Symphony of a Thousand because of its enormous orchestral and choral requirements, in addition to its eight soloists. All the soloists were living together in a kosher "guesthouse," and while we each had our own room and bathroom, we were expected to take all our meals together. When you accepted a gig there, you knew it was going to be a little bit like camp—a very communal, dormlike atmosphere.

But there was one mezzo-soprano, let's call her "Mezzo X." She was a stunningly gorgeous woman who was having a lot of success based on the fact that she looked the way she did. She had a lovely voice, too, but it was limited to essentially one role, which she sang all over the world. She was very sexy, and I admit I may have been jealous of her to a certain degree.

During our time in Israel, Mezzo X had all her meals brought up to her room and never ate with the rest of us. There was just one practice room in the house, and you had to walk past the kitchen table in order to get to it. We'd be sitting in the kitchen, eating, and Mezzo X would walk right by us without saying hello.

Every day, they'd pick us all up as a group in a van and take us to the concert hall to rehearse. Strangely, there was only one room to warm up in at the hall, so with eight soloists that's tricky. Most of us would warm up in our rooms back at the guesthouse and then do a little something before the concert. To be "proper," they'd set up a screen running down the middle of the room so that the men would be on one side and the women on the other—sort of like an Orthodox Jewish wedding.

The room at the concert hall had only one piano, and as soon as we'd arrive, Mezzo X would go over to that piano and warm up. And warm up. And warm up. Incidentally, she had the easiest part in the whole performance. Two lines, to be exact—which she could have burped out and she would have been fine. But she rehearsed these two lines over and over again, and did these funny tongue-twister exercises (*Round and round the rugged rocks the ragged rascal ran . . .*)—to the point where the other mezzo-soprano in our group was ready to bite her head off.

After several days of this, a few of us went to administration and complained: "Look, isn't there another room with a piano so that if *someone* feels they need to warm up *extra* long, they can go there. And the rest of us, who would like fifteen minutes of quiet before the performance, could have it?" The next day during rehearsal while Mezzo X is hogging the piano, someone comes in and announces that they've set up a second room for those who want longer rehearsal times.

But Mezzo X stays at the piano, going on and on, running her ragged rascal round and round . . . until I finally had enough.

"Mezzo X, did you not hear the announcement that was made a little bit earlier?"

"Announcement? What do you mean?"

"About there being another room to warm up in."

"Oh, do you need the piano?" Mezzo X was born and bred on the East Coast, but she talked with a trace of an affected British accent.

"No, I don't need the piano, but I would like to have a little bit of quiet before the concert, and there's another room where you can—"

BANG!!!!!!!!!!!!!

She slammed the piano shut, picked up her music, and stormed out of the room. *Oh shit.* Two days later I got a call from my manager.

"How are things going in Israel?"

"Fine, why?"

"Well, I got a call from guess-who's manager saying you were picking on her."

She never spoke to me again—until we worked together a year or two later and she was absolutely forced to. We were doing several concerts together with two other vocalists, and as luck would have it, she and I were set to share a dressing room. When I arrived on the first night, her stuff was everywhere—makeup all over the counter, hair all over the sink, clothes taking up all the hooks. And she had a camera crew following her around all week, even in our dressing room as she kept popping in and changing her outfits. We did a week of performances, and every night her dresses got more revealing until the last night when her breasts were barely covered by a skimpy halter top. The audience ate it up.

Apparently, certain figures *can* be held against you on the opera stage. But if you have the right sort of figure, it can work to your advantage.

THE OTHER DIVA I had a conflict with was a mezzo-soprano from Germany—Mezzo Y, I'll call her.

Skipping ahead several years, I was singing Isolde in Wagner's *Tristan and Isolde* and she was singing the part of Brangäne, Isolde's handmaiden. For the entire run in this midwestern city she was a troublemaker.

In rehearsals, she started off by saying "there was something in the air" that was making her sick. She was faint, she was nauseous, and it was "something in the air" that was doing it to her.

We managed to get through rehearsals, for a while, until she began challenging me on the staging.

"You shouldn't be doing that there," she'd say, "the line says to do this."

After a few more days of her comments, I finally blew a gasket.

"Listen, we have a director. When you sing Isolde you will make decisions you want to make, but for the moment I'm making mine and I don't want to hear another word from you."

I went off to the side of the stage and broke down in tears and . . .

"Break time!" the director called.

A few minutes later I was in my dressing room and the general manager, who knows me well, knocks on my door.

"Look, I know what you're dealing with, I've heard it from other departments. I'm very sorry that this is happening, and we've had a talk with her and told her she can't behave this way."

For a while, Mezzo Y's behavior did improve. But she could not sustain it. A few days later we were performing the final scene in the opera that ends very dramatically. She was already onstage and I was to come running into the scene to perform the final aria, "Liebestod" (it means, literally, "love-death"), which I sing over the dead body of my love, Tristan. I ran in and begin to sing the sad, sad aria, and she looks at me and laughs! In the middle of the performance! I ignored her as best I could and carried on, but as soon as we took our bows and the curtain went down, I turned to her.

"What were you laughing at?"

"Oh, your lipstick. It was so red, it was silly."

The next performance, we went out onstage for Act I, which is primarily between me and her, in which I sing Isolde's "Narrative and Curse"—a powerful, rage-filled aria—and I nailed it. It was one of those nights when I was really "on," and I knew it, and so did the audience. At the end of the act, my character faints in her handmaiden's arms and then the curtains close. Mezzo Y immediately pulled away from me roughly.

"You're wearing too much perfume!"

"I'm wearing the same amount of perfume that I've been wearing every day for weeks and you never said a word about it before."

I knew what was really going on. I had sung well, very well, and she couldn't stand it.

"No"—she shakes her head—"something's different. Maybe it's your wig. Maybe they put something in your wig, but it's really affecting me. I don't know if I can sing. I might have to cancel. . . ."

We're all onstage—the cast, the crew—and everybody is hearing this entire exchange. I looked at her, amazed that she'd threaten to cancel in the middle of a performance.

"Look, I'm not wearing any more perfume than I've been wearing before. You must be coming down with something, I'm really sorry to hear that." I turned to leave the stage, then turned back—

"—and if you *ever* walk onstage and laugh at me again, we're going to have a serious problem."

I marched offstage and went to the general manager's office. This was all happening during the break between Acts I and II, mind you.

"I just had another incident with her. She threatened to cancel tonight and everybody heard her. Maybe she didn't mean it, but maybe you want to call her cover, just in case."

And as I've said, the way to get a diva onstage is to call the cover.

Moments later as we were getting ready to go on for Act II, she caught a glimpse of her cover backstage and, of course, she went on with the show.

The end of this diva episode wrapped up with an odd and creative *tour de force* offstage. A few weeks later, on the last day of our run, the assistant stage director, whom I'd known since my early San Francisco days, came to my dressing room, holding something behind her back.

"I have a gift for you, but you can't tell anybody what it is and you can't show it to anybody." I promised, and from behind her back she pulled out a voodoo doll of the diva in character, dressed in her green costume from the show, with the face painted and needles stuck up and down her body.

"She was so unpleasant," said the AD. Seems no one likes a nasty witch of a diva.

How do you get to Carnegie Hall?
Practicing my scales while still in
diapers, age two.

One of my early acting roles at age
seven: a Southern Belle in Mom's
homemade costume.

A churchgoing family, on our way to "dedicate" baby Kevin in the
Southern Baptist faith, circa 1968.

By thirteen, my new repertoire included ballads by my idol, Karen Carpenter, and Broadway show tunes.

Hiding my braces in my grad photo at El Dorado High, the year I performed in *The Music Man*.

Size 24 wedding dress and Jane Paul (far left) as my matron of honor. Melinda is on my right and Marianne on my left.

The "cover" gets her big
break: my stage debut singing
Amelia in *Ballo* in San
Francisco, November 1990.

Marty Sohl/San Francisco Opera

Emoting—with hair—and the
wonderful Hildegard Behrens
in *Elektra* in 1992.

Winnie Klotz, courtesy of the
Metropolitan Opera Archives

A big Italian hug from a big, beautiful soul—with Luciano Pavarotti in his
dressing room, after a performance of *Ballo* in 1997.

Up close and personal with President Clinton,
Chelsea, and Luciano (far right) after Act Two
of *Aida* at the Met in 2001. *Janet Koltick*

Plácido Domingo and I, pre-kiss,
in *Die Walküre* at the Met—
the month I met Mitch.
AP Photo/Richard Drew

Tightly corseted in the sweltering heat for my role debut as
Isolde in Vienna, 1993—we got a twenty-three-minute standing
ovation on opening night. *AP Photo/Stephan Trierenberg*

Skewering the little black dress "mess" at my
Carnegie Hall debut recital, 2004. *Richard Termine*

Manhandled by the Executioner in *Salome*
in 2006, where I revealed my svelte, postsurgery body. *AP Photo/Charles Rex Arbogast*

My drinking was out of control when
I sang Maddalena in *Chénier* in
Barcelona, 2007. *Antoni Bofill*

With fellow winners at the *Opera News* Awards gala in 2007—(from left) René Pape, Renata Scotto, James Levine, and Ben Heppner. *Dario Acosta*

Paragliding in Zurich—weightless and freeing, a sport I never would have attempted in my heavier days.

Paired with Ben—finally!—in the plagued production of *Tristan and Isolde* at the Met in 2008.

Ken Howard/Metropolitan Opera

Fitting into that little black dress in my triumphant return as Ariadne at the London Royal Opera House in June 2008. *Clive Barda / ArenaPAL*

The role of my career; the fearless Brünnhilde in *Die Walküre* (with Bryn Terfel) in spring 2011.

Ken Howard/Metropolitan Opera

Interviewing Plácido for a Met *Live in HD* broadcast; transmitting opera to audiences around the world.

Ken Howard/Metropolitan Opera

My constant companion and faithful sidekick, Steinway, helps out with an *Annie Get Your Gun* photo shoot. *Luke Ratray*

Lifting my spirits—and perspective on life—during a recent break in the mountains of Kamikōchi, in the Japanese Alps.

A difficult year ends on an exalted note; singing with the Mormon Tabernacle Choir, December 2013.

Intellectual Reserve, Inc.

10

Amelia and Ariadne:
Luck Be This Lady

JOHN AND I awoke to gunshots. It was 1990 and we were now living in a little apartment in New York—in Inwood, the northern most part of Manhattan, and the last stop on the number 1 train. I hated it. I was making no money at the time, and I'd gotten John a job working in the office of my new agent. The neighborhood was scuzzy and our stairwell was a hangout for drug dealers. In our first few weeks on Dyckman Street, there'd been one mugging and, as we were soon to discover, a murder in our building.

We'd heard the BOOM! in the middle of the night, but had no idea what it was. At seven a.m. someone pounded on our door: "Police! There's been a murder on the fifth floor. Didja hear anything, ma'am?" We answered a few questions and they were on their way, saying, "Thanks for your time, Mr. and Mrs. Leitch."

After fourteen years of "dating," John and I took the plunge and got hitched a few months earlier, in California, and then relocated to New York. Why New York? Well, just as the TV world has "pilot season," when actors audition for all the new TV shows in production, the opera world has a season in New York when managers and artistic directors from opera houses all over the world come to audition singers.

And now our first abode as husband and wife was a dump that looked like a *Law & Order* murder scene. But it served me right, because I had gotten married for all the wrong reasons and I knew it. I was getting ready to go to Moscow to compete in the prestigious Tchaikovsky Competition and I was in a panic—not about the competition, but about John. I sensed I was losing him, and that made me want to cling.

That I was prepping to go to the Soviet Union, which was like a distant planet to me, only made me cling more. I suddenly decided, I have to marry him, there's not going to be anyone else, I'm too fat. I might be talented but I'm not smart, I'm not pretty . . . who else would want me?

There was no romantic proposal or anything like that. I basically told him it was time and I sold some of my jewelry and we combined our meager sums together to buy a diamond wedding ring. But there was one detail I wanted to do right, and traditionally, and that was to get married at our Evangelical Free Church. After all, my family had been members of the congregation since we'd moved to California, sixteen years earlier. It was the house of worship where I'd been the pianist and soloist, where my mother had been the Sunday school and vacation Bible school teacher, and where my dad had been a deacon. My entire family had a deep and longstanding relationship with this church.

When the day came to speak to the pastor about my upcoming wedding, Mom and I walked into the church like it was our second home. The pastor, an old family friend, greeted us and made chitchat, asking about my brothers.

"Oh, you know . . . Rob is doing this and Kevin's doing that," Mom said, "and Debbie and John are moving from San Francisco to New York. . . ."

The pastor's face paled. "Am I to assume"—he looked at my mother—"that Debbie and John are living together?"

"Yes, we are," I piped up. What was all this now? I was standing right there, why didn't he just ask *me*?

The pastor cleared his throat, and this time he did look at me.

"You are living in sin. You cannot be married in this church."

"What are you talking about? Is that church policy? I mean, we've seen plenty of girls walk down the aisle very pregnant."

"It's not a policy of the church," he said. "It's just the way I feel."

Mom, meanwhile, burst into tears while I stood there in shock. The pastor hadn't asked me about my or John's relationship with Christ or if we wanted to do premarital counseling, none of the more important questions that really counted. If he had been just a bit compassionate, I would have told him that John and I intended to spend the next few months before the wedding living apart. (It was due to my busy schedule, but still . . .) But he was cold and immovable. I remember how disapproving he was ten years earlier when Mom and Dad got divorced and there was a bit of scandal in the church about that. It was payback time, I guess.

The pastor's shunning of my mother and me at that moment affected me so deeply, it took many, many years before I could embrace the idea of going back to church again.

His refusal to let us marry in our church wasn't the only omen before the wedding. A few weeks earlier when I broke the news to Rob that John and I were getting married, his reaction was less than congratulatory.

"Yeah, I've heard," he said, rolling his eyes. "Everybody is wondering why."

"What's that supposed to mean?" I asked.

"Well, John doesn't work or do anything. And you're so . . . heavy."

I froze. I looked at my brother, astounded by the words I'd just heard come out of his mouth. Did he feel I was somehow unlovable or not worthy of getting married because of my size? I knew he just wanted me to be happy and hadn't meant to hurt me. What he was really trying to say was: "You have a problem, and this man is maybe not the right man for you."

Still, hearing his words hurt.

*   *   *

JOHN AND I got married at another church in Orange County, where the pastor didn't ask if we were cohabitating and/or fornicating. My dear voice teacher Jane was my matron of honor (and her band played at the reception!), and at age thirty I walked down the aisle wrapped in so much virginal-white embroidered fabric, I looked like a walking tablecloth. I can't remember how much I weighed, but I remember the size of the dress: 24. Still, against all odds, we managed to pull off a romantic do, and I remember feeling happy and excited. Although it's a wedding taboo and bad luck for the groom to see the bride before the ceremony, we took all our wedding party photos before the ceremony instead of after. So the wedding planner devised a plan so that we could still experience our own version of "the big reveal"—that first moment the groom sees the bride in her dress. Before the photo sessions and ceremony, she put John up by the altar and flung open the front church doors for me to fake-walk down to him swaddled in my hundred yards of taffeta, twenty yards of tulle on my head, and a garden of lilies in my hands. He looked devastatingly handsome in his tails and even though he'd seen me in dozens of glamorous gowns before, when I reached the altar he was beaming and said, "You look very beautiful."

The wedding was a fairytale moment, and for a brief time I did feel beautiful. Until a woman I didn't know approached me during the reception to applaud me on my political statement.

"Debbie, I want to tell you how proud I am of you! You look so beautiful."

"Oh, thank you. It's such an important day, " I said with a smile, trying to remember who she was.

"I think it's just wonderful the example you're setting for heavy women," my unknown wedding guest continued, "by having this wedding, and even wearing a wedding dress."

Her words rang in my ears with the echo of my brother's words weeks before. *How brave of you to display yourself like this*, she was saying, between the lines. And, furthermore, *How brave of him to love you, even though you are a big, fat person. Lucky, lucky Debbie to have found a man to love her.*

I did my best to brush her comments aside and joined my bridesmaids—which included Lynn's daughters, Melinda and Marianne—who were motioning for me to pose with them by the three-tiered cake. They surrounded me in their poufy pink-and-white Jessica McClintock creations like a cloud of cotton candy. The barrier was not so thick, though, that we all couldn't hear Grandma Gruthusen, my mother's mom, whispering (or so she thought) off camera a few feet away in her wheelchair.

"Debbie always insisted she'd never get married!" she said, loudly, to my grandpa, sitting next to her in his own wheelchair.

"We can hear you, Grandma!" I called out to her, as we all burst into laughter—especially me. But her comment, and that of my anonymous guest, lingered in my mind well beyond the wedding night.

THE INTERNATIONAL TCHAIKOVSKY Competition is one of the most prestigious classical music competitions in the world and taken very, very seriously by the Moscovites. It gained fame in the United States at the height of the Cold War when American pianist Van Cliburn won the very first quadrennial competition and came home to a ticker-tape parade in New York. It's most famous for its piano division, but it also awards prizes to violinists, cellists, and singers.

A colleague of mine who'd entered the competition in the past and placed second with a silver medal gave me advice on the most important items to pack: cans of tuna and toilet paper. Food was scarce, and their toilet paper consisted of little waxed squares. "It's a smearfest," she warned me. I also went to the nearby dollar store and bought loads of nylons, Tic-Tacs, bubblegum, cigarettes, lipsticks, and condoms—everyday items that were impossible to get over there—and made up little packages as gifts to give to house-keepers or people working at the competition.

Unfortunately, my luggage took a wrong turn and didn't get to me for days. For once in my life, I'd decided to travel comfortably and had only sweatpants to wear. So that's what I arrived in for the first day of competition—stretched out, navy-blue Gap sweats and a T-shirt that had been slept in and spilled on during the long flight. I couldn't buy anything to wear because . . . there was nothing to buy. To make matters worse, what scant clothes or food that might have been available for purchase had been scooped up by the La Scala Ballet troupe, who'd been there weeks before and cleared out any bottled water, potato chips, chocolate bars, and T-shirts. I did my best to tart myself up with the curling iron in the bathroom—a tiny room with a shower in the center, out in the open without a screen or curtain, and two towels that had holes in them and were rough as sandpaper.

On the first day, we had to draw numbers to decide what order we'd compete. The competition took place at the Bolshoi Theatre and at the Tchaikovsky Concert Hall; and it was broadcast live on TV all over the country from start to finish for the entire two weeks.

Picture me there, surrounded by beautiful girls in silk dresses and every hair in place, while I look like a lazy American couch potato.

"Deborah Voy-yeeeeeeeeeeeeet!" someone calls. I go up on to the stage like a shlump, reach into the barrel, and pull out my number . . . 13. *Oh, hell. I should just go home right now. . . .*

A moment later, I hear the theater of over a thousand spectators burst into cheers and applause. "It is good luck here, the number thirteen," a theater page next to me whispered. Well, that was the first bit of good news I'd had in days.

The competition was very thorough, in that the first day you offered them five opera arias and they pick one and you pick one, and you sing those two—that's normal competition procedure. Then there was a section where you had to do a forty-minute recital, which had to include songs by Tchaikovsky and another Russian composer (I chose Rachmaninoff) plus a folk or pop song from your own country. All I could think of was "Beautiful Dreamer" which I'd heard Bing Crosby and Roy Orbison sing when I was a kid, a song my mother dreamily sang at the piano when I'd sat next to her.

Beautiful dreamer, wake unto me,
Starlight and dewdrops are waiting for thee . . .

The next day at the hotel I'm primping in the bathroom with my curling iron (my luggage finally arrived!) and the black-and-white TV set is on in the other room, when all of a sudden I hear myself singing "Beautiful Dreamer." I look at the TV and see the gauzy, slow-motion image of little girls running through a park with big bows in their hair, and couples lovingly looking at each other, and my voice in the background. Someone had turned my audition song into a music video! To this day I have no idea who—I assume it was the people involved with the competition. But there on the television was a bootleg recording of me paired with a video, or maybe it was some sort of commercial, I don't know. It was hysterical!

By the second week in Moscow, John and my brother Rob—who had joined us in week two for the semifinals—suspected we were being watched. Our hotel stood kitty-corner from the theater, on the other side of a huge, busy, six-lane boulevard. To get across, we were sternly warned, we had to use the underground pedestrian walkway. One night John, Rob, and I left the theater at two a.m. and were feeling a bit loopy. It was a beautiful summer night and the boulevard was completely empty.

"Oh, fuck it! Let's just run across the damn street!" Rob yelled. We started running and laughing . . . until we heard a booming Russian voice from above—from loudspeakers—scolding us. "Oh my God, we're going to get shot dead right here in the middle of Bolshaya Sadovaya Ulitsa Smirnoff . . . or whatever the hell it's called," I yelled to the guys. "Run!"

The next week was July Fourth, and as much as we loved standing in food lines and searching for borscht, we were aching to do something embarrassingly and thoroughly American. We hopped a cab over to Red Square and threw a Frisbee around for a few hours under the statue of Vladimir Lenin. Back at our hotel room (John's and mine), the three of us sampled every vodka known to humankind—that was one thing that was easy to get in Moscow. And we got tipsy, and rowdy, and we started mouthing off about how bloody hot it was, and why is no place here air-conditioned, and why are these wool blankets in our hotel rooms so itchy and horrible.

The next day, when we returned to our rooms after being out all day, the heavy wool blankets were missing, replaced by lightweight summer ones. How odd, and what a coincidence, we thought. But we didn't want to get all paranoid. Besides, we were hungover and couldn't trust our perception skills. But the next night, we were sitting around in the room when Rob tried to turn on the radio on the desk. The knob wouldn't budge. He picked up the radio to look behind it—the back part of the radio was hollow except for a cord coming out of it leading into a wall—no outlet, no jack, no nothing. John and Rob couldn't figure it out, and went out to the balcony to get some air.

"Debbie, Debbie! Get over here!" I rushed out and looked. Across from us was a huge government building, and lining the balcony directly opposite our room were rows of guards with binoculars to their eyes, staring right at us. We kept the curtains closed for the rest of our stay there.

The civilians, though, could not have been more warm and welcoming and passionately devoted to their music and to this competition. At least a thousand of them would line up every morning to buy a ticket to the competition that day, which would start at ten a.m. and often go till one a.m. They treated us like rock stars and brought flowers for the singers.

After more than two weeks of singing, I won the gold medal and first place in the female vocalist category—very rare for an American. I was the second American to have ever won it at that point.

To celebrate, we took my 5,000 rubles of prize money (which equaled somewhere between $140 and $480, depending on the day) and went out to eat at the best restaurant in Moscow. By this time, we were starving. We'd run out of tuna and Lipton Chicken Soup packages.

They didn't speak any English at the restaurant, and we couldn't understand the menu, so John attempted to draw a picture of what we wanted to eat with a pencil and paper. He was trying to draw a chicken and potatoes, but John's no artist. His potato looked like it had a head growing out of it; and he had placed it under the ass of the stick-figure chicken so that it looked like some sort of mutant egg alien monster.

"*Da, da, da!*" the waiter said, nodding. That worried me; what the heck was he going to bring? Thank goodness he arrived at our table with two of everything on the menu, and we devoured it all. The day before we left, I gave the rest of the rubles to Katja, the very sturdy woman who had been my translator for the duration of the trip. There was nothing to buy, and I couldn't exchange them for U.S. currency. The girl was in tears and hugged me; you'd have thought I'd given her a million dollars.

Back at home, I got the modern-day version of Van Cliburn's ticker-tape parade—an interview spot on *Good Morning America* with Joan Lunden. The *L.A. Times* even called my mother for a quote: "I'm thrilled," said Mom. "I'm so excited for her. This is the highlight of her career. I'm sure it will open many doors for her."

The win was a very big deal because the Russians really don't want to give it to an American. After that, I was off to Fort Worth, Texas. I'd gotten a phone call at home from Van Cliburn himself as soon as I returned to New York; he wanted to hire me to come sing at his mother's seventieth birthday party a few days later, which I did. I sang my one-hit-wonder, "Beautiful Dreamer," now famous on late-night Russian television. After the party, he invited me to his home for a private soirée and showed me his souvenirs from his many travels. Every table top, every wall, in every room was adorned with memorabilia.

I was particularly drawn to a framed photo atop the piano of two little boys, around age five, wearing shorts and sitting side by side at a piano, playing together.

"Do you know who that is?" he asked. I shook my head. "It's me and Jimmy Levine." Soon enough I would get to know Maestro Levine's face very well.

WINNING THE GOLD medal at the Tchaikovsky Competition was a major turning point in my career and attracted a lot of attention. What followed for Lucky Number 13 was a lucky break that sealed the deal for my destiny.

That November I was covering Amelia in *Ballo* for Aprile Millo at the Met—I was already cast in the role for the New York Metropolitan Opera Parks Concerts the following summer—when I got a call from my agent one Friday night. Susan Dunn was singing Amelia in San Francisco and had taken ill and wasn't sure if she'd be able to do the upcoming Sunday matinee. San Francisco wanted to know if I'd fly over, just in case she couldn't go on.

Well, the San Francisco Opera was like family to me after my years there, but I didn't want to go all that way for nothing. I had flashbacks of my Margaret Price and Carol Neblett situations a few years earlier when I'd rushed over thinking I was going on, only to be left standing there in wig and makeup, like a stood-up bride at the altar. I went to bed, restless over what to do; around two a.m. I noticed the light flashing on my answering machine. My agent had called: Dunn was definitely canceling the Sunday matinee, and probably several more after that. Early next morning, John and I were on a plane, and shortly after landing I was shuffled into a quickie two-hour stage rehearsal, a one-hour rehearsal with the conductor, and a rushed costume fitting for my full skirt and heavy cape.

John was traveling with me steadily now, in the role of "taking care of the family business." But it was really because he had no other work—his job with my agent didn't last and I was tired of traveling alone. Mostly what he did on the road was feed me. We'd go out to fantastic dinners after performances and cap the evening off with a huge dessert at two a.m. Or John would cook incredible, fattening meals if our lodging had a kitchen. Both of us always made sure that, wherever we were, our hotel room was well stocked with munchies for late-night snacks. I was a closet eater and never overate in front of other people. Judging from what I ate in public, you'd think I'd be half my size. By now my five-foot-six-inch frame was carrying about 290 pounds.

It could have been emotional eating. Three months after we got married, I found out that John had carried on a year-long affair back when we were living together. Even though I knew we weren't madly in love with each other, it still broke my heart, and I'd like to think that had I known before we got married, I wouldn't have gone through with it. I'd like to *think* that—but I also believe part of me did know it, sensed it on an unconscious level, and that that was why I'd felt such a panic to marry him quickly.

I called Mom from the opera house and she alerted the whole family: Debbie was going onstage! They all planned to be there— Mom, Dad, their spouses, my brothers, Grandma Voigt, Jane. I was thrilled and terrified, and was surviving on no sleep and plenty of adrenaline. Which may have contributed to what happened next.

Onstage at the next day's matinee, all was going great . . . until the singer playing the role of the fortune teller shoved me a bit too eagerly during one scene as I left the stage. I could feel myself hurtling toward the floor, half onstage half off, falling in slow motion. The words shot out of me like an unstoppable cannon shooting a *ballo*:

"*Oh, SHIT!!!!*"

I was hoping only the first few rows heard me. My family and friends were in row ten, so they were safe. But everyone for sure saw me fall flat on my face just offstage, and the critics were none too kind:

> . . . now diva sized and hardly nimble to begin with, [she] tripped and seemed to go headlong down the stairs that led offstage.

> Superior direction may yet mitigate her unwieldy stage demeanor. At one point she flopped and floundered on the floor, thanks to a shove. . . .

But my hometown audience knew me and they were rooting for me. It was the first time my parents saw me in an important role and I caught a glimpse of them from the stage; they looked happily astonished. And, thankfully, the local newspapers focused on my voice, not my weight.

> [She displayed a] genuine spinto sound, gleaming and urgent at the top, imbued with a long line and supple breath control.

Sometimes, I have learned, people are in the right place at the right time. Call it fate, call it destiny, call it coincidence—but making the right move at just the right moment can change a person's life.

Two months after Amelia, I was making my debut in the title role of Ariadne in Strauss's *Ariadne auf Naxos* for the Boston Lyric Opera, a small opera company that was paying me very little, but they were giving me an apartment for free, and it was a great role for an anti-diva like me. The story is an opera-within-an-opera, and in the first half my character is an operatic prima donna who displays wild, diva-esque behavior. In the second half, she becomes Ariadne, a woman stranded on an island, pining for her lover who deserted her, before she is finally rescued by Bacchus—the god of wine.

JOHN AND I arrived in Boston in December, and it was, of course, one of the worst winters Boston ever had.

Our apartment was half basement, half aboveground, and it was freezing because the furnace kept breaking down. Since we were going to be in Boston for a month, we'd brought our cats with us— Tiffy and Ballo—and in our wisdom, had drugged them for the flight. Well, the flight was less than an hour from New York and the drugs had kicked in when we got to Boston; once we let them out of their cages, they were bumping into walls and rolling their eyelids like drunken sailors.

Taking a cue from the cats, we threw a wild party at the apartment and invited friends from the cast and in the process of our riotous revelry, we accidentally set off the fire alarm in the middle of the night and could not figure out how to turn the damn thing off. I teetered on a skinny metal folding chair and ripped the thing out of the ceiling.

Since I was at my all-time high in weight at that point, my costuming was becoming a problem, just as Jane's vodka-swilling colleague back at Cal State had predicted. Nothing they had in the wardrobe department fit me—there's only so much a seamstress can do—and they couldn't find a size 26 Ariadne costume for rent. An angel came to my rescue when one of the financial patrons for the company, a really wonderful (and wealthy) woman named Lee Gillespie, donated the money for costumes to be specially made for me. Lee had just had back surgery, but was such an opera fan she'd come by rehearsals and lie down on the floor under the piano, close her eyes, and listen to us.

We had a great cast and we grew very close to one another. One reason was because we were all young and hungry together—relative beginners being paid very little, working really hard, and loving what we were doing. We were in the trenches, the orchestra pit, together. Another reason we bonded was because we could all feel a bit of magic surrounding the production, the feeling that everything was clicking, and that was exciting.

Before I even got to Boston, I had an inkling this role would be important for me. I was studying with a well-known Manhattan pianist and voice coach, Levering Rothfuss, to prepare—he had worked with such greats as Marilyn Horne, Tatiana Troyanos, and Carol Neblett. We'd meet in his apartment and work on Ariadne's arias. Lev had a jaded side to him, having been in the business for a long time, so I knew if something moved him it had to be really, really great and true.

On the day I sang through the entire opera for him in his living room, I looked over to him after I'd finished and he sat on his piano bench with tears running down his face.

"This is exactly where your voice is supposed to be at this moment in time," he told me, wiping his face. "This is your role. There is no one—*no one*—right now who sings it as well as you do." His words made me shiver.

Maybe I sang it so well because I understood her. Ariadne had a melancholy I related to. And yet she was hopeful, too. She sits on a rock, having been abandoned, and suffers great emotional turmoil as she waits for someone to rescue her, but she doesn't give up.

Playing the other side of the role, the "prima donna," is some of the most fun I've had singing opera. It's one of the few roles I've ever played that allowed me to show my humor and really lampoon the opera diva caricature; it's so over the top. I even put a little humor and levity to the mournful Ariadne when I played her later in the Met Opera production. In one scene I added my own little stage business that has lived on with other sopranos. There's a moment when Ariadne is surrounded by a group of clowns juggling and throwing scarves in the air and she's upset. In the middle of the scene I reached out, grabbed one of the scarves, and blew my nose in it. It was ad-libbed, and the audience roared.

AS A FLUKE—OR was it destiny again?—a prominent opera critic, John Rockwell, was in the audience on our opening night, January 16, 1991. He'd come to Boston to write an article for the *New York Times* on the little opera companies that were lately sprouting up in Boston, and he found himself, by chance, in our audience at the Emerson Majestic Theatre. Two days later I got a call from my agent.

"Did you see your review by John Rockwell in the *New York Times?*" he was yelling into the phone. He didn't wait for an answer; he read it out loud to me:

> . . . it introduced one truly remarkable singer in Deborah Voigt. . . .
>
> Friday's performance, her first of Ariadne, revealed one of the most important American singers to come along in years. It is wise to counsel caution, but foolish to stifle enthusiasm. Miss Voigt's voice seems huge. It was hard to tell just how huge in the roughly 1,200-seat Majestic Theater—but it rang effortlessly in the ears.
>
> More to the point, it sounded warm and solid and musically shaped. The obvious comparison among earlier American dramatic sopranos is Eileen Farrell. If Miss Voigt does not soon become an important Wagnerian soprano, she will have taken a wrong career turn.

I had to sit down. This critic had written a love letter to me but I could barely absorb the magnitude of his words. I didn't know if I deserved such praise, and I had no idea how to embrace the success of the moment. It was my first major, major exposure in something that really mattered. It was pretty heady for a young singer to be singled out like that in a review, and to have it in the *New York Times*, and written by their chief classical music critic.

My phone rang off the hook after that, with friends and colleagues calling to congratulate me. Of course my family called, too.

"Congratulations, honey, we're so happy for you!" my mother said over the phone. And she was. But I don't know if my family understood the enormity of what this review meant, and what it was leading up to. They were still very innocent about the opera world, and still a bit of the mindset like, "Oh, Debbie sings, and it's so easy for her, and she's having her fun."

The two roles I played within those few months—Amelia and Ariadne—would become signature roles for me over the next two decades of my career.

A career that, in one moment on the phone in an ice-cold basement apartment in Boston, took a monumental leap forward.

11

Leona, Leonie, Luciano: Breakthroughs and Breaking Up

FIFTEEN MINUTES BEFORE showtime and I'm singing under an oak tree in the Bronx.

It was the summer of '91 and I was about to make my Metropolitan Opera debut as Amelia in *Ballo* in Van Cortlandt Park for the Met's five-borough recital series, but I had one delicate problem: there was another diva sitting in my makeshift dressing room, prepping to go on and steal my debut.

My very first contract with the Met was to cover Amelia and Ortlinde (one of the Valkyries in *Die Walküre*) in the annual summer concerts performed in various parks in New York. I was the understudy for Leona Mitchell, a Grammy Award–winning soprano who sang for eighteen seasons as a leading spinto soprano at the Met. My contract stipulated that of the six performances I covered, I would get to sing one for sure, and this was arranged to be my night. We'd had a lot of rain dates that summer, and quite a few postponements and cancellations—but finally my time had come. They had sent a glass carriage—a Town Car—to pick me up to ensure I'd be there.

I arrived at seven p.m. to give myself time to change into my dress (these were noncostume concerts) and fix my hair and makeup in the trailers that were set up as dressing rooms. I walked into the trailer and . . . there's Leona, warming up.

"Oh!" I said, surprised. "You're warming up?"

"Yes, of course," Leona answered quickly, getting back to her scales. Another singer in the recital, Erie Mills, who was singing the part of Oscar, was also in the trailer, getting ready. She exchanged a look with me that said: *You and I know it's your day to sing, but Leona doesn't.* But could I have been mistaken? Clearly, if the great Leona Mitchell is warming up, Leona Mitchell is going to sing. I stowed my bag in the corner of the trailer and tippy-toed out, heading two trailers down to find Jonathan Friend, one of the artistic administrators.

"Mr. Friend, am I singing Amelia tonight?"

"What do you mean? Of course you're singing Amelia tonight. Why are you asking me this?"

"Because Ms. Mitchell"—I pointed to the other trailer—"is in there warming up. She thinks she's on tonight."

His face dropped. It was surely an honest mistake on Leona's part, but this who's-on-first soprano confusion had to be fixed, and quickly. By now it was 7:45, and time was running out—I had to warm up and get dressed. I moved as far away from the trailer as possible and hid behind a row of trees so that Leona wouldn't hear or see me do my own scales while Jonathan handled this. I kept my eye on the trailer door, though, waiting to see signs of Leona descending.

I had worked with her a year before in a concert performance of *Aida* where she was singing the lead and I was singing the voice of the High Priestess, an offstage role. She was friendly, a lovely person—and this must have been an awkward and humiliating situation for her, to be bumped by this unknown young soprano whom she met a year ago singing a disembodied voice and now . . . the main role.

I felt terrible, but by now it was 7:50, and I had to get in there.

In the trailer, Leona was gathering her clothes and bags with the help of an assistant when I slipped in and began doing my makeup.

"Do you have all your things, then?" the assistant asked her.

"No," said Leona, "one of my bags is behind *her*." She pointed at me. Yikes.

She left, and ten minutes later I was onstage.

Amelia's first scene in Act I is the most difficult part in the entire opera—she enters with a great deal of urgency to meet with the fortuneteller to get love advice about her husband's best friend. Not only is she desperate, she's also afraid to be observed meeting with the seer in her hut. Her first few lines have to be whispered, with a tremor in her voice. By the end of the trio (unbeknownst to her, her husband's best friend is also present but hidden from view, overhearing the women's conversation) Amelia is singing long, arching Verdi phrases that give the audience their first opportunity to really hear the voice of the soprano. But I wasn't nervous. It was a role I absolutely adored, and I could sing it in my sleep—I probably did—and I was in the bloom of my career and voice. I was more worried that the bugs swarming around the surrounding stage lights would fly into my mouth when I opened it. As I hoped, the performance went very well—smooth sailing, and singing.

EVEN BEFORE MY strongly reviewed Boston Ariadne, I'd already auditioned for Met conductor James Levine and General Manager Joe Volpe and from that had gotten my summer parks contract; so you could say my foot was already in the door before Ariadne. But the day John Rockwell's *New York Times* review landed on Jonathan Friend's desk, they happened to be looking for someone to sing the part of Elektra's sister, Chrysothemis, in their new production of the Strauss opera, to premiere in March 1992. I was singing a similar repertoire by the same composer, so everything came together at the right moment.

They had already cast the well-known Hildegard Behrens, who was in her prime, in the lead role, and Leonie Rysanek as the mother, Klytämnestra. Rockwell's review had prompted Jonathan to come to Boston to see me perform as Ariadne and arrange a stage audition for the role of Chrysothemis. What made this such a turning point for me was that it was a new production. For singers, especially when you are starting out in your career, performing in a new production is really important because it comes with a new director, new costumes, new staging, new set—and leads to more press attention than if it was a revival. And the director for this one, Austrain-born Otto Schenk, was already known for his lavish, realist, traditionalist stagings that always garnered attention.

The character of Chrysothemis is a great part. She wants to leave home and marry and have children, but her sister, Elektra, who is trying to exact revenge against their stepfather for the murder of their father, wants her to help in her plan to kill him. At this point in the libretto I had my first panic attack while rehearsing. In the scene, Elektra is trying to convince Chrysothemis to sneak into the palace with an ax by saying, "You're so thin, you could move between the crevices in the walls of the palace without being observed."

I flipped out. The Met wasn't using surtitles yet at that point— English translations on screen—but those who were familiar with the opera or understood German would understand and be laughing their heads off. There I was, this gigantic woman who couldn't slip through anything. I crossed my fingers that no one in the audience would understand the line and laugh.

My next anxiety attack came when I first saw myself in hair and costume.

Standing in front of the dressing room mirror with costume designer Jürgen Rose, I burst into tears. My costume was basically a muumuu, which made me look even bigger—like throwing a tent over an elephant—and he'd stuffed my hair into a skull cap to make me look bald. Apparently the lavish director was taking a decidedly nonrealistic approach this time around, and within his concept of the show, I looked like an enormous body with a tiny, hairless head— like an overgrown alien.

"I can't go onstage like this, I look like a pinhead! Can't you . . ." I cried.

"It's your job to sing," Jürgen snapped, "not tell me what to do with your costume."

I was horrified and mid-sob when in walked Met Artistic Director Sarah Billinghurst, who used to be at the San Francisco Opera in my Adler Fellowship days. Sarah's known me longer than just about anybody in my professional life, and she's used to hearing me cry— she's the one I cried to on the phone that time from Munich during my Euro sojourn with Grandma Voigt.

"What's the matter, darling?"

"He said . . . I can't . . ."—I was sucking in gusts of air between sobs and words—"have any hair . . . and I'm . . . going to . . . have my head wrapped. . . . And I can't go onstage looking like this!"

Sarah handed me a tissue and ushered Jürgen out the door.

"There, there. We'll put hair on your head. Don't you worry."

And Sarah arranged it, God bless her.

I was more sensitive about my size than usual because I kept growing and was now 320 pounds. And a conversation I'd had recently with John about my weight had lodged in my heart like a shard of glass.

John usually sat in a house seat during my performances to get the audience's reaction firsthand as I'd walk out for the first time. In our conversation, he was very delicately trying to tell me that there were times when I'd walk onstage with my 320 pounds cinched in by a corset and the audience would laugh at me.

"Honey, you know that you're a big girl—bigger than most of the girls onstage. And you know that there are certain angles that are not going to be flattering to you in any way, shape, or form. And there are moments when you come onstage and there is a tittering of laughter. For some people, it's shocking to them to see someone of your size walk out there. It takes them a little while to get used to it."

I started to cry. John was not a malicious man, I knew he was telling me the truth, but the truth in this case was hard to hear. It was my job to play characters who were in love and loved by men; but if people were going to laugh at me as soon as they saw me, how were they going to believe me onstage? John, I was sure, loved me no matter what my weight was. In fact, I assumed he rather liked my size.

"John, if you were going to marry someone else again, you'd choose a big girl again, wouldn't you?" I was obviously trying to make myself feel better. The one person in the world who is supposed to accept and love you as you are is your husband. But my plan to get John to admit this backfired right in my face.

"I'd . . . you know, Deb"—he was tripping over his words—"I guess I'd probably choose a thinner woman."

At that, I went beyond crying into silence. I didn't have any words, or any tears, just numbness.

The soprano singing the part of the mother and murderous Queen Klytämnestra, Leonie Rysanek, was the major Strauss-and-Wagner diva for decades at the Met along with Birgit Nillson. Leonie was especially known as the leading Chrysothemis of the day—maybe of all time—so I was doing a role she'd done for years, and was, in a way, taking over her role. Leonie had been a dramatic soprano her entire career but now, well into her sixties, she had moved a notch to mezzo-soprano.

It was pretty daunting, and I was very nervous and wondered how she was going to react to me. On the first day of rehearsal I tried to let her know I was humbled to be following in her footsteps.

"This is my first Chrysothemis," I said, during a break, "and

I'm excited, but nervous. Please, give me any advice you want to give me."

She smiled graciously. "Don't worry, I will!"

For the rest of our production she was completely supportive, she never said to me, "This is how I did it," or "You should do this," and never advised me to do anything different from what I was already doing, encouraging me to go further with it. "You're on the right track!" she kept saying. I adored her and admired her, as a person and an artist.

I had met her once before, back in my San Francisco Opera days. She'd come to sing a lead in an opera in which I had a little part. I had a photo that was taken during one of the rehearsals that pictured her in the foreground, and me, standing in the shadows, in the background. Now, years later, she surprised me with a memory from back then. She had heard me sing from backstage, she said, "and I wondered . . . who does that voice belong to?"

I learned a lot from Leonie and Hildegard Behrens during that run. One bit of acting advice I got from Hildegard I still use to this day. Back then, opera singers weren't expected or required to "act" their roles much. We used to call it "park and bark"—just get onstage and sing great, no need to do much more than that.

Hildegard and I had a very dramatic scene together—my big singing scene—where we are sitting on the floor and I'm wailing to her about how we sit there, day after day, in anguish. As we rehearsed the scene, I'd reach out to touch her to try and convey Chrysothemis's pain.

During one rehearsal, she gently stopped my hand and said quietly:

"Why don't you reach for me but not really touch me. It's stronger, lonelier, that way." She was right. The director loved it. Opera singers were so used to playing it big back then, we didn't know yet that a subtle gesture can move an audience even more than a grand one. For the first time in my fledgling career I felt like I was entering the Big League. Backstage, in my dressing room, I had a piano, a shower, a fabulous chaise longue. I kept my door open as people ran by in the hall, pushing costume racks, running in and out of dressing rooms, wishing each other "Toi, toi, toi!" (opera-speak for "break a leg"). I could hear the other singers warm up in their dressing rooms and the director and conductor giving last-minute notes. Fifteen minutes before showtime for opening night, I did what I always do: I shut the door and sat quietly for a moment and said a prayer:

Dear God. Please help me sing well for you tonight.

And He did. At the end of the evening when we came out for our bows it was clear from the applause that it was my night. One review described the response as "a roar in the opera house," and Peter G. Davis of *New York* magazine wrote, "her shining soprano was balm to the ear and soared easily through the music."

The best review I got, however, was for my acting—and from one of the finest actors of my generation. My dear friend the casting director Jack Doulin, with whom I'd worked a few years earlier, was doing a play with actress Julie Harris at the time, and he'd brought her to opening night as his date.

The next morning, he woke me up with her thespian critique: "Debbie, Julie thought you were amazing!"

"What?" I nearly dropped the phone. "What did she say?"

"She said, 'She conveyed so much of her character's complexity in her voice. She inhabited her character beautifully!' "

As far as I was concerned, that was as good as an Academy Award.

The run was a success and a boon for my career, but what I treasured the most was gracious Leonie. We kept in touch until she died, six years later, at age seventy-one, of bone cancer in a hospital in her beloved Vienna. A few months later I received a small package in the mail from her husband, Elu. In it was the black enamel, pearl, and gold filigree brooch that Leonie often wore. It was very old and quite fragile, nothing extravagant or expensive, but understated and suffused with heart and sentiment. It was a beautiful goodbye.

MY CAREER WAS just taking off, and to take advantage of the momentum I'd hired a publicist. Not just any publicist, but the notorious Herbert Breslin, whose claim to fame was that he was Luciano Pavarotti's longtime manager. Herbert was much despised in the business because he could do and ask for whatever he wanted and people had to do it, because he had Luciano. When he met me, he was bewildered, then annoyed, and finally amused by my undivalike behavior—he was not used to it.

"Kid, we have to create some kind of mystique for you," he told me during our first meeting in his office. Herbert always talked like he was in a forties film noir. He slammed phones and swore at everyone and their mother and I'd heard he had the best table at Sardi's reserved for lunch every day. He didn't understand my good-girl suburban shtick, and he wanted me to bitch it up.

"You're too open. You're too sunny!" he said, accusingly. "We've got to find some way to make you more . . . more . . ."

I burst into tears, as usual.

"Herbert, how am I going to do that? How am I going to create something and maintain it for the rest of my career? Something that's false and not true?"

He handed me a tissue. At least *own* my diva stature, he urged.

"Come on, Voigt. After all, you're Deborah Voigt. You're not Miss Scratch-your-ass!"

A few weeks after my *Elektra* premiere, I got a call from Herbert. "Hey, kid."

"Hey, Herbert. Um. What's going on?"

"I'm calling to tell you you're the new Tucker winner."

The Richard Tucker Award was a coveted award for up-and-comers. Named after the famous American tenor, it was awarded to an American singer every year who was "poised on the edge of a major national and international career" in the hopes that the award money—a cool $30,000—could help the artist continue to great heights. For the award presentation, the Richard Tucker Music Foundation throws a big gala every year, aired live on PBS, and the recipient sings duets with other illustrious vocalists. It's a major black-tie event.

Herbert wanted me to embrace my inner diva-ness? I may have been too sunny and approachable to be a real diva, but I knew how to dress like one, and I planned to go to this gala looking like a queen. I contacted one of the best operatic gown designers in the country, Barbara Matera—famous for the dazzling dresses she'd made for Joan Sutherland—and we got to work several months in advance, with measurements and muslin fittings in her Hell's Kitchen showroom. I was so huge that I couldn't buy anything off the rack; but, anyway, this sort of gown had to be custom made.

It was a wine-colored velvet with pieces of pink chiffon and georgette built into it and sleeves that puffed out, with gorgeous little crystals sprinkled down the front of the dress. The neckline was open, and there was a *Flying Nun* cap thing around my shoulders. The sleeves made me look like a linebacker, but the dress was, in the best diva tradition, truly over-the-top . . . it was spectacular. To this day it was the most I ever spent for a dress: $5,000. But that night, I felt like a million bucks.

THAT FALL OF 1992, John and I went to the City of Light for my debut at the Paris Opera Bastille, where I reprised my Chrysothemis in *Elektra*. I was feeling good about my year so far. A month before, *Vanity Fair* had published a reportage about the upcoming opera season, and I was one of the handful chosen to be photographed and interviewed. The photographer tried to do whimsical, offbeat, fairytale-like setups for each portrait—and for me, they dressed me up as an angel. I was at my all-time high in weight so far (325) and they gave me this big, drapelike blue *shmatte* to wrap around my body and a pair of really cool gold wings. The hair stylist piled my hair up high into a Grecian do, to look proportionate to my hips, and for the final touch—a dripping adornment of pearls. It was a pretty picture, but no matter how you draped me, you couldn't hide the fact that I was a huge woman.

So now I was in Paris, getting ready for my first rehearsal with Eva Marton, who was singing Elektra, and who wasn't known for her politeness. I walked into the rehearsal room and the first thing she said to me was:

"Oh my, I saw that picture of you in *Vanity Fair.*" Pause. "I couldn't believe how fat you looked."

And then she laughed it off. I couldn't tell if her remark was meant to be nice or catty. Was she paying me a compliment, saying I looked thinner in person and that the wide-angled lens made me look bigger than I actually was? Or was she just telling me I looked fat? Either way, I used the remark as fuel for my singing, and during rehearsal that day I sang like a goddess.

In between the busy rehearsal schedule, John and I attempted to have a romantic time in Paris, but we weren't doing a very good job of it. I vaguely remember having dinner at the top of the Eiffel Tower. We'd been married only a few years but had been together since I was sixteen, so whatever romance we'd had was long gone. I felt more excited about the pâtisserie next to our Left Bank hotel than I did about John.

The truth was, I was angry and losing patience.

Throughout the years, as I was climbing in my career and he was doing odd jobs, driving buses or working behind the counter at stores, I tried to get him interested in a career of his own, but nothing clicked for him. Every time he started something new, he'd fizzle out after barely beginning. Once we got married, we decided he'd try being my manager for a while and take care of me, the family business, so that we could travel together. But he wasn't doing that so well, either. He didn't have a business head and he had trouble getting organized. One of his ideas was to take over my website and spiff it up, so we bought a computer and he did some research and then . . . that, too, fizzled out. Next, he decided he wanted to be a photographer, so he bought camera equipment, top-quality stuff and the most expensive kind. He liked nice things—designer suits and only the best cigars. After he purchased the cameras, lenses, flashes, motor drives, and filters, we made a darkroom at home so he could develop his own film and print his photos. But what photos did he take? All he wanted to shoot was inside the opera houses, where they already had their own staff photographers.

"John, we go to all these incredible cities," I said. "Why not get out there and take pictures and try and sell them to travel or airline magazines?" He nodded, but he never did it. Where was his drive? Where was his ability to do a job, any job, with commitment? I couldn't even depend on him to pay our electric bill on time.

It all came to a head for me over something so simple as that. A year or more after Paris, my mother was visiting us, and when she and I left to do some errands together, I asked John to pay a few bills while we were gone. They needed to be taken care of right away because they were overdue. When we got home a few hours later, the bills were still sitting on the kitchen table, unopened, and John was in the middle of one of his favorite hobbies—having a beer. It's not like he didn't take care of those bills because he was busy doing something; he didn't *do* anything. (My brother's words before our wedding came back to haunt me more than once.)

Later that day as my mother was getting into her car to leave, she stood on the driveway and hesitated before getting in. She'd watched John and me for two decades and seen him coast along aimlessly, even when it came to me. He wasn't a bad guy, he was just . . . inert.

"Listen, Debbie. I'm going to say this to you and I'm only going to say it once."

I braced myself.

"If you decide to divorce John, you have my complete support."

It was probably the first and only time in my life that I actually listened to my mother about my love life. I thought about her words seriously, instead of automatically rebelling against them. But still, I lingered. I was unhappy, but I didn't know what to do about it. When it came to John, *I* was inert, too.

IN APRIL OF 1995 I had my second Pavarotti experience; and this time I was singing with him, sort of. We were in London, at the Royal Opera House, for a performance of *Ballo*, and in the middle of our love duet in Act II, he disappeared. There we were, singing and singing, and then came the part where I'm to sing alone . . . and suddenly I was feeling very, very alone. I look to my right and no Luciano. I look to my left, no Luciano! Panicked, I glanced over to the wings and there he was. He had left the stage to get a glass of water. I remember thinking: *Is he gonna come back?*

Apparently he was known for this, but no one had warned me. I gamely kept singing, and a few minutes later back he came onstage . . . entering backwards, as though he'd been looking for conspirators in the wings and was returning from his search. It was quite hilarious. When we performed *Ballo* again at the Met, he did it again during the same love duet (there must be something especially dehydrating about his part in the duet), but at least this time I knew he always came back. And he's Luciano Pavarotti, so he can do whatever he wants.

When we were in London, I recall, he'd just come out with a new scent for women called "Pavarotti Donna." David Letterman had a joke about it that he was repeating constantly—"Luciano Pavarotti has released a new perfume and it's called 'Sauce', as in 'spaghetti sauce.' " We had a dinner party after the show one night, and Luciano, as he often would, showed up still wearing his costume and his wig and in full makeup. He was quirky and everybody adored it because he's Luciano!

So we're having this dinner party and we all start eating, and that's the moment that he decides everyone should have a whiff of his perfume. So he gets up and he walks around the room and while we're eating, he sprays everyone with the stuff! And, well, it wasn't what I'd call a beautiful scent. John and I went back to our hotel reeking of it.

IT'S FUNNY THE way art really does imitate life, or maybe it's the other way around. All I know is that somewhere along the way, the operatic roles I delved into onstage began to eerily parallel the dramas playing out for me offstage, in my own real life. I had gotten Mom's blessing to split from John—I imagined she and my father had been waiting twenty years for my relationship with him to end, thinking it was a flash-in-the-pan, teenaged rebellion from the beginning. It probably was. About a year after Mom's big statement in the driveway, I finally pulled the plug on my marriage and two-decades-long relationship with John.

In November '95 we were in Dresden, where I was singing Strauss's *Die Frau ohne Schatten*, which translates into English as "The Woman Without a Shadow" (though I've seen the title rendered elsewhere, ironically, as "Your Man Is Always on Your Side"). The role was new to me and it was a very, very serious role and I found it emotionally draining.

My character, the Empress (Die Kaiserin), lives in an otherworldly realm with her husband, the Emperor, beyond earth. She is only half human, and because of that, she has no shadow—which also symbolizes her inability to have any children. She's having trouble with her husband, who has gone off hunting, and she doesn't understand what's going on between the two of them. Her nurse, who has cared for her since infancy, suggests they go down to earth to observe the mortals and perhaps learn from them. They follow a couple who are also having problems because the husband is a very simple man and his wife is unhappy and bored with him.

On Thanksgiving Day we had a grueling eight-hour rehearsal where no one spoke any English, and so for me, with my scant German, it was a major effort communicating with anyone about anything. As I walked home from the theater to the little apartment where John and I were staying, my mind was spinning. I was playing a character going through all sorts of questions about her relationship with her husband just as I was questioning mine. My marriage had been falling apart for a long time—John and I weren't even sleeping in the same room or bed together anymore. I was cold, tired, and upset; I just wanted to get inside and curl up in bed.

John, on the other hand, was eager to talk, or to go out and have fun after being stuck all day in the apartment. He was suggesting we go out for a faux Thanksgiving dinner, but in those days, not so long after the Wall came down, Dresden was still very much *East* Germany. Hardly anyone spoke English, and there was very little in terms of service or restaurants. And besides, I was pooped.

"John, I really need to rest, and I need some time alone."

"You've been alone all day."

"No. Actually, *you* have been alone all day. I've been working and dealing with dozens of people and problems and—"

"Well, maybe I'll go out for a walk, then."

As I stood at the window, watching him as he roamed aimlessly along the Elbe river, smoking one of those expensive cigars he liked, a question popped into my head:

Do you want this man to be your life forever? Is this all you want?

I had married John for all the wrong reasons—out of insecurity, because I didn't think I was good enough, pretty enough, thin enough, or deserving enough to have a real, true love of my own. Because I was scared to be left alone.

When John returned from his walk, I told him it was time for us to be apart for a while.

At that moment, far away from home and stuck in a barren marriage, I decided that I wanted more.

ACT III

CRESCENDO

12

Dangerous Liaisons and
Plácido's Kiss

THE SNOW FELL softly on Johann Strauss's statue. A few months after I told John it was over, I was walking alone through the Stadtpark
in Vienna in the wee hours and came upon a beautiful gilded likeness
of the famous Waltz King. I had come to the city in early 1996 to record *Elektra*, composed by that *other* Strauss, Richard, and after a long
day at work I needed some air. In the early-morning quiet, surrounded
by old-fashioned gas lamps casting light onto the park's white canvas,
I felt like I was in a painting. I brushed away the snow from the stone
and looked at Strauss's name, in awe of his brilliance and grateful that
I was part of the classical world of artists and music.

It was a magical moment—and a rare one of stillness and con-
templation amid my new, frenzied life since leaving John.

I was recording *Elektra* with fellow soprano Alessandra Marc,
who was considered one of the biggest opera singers, weight-wise,
until I hit the scene. The joke going around opera circles was that
she and I and another larger-than-life soprano, Sharon Sweet, were
going to go on tour together as "The Three Ton-ers." Very clever,
but a little hurtful, too.

Alessandra was a colorful, boisterous character famous for throwing wild pool parties where opera singers—especially Alessandra
herself—got tipsy and flung off their bathing suits. She was also

one of my first cautionary tales when it came to weight and work. At that time she was still Queen Bee of the stage, but a few years later she would become so big in size, people simply stopped hiring her. That made her furious. She was an in-your-face kind of woman and if you ticked her off, you knew about it. I remember hearing she had a concert in Berlin that didn't go so well and the audience booed, after which Alessandra defiantly gave them the finger.

But, oh, we did have fun together. On our last night in Vienna, we sat in a smoky little bar at the fancy Hotel Johann Strauss all night and drank dirty martinis (an homage to my olive-juice bender at age five) and smoked Cuban cigars (Montecristos). But although I was her drinking and cigar buddy, I wasn't her eating buddy. In Vienna, I ate like a bird—a cliché I never thought I'd use to describe myself. It was around the time when I told John it was over that I discovered the dynamite weight-loss cocktail fenfluramine-phentermine (street name: fen-phen). It was all the craze in the diet world and *I was in love with it.*

It zapped away my hunger, jacked up my metabolism, and in four months I had lost sixty pounds. Sure, I didn't sleep much and was up at three in the morning doing calligraphy. But I got down to 240 pounds—which was still well above "normal," but it felt more normal to me. For the first time in a long time, I bought clothes off the rack in a "normal" store, and I was feeling good, I was feeling energized, I was feeling . . . sexy.

John had been the only man I'd ever been with my entire life, and now that I was a free woman—free from the constraints of marriage, my parents, and the church that had turned me away—I unleashed all my inhibitions and went looking for love in all the wrong places, with all the wrong men. If my parents thought John was a bad boy, they hadn't seen anything yet. I found out later that fen-phen affected your libido by either killing it or launching it out into orbit. Clearly, mine was going the orbit route and I went along for the ride, embarking on a year of living dangerously.

Pumped up and armed with a new, flirty wardrobe, I went online and scanned the dating websites. I don't even know if you can call it dating—I created a fake name and persona and went directly to sites that catered to men who liked larger women. The men I met didn't have old-fashioned "dating" in mind.

At one of those sites I hooked up with Tim, who lived in Manhattan and had placed an advertisement seeking "some company this afternoon to go skiing with me." I knew he didn't mean the kind of snow you find on the slopes. I'd tried cocaine once or twice with John and wasn't into it, but I went over to see this guy anyway. Why? I'm not even sure I knew. I needed . . . something, I didn't know what.

When Tim opened his apartment door, I was immediately *not* attracted to him. He was blondish, chunky, and short—the opposite of my type. But I was feeling high and pretty and bold, so I fooled around with him anyway and enjoyed the attention. I also enjoyed being this anonymous someone, acting out a secret, bad-girl fantasy life. But here's the kicker—as I was getting my things together to leave Tim's apartment, I glanced over at his coffee table and saw that day's *New York Times* opened to the Arts section with a review of my current Met performance and a photo of me splashed across the page. Oh, hell! Tim didn't even realize that the woman he just *shtupped* was the same woman he'd been reading about moments before I arrived. I hurried out before he had a chance to make the connection.

I'm not proud of it today, but I sought out a lot of nameless one-night stands like Tim as I watched myself go from one lover in twenty years to a woman diving into the deep end of promiscuity. Why was I doing this? I didn't, couldn't, stop to think about it because I was too pumped up and exhilarated. Later, I would understand that these one-night stands provided the same function for me as too much food and too much alcohol did—they anesthetized me, they took me out of myself, they were a drug.

I found Dane on the "Big Woman" site, too. His personal bio read: "Lonely, married Harvard law student seeks pen pal." Pen pal. Right.

"Why are you lonely?" I wrote back. And we were off and running—two lonely people trying to beat back our respective inner demons. Dane was moody and dark, he read poetry and Latin, he was a former heroin addict who went to Narcotics Anonymous meetings religiously, and he introduced me to Joni Mitchell's sad and soulful album *Blue*. But here's the catch with Byronic Dane— when we had sex, he was so tender and adoring, he made me feel like he loved me, it wasn't just boom-boom-boom. Therein lay the problem. Most women would have found this a plus in a man, but to me it was confusing—which, I realize now was a sign that I wasn't looking for love, or maybe thought I didn't deserve it. Dane was passionate, and he would make several appearances in my love life over the years to come. But he wasn't the kind of guy who'd grab you, flip you over, and give you a spanking, and, for whatever reason, that's what I was craving.

AND THEN MITCH swaggered into my life.

It was the spring of '96 and I was singing Sieglinde in *Die Walküre* opposite Plácido Domingo, at the Met. Despite the incredible high of that situation, I was having a bad night at home alone on one of my days off.

It was a Friday evening and I was feeling the way I get when I'm left alone with my thoughts; I wasn't comfortable in my own skin, I needed a diversion. Then a totally impulsive thought popped into my head: *I wonder if I could pick a man up? I wonder if I'm alluring enough to attract a man just by how I look, with my face and body?* All my friends had gone through that phase in their twenties, when they hung out at bars and danced all night and had guys telling them how pretty they were, something I skipped entirely. Now I wanted to see if I could do that, be like everyone else. I knew it wasn't the way a proper Christian girl thought, but then again, I hadn't been acting like a proper Christian girl for a while. I was running on a hamster wheel of addiction—at this moment it was men and sex—and nothing was going to stop me.

I got glammed up in a black skirt and snug sweater, blew my hair out, and went over to—*what was I thinking?*— the restaurant across the street from the Met, where I took a seat at the crowded bar. I had barely sipped my first drink when I saw him—strutting across the room while rapping a pack of cigarettes against his palm. Mitch spelled Trouble. *Ding, ding, ding!* Within a few minutes I was making eyes at him after he sat down, alone, across from me at the bar. I was having a Long Island iced tea, the dead giveaway of the novice drinker. It was all I knew to order—but Mitch, in time, would educate me on how to drink like a pro.

"The guy over there would like to buy you a drink," the bartender told me. "You can say no if you want."

"Why in the world would I say no? Of course I'd like the drink!"

A seat opened up next to Mitch, so I sidled over.

"Hi, I'm Debbie."

"Hi, I'm Mitch." He was my type: tall, dark, thin, and a little rough-looking—like a cowboy outlaw who'd been riding out in the sun too long. Our drinks turned into dinner, and he told me he was a former car salesman who was now in the mortgage business. He asked me what I did for a living.

"I'm a singer."

"Really." He took a drag off his cigarette and squinted. "What do you sing?"

"I'm an opera singer."

"Well, that's interesting. Because the friend that I'm waiting for is at the Met, across the street, seeing something called . . . *Gudda . . . Gadda . . .*"

"*Götterdämmerung?*"

"Yeah, yeah."

"That's the fourth opera in Wagner's Ring Cycle. I'm not in that one. I sing Sieglinde in the second opera." He had no idea what I was talking about.

"Well, you should stay and meet my friend. He's coming to join me after the show. He's a big opera fan."

Well, this oughtta be priceless, I thought.

A minute later, in walks the friend.

"Hey, Fred," says Mitch. "I just met this lady, Debbie . . ."

Fred looks at me, stunned.

"That's Deborah Voigt, the opera singer! She's singing with Plácido Domingo, for God's sake!"

Once you were paired with Plácido, I had learned recently, you entered the solar system of stardom yourself.

I could see stars in Mitch's eyes; he was hooked. Mitch was a sucker for a woman who could offer money and fame. He told me later, though, that at first he'd thought I was a high-class hooker, which, strangely, flattered me. *He must have thought I was attractive,* I thought. How twisted is that? I was charmed by him in a sick, bad-boy way, and he supplied what I needed—someone who made me forget myself. So I took him home with me. He picked up liquor on the way and stayed until five a.m.

"Where's your next engagement?" he asked, before taking off in the dark.

"Lisbon, Portugal."

"I'll meet you in Lisbon."

A FEW WEEKS later, he arrived at the Lisbon Portela Airport. He emerged out of immigration control drunk, and spectacularly so.

"I have a gift for you," he slurred, through the cigarette dangling from his lips. "I feel our relationship could be something significant, and I want you to know I'm serious about pursuing you."

He opened my right hand until my palm lay flat, and dropped a diamond into it. This was something Aristotle Onassis was famous for doing with Maria Callas, handing her a loose diamond all by itself, so I swooned. (I would find out later that most of Mitch's romantic gestures had a seedy underbelly—but not just yet.)

Mitch loved to do everything to excess—sex, food, drinking, and partying—and he encouraged me to do the same, so I tried to keep up. I'd never drunk so much in my life. Mitch wined and dined me and threw money around at the best restaurants in Lisbon and showed up at my door with bouquets of red roses and the best champagne. In the beginning, I never spent a dime—he took care of everything (his money, I'd later find out, came from his illegal pot farm in Tennessee). We'd still be awake when the sun came up, after being up all night taking tequila hits straight from the bottle. At dinner, he held my chair for me. He was fucked up, and he was a criminal, and I was his willing prisoner.

"I like you big," he'd tell me, "I want a woman with meat on her. If the Jacuzzi doesn't overflow when a woman gets in, she's too small. But listen, baby"—he'd take a long drag on his Marlboro—"if you want to lose weight, I'll help you lose weight. If you want to gain weight, I'll butter your bread." It was one of the best lines I'd ever heard.

"Mitch, do you drink like this all the time?"

"Only on days that end in a 'Y,' baby."

God, he was fun. Mitch was a perfect man-drug for me—his wildness got me out of myself immediately, completely, and I needed him intensely. And he knew how to make my codependence grow. He kept me in an ever-tipsy state when I wasn't working, and pushed me beyond my comfort levels—often in unhealthy ways, but sometimes in good ways, too. One night in Lisbon we decided to go nightclubbing (for the first time in my life!). It was one a.m. when we arrived at a very chic-chic disco filled with dozens of fantastic-looking transsexuals standing around in their high heels, showing off their sculpted legs.

"Why isn't anyone dancing?" I wondered aloud, as we got drinks at the bar.

"They're waiting for somebody to start. You want to see?" He jumped off his stool. "C'mon, come with me!"

The idea of getting on a dance floor in general was nerve-wracking to me, let alone being the first one out there, where everyone would be watching me. But Mitch never took no for an answer. He pulled me off my stool and dragged me to the middle of the room.

Within five minutes we were surrounded and the floor was packed and moving. Mitch's daring personality constantly energized me. We'd go up onto hotel rooftops and dance at ungodly hours and he'd call me his little vampire because I refused to go to sleep, I was so "on."

MITCH CONVINCED ME to do things I would have never done, like get naked in a coed sauna. At our next rendezvous, in Germany, I was performing concerts with the Staatskapelle Dresden, one of the greatest orchestras in the world. We were staying at a beautiful five-star hotel and after my concert we went back to the hotel, had a few cocktails, and Mitch lured all 250 pounds of me into the coed sauna. As I lay on my back, topless, with a tiny towel across my lower lady bits and my flesh flopping about everywhere, two guys came in.

"*Guten Abend, guten Abend,*" we all murmured to each other. The two men continued to talk in German as I shut my eyes and relaxed . . . until I started to recognize some of the words. *Konzert* . . . *Staatskapelle* . . . Fuck! They were asking me, "Are you Deborah Voigt who just sang with the Staatskapelle Dresden?" I must have blushed from head to toe, and surely they could see it; meanwhile, Mitch was ripping his guts out laughing.

Other times, he could be moody, rude, and selfish. Mitch never watched me perform; he wasn't interested in that side of me, and couldn't give a shit about opera. He'd sit through a few minutes and then take off at intermission to wander through the silent, empty opera house lobby. He'd stop at every bar on every level, downing drink after drink, smoking like a chimney when it was still allowed. If it was Wagner, the added hour or two meant at least four extra drinks. When the opera was over, I'd be back in my dressing room, relieved and happy, with friends popping in to offer their congratulations. Mitch would arrive with two pints of chocolate-chocolate-chip Häagen-Dazs and two plastic spoons, impatiently circling the crowd of well-wishers, wanting my attention on him. It didn't occur to me that his behavior was disrespectful. I'd just been married to someone who had spent his entire life, all his energy, on me and my career, so I was ready for someone who wanted nothing to do with it.

He was, however, very interested in how people fussed over me, and the fact that my photo was all over the place, and that he was dating the on-the-verge-of-big-big-fame opera star Deborah Voigt and all the celebrity that surrounded that. So when an opera I was singing had a celebrity onstage, and paparazzi at the stage door, Mitch made sure he was there.

BUT BACK TO that spring of '96, when I first laid eyes on him. At that time I had also just met the famous tenor Plácido Domingo, a man as different from Mitch as you can get. I was singing Sieglinde in *Die Walküre* opposite Plácido for the first time, and do I even need to mention that I was oh so nervous?

"You're going to *love* him, you're going to *looooove* him," my director, Phebe Berkowitz, kept saying.

"But I'm scared because he's Plácido Domingo!"

"Debbie, he is the nicest and most workmanlike guy ever. He shows up, he doesn't know his part most of the time but he works hard and he gets through it. He's kind to everyone and he's Plácido Domingo, so the theater goes crazy to have him there."

That turned out to be exactly my experience with him. At first, when he walked into the rehearsal room at the Met, my heart pounded out of my chest.

We were rehearsing in the basement, on the C-level, three floors underneath the Met stage, and it was like being in a dungeon. There was no air in the room and it had crappy lighting so everyone always had a headache by the end of the day because it was so stifling and we're all squinting. New productions always rehearsed there because the area is the exact size of the Met stage; also, a mock-up of the set is usually provided, or at least the floors will be taped to show the edges of platforms and scenery.

Plácido walked into rehearsal a few days later than the rest of us, like most of those famous tenors did—that was usual. He looked handsome, he smelled great, and he had no entourage. He went out of his way to show everyone he was one of the gang and, just like Phebe promised, he fumbled just like the rest of us, too.

His English was fluent but his German, not so much. I don't speak German well, either, but I've always had a voice that was more naturally placed to sing German music—it's a brighter, more forward sound. Plácido's is rounder, more Italian, so getting those German words out is harder for him.

During rehearsal, he'd forget words or stumble, but he always stayed calm, and his difficulty endeared him to me. He was both sweetly apologetic and complimentary as we worked together, saying: "Debbbbeeee . . . that phrase . . . your phrase, she is beautiful. . . . Please, excuse my mistakes."

He had a very quiet spirit about him—unlike me, who wanted to crawl into a corner and roll up in a little ball if I made a mistake or couldn't remember the words.

All my life, except for my childhood musical period, I've had trouble memorizing, and I've always been very, very good at procrastinating. The combination is not so convenient for someone whose job it is to memorize three-hour-long operas in several foreign languages. When prepping for a new role, the usual routine is to start rehearsing on your own, weeks or months in advance, but I agonize at the thought of it, worried *it's going to be hard, it's going to be boring, it's going to take so much time.*

Once I finally get my ass on the piano bench and concentrate, I'm always surprised how not difficult it is and even enjoyable. It's my pattern, and after years of trying to improve it, one of my coaches finally said to me, "Debbie, you've been doing it this way all your life. What makes you think you can change now?"

I try not to beat myself up about it and accept the fact that I'll usually arrive at the first rehearsals feeling woefully unprepared and filled with angst.

Not Plácido. He was always in good cheer, knowing he'll get it done somehow. It's one of the things I loved best about him—he didn't let any mishaps faze him. He doesn't complain, he doesn't cry (like me) if he screws up a word; he sings that messed-up word with conviction, beauty, and passion and he sells out the house.

I loved playing Sieglinde with Plácido.

As my career progressed, I was beginning to understand and respect these women I played onstage, especially Sieglinde in *Die Walküre*. She was sad but gutsy—a lot like me, I think. As I've said, I wasn't a born opera fan, but I did love playing these great, passionate women.

In the story, Sieglinde is taken by a man from a warring tribe, a man she doesn't love, and, forced to basically be this man's slave, she lives in constant sadness and despair. She's a woman living in an unenlightened era, what's she going to do? Where is she going to go? How would she survive on her own? I could relate to her sadness; it touched something deep inside me. She's trapped and isolated, which is how I've often felt. And yet, in the core of her being Sieglinde is hopeful—she doesn't give up hoping that something better will come along.

When I sing her, I get choked up at the words and I have to remind myself to act it, not really feel it myself, or the emotions will clog up my vocal cords. Actors onstage or on film can afford to feel the emotions their characters are experiencing because they don't have to belt out a Wagnerian aria at the same time. But an opera singer has to act it on the surface without feeling it too much or they won't be able to sing. With Sieglinde, especially, I sometimes catch myself holding my breath from the emotions, robbing myself of oxygen I'm going to need. I have to pull myself out of her sadness so that I can do my job. I can't let myself get carried away.

It wasn't too difficult to pull myself out of Sieglinde's melancholy when I was playing opposite Plácido.

One of the greatest memories I have with him is when we walked out onstage after the first act of *Die Walküre*. I knew it had gone well, the chemistry between us was palpable. There's a scene where Sieglinde passes out and Siegmund must hold me in his arms— Plácido is so romantic and tender in the scene, gently stroking my face and hair. He makes you feel so present in the moment, because he is.

When we went out for that first curtain call it was like the breath being knocked out of us. The energy that poured out of that audience and the way they applauded and yelled . . . it was astounding. It was applause for Plácido, but I realized it was for Debbie, too. I was very proud of myself—especially because four weeks earlier, I had felt so intimidated.

THE REVIEWER FOR the *New York Times* wrote:

Deborah Voigt, also rarely heard in Wagner, sang her first Sieglinde in the house, and gave an account that matched Mr. Domingo's Siegmund superbly. Like Mr. Domingo, she offered a personal rather than monumental approach, for which her fully powered, clear-textured and sharply focused soprano was well suited.

And if all that wasn't enough, I also had The Kiss.

There's a moment in the opera where our two characters kiss, and every beat of our acting is timed perfectly to Wagner's music: the orchestra ascends, then it settles on a chord, and then . . . The Kiss. On the night of our first kiss, as I watched him move toward me, I was jolted out of character and thought to myself: *Oh my God. I am onstage, singing with Plácido Domingo! How did this happen? In what universe and with what luck did I end up here?*

I wanted to laugh. True, it was a "stage" kiss, but there was definitely lip-on-lip contact for several seconds, and it was magic. In that moment, I wasn't Sieglinde anymore. I was Debbie Voigt from Wheeling, Illinois, onstage in front of thousands of people, being kissed by Plácido Domingo.

It was real, and it was spectacular.

13

Blood, Death, and Grace

I FELT THE sharp edge of Mitch's hard boot smash against my browbone, barely missing my left eye. Mitch and I were having one of our take-no-prisoners arguments and this time it had gotten physical and I was left bloodied and bruised.

I was staying with him in Miami in 1999 while singing the role of Lady Macbeth in Verdi's *Macbeth* at the Florida Grand Opera, a character known for her bloody motives and morbid end. The drama offstage between Mitch and me was just as fiery as that between the Scottish king and his queen.

We'd got into some big argument—I'm sure we were both drunk at the time—and we were sitting by a big glass coffee table. We were both ready to explode. I was getting up from the couch, and at that same moment, Mitch, who was standing, moved to give the coffee table a swift kick—his steel-toed boot landing full force above my eye instead, nearly knocking me out cold. It was an accident, but the reality of how serious it could have been stared back at me when I looked in the mirror minutes later and saw my eye turning purple.

I'd been with Mitch for over three years now (too long), and gone were the days of roses, chair pulling, and him paying for things. And that diamond he had so ceremoniously given me at the airport in Lisbon, which I had made into a necklace? It was now an instrument of warfare. On at least three separate occasions when he'd gotten angry he'd ripped it off my neck. (I found out later that the diamond had belonged to a guy who owed Mitch money and that he'd pried the stone out of his wife's engagement ring to pay the debt.) My therapist warned me that if I didn't leave him, I'd end up seriously hurt.

I had begun to see a therapist to talk about my food and weight issues: I was gorging and topping the scales again since my beloved fen-phen had been yanked off the market after giving people heart-valve problems. Inevitably, our therapy sessions about emotional eating quickly led to talk of the men in my life, and the therapist warned me that my way of dealing with men, specifically Mitch, was more dangerous for me—emotionally, physically, financially, and mentally—than my uncontrollable eating and obesity, and that's saying a lot. Mitch had acted as my "assistant" for a few months while I was looking for a new one, and he'd racked up $20,000 in restaurant and strip-bar bills in two months with his no-goodnik buddies. When I saw the credit-card bill, I was shocked and took the card away from him. After that, he turned mean and drank more. The more he drank, the meaner he got.

After he kicked me, I grabbed my keys and purse and ran out of the apartment. But I'd left one very crucial item behind—the new antidepressant I'd been prescribed to elevate my lows and soften my anxieties. Those pills had been keeping me sane during the last stages of my so-called romance with Mitch, and they were sitting on the kitchen counter. I parked across the street, waiting to see if Mitch would leave so I could go back in and get my meds, and called my therapist for advice.

"Do not go back in there," the doctor told me. "I'll give you a new prescription." But I also didn't have the clothes I needed for re-hearsal the next day. By this time, my eye was swelling up so much it was nearly shut. I waited for a while more, then took a chance and slipped back in. He had ransacked the place and gone through my drawers looking for money. When he didn't find what he was looking for, he'd taken my antidepressants, just to hurt me. And if there was a time this woman needed her antidepressants, it was now.

At rehearsal the next day the makeup artist was able to cover my bruising (I told him I'd slipped and conked my head on the nightstand, and he bought it), but when the manager of the opera house saw me after I'd washed it off, he made me go see a doctor, who confirmed a hairline fracture.

And still I went back to Mitch. We dragged each other into the new millennium together, kicking and drinking.

IN JANUARY 2001, I took the stage again with the world's most famous tenor, Luciano Pavarotti. We were singing Verdi's *Aida* together at the Met, and he arrived like a star, with an entourage of a dozen and an endless supply of white silk scarves. You could never get Luciano alone, he was constantly surrounded. He was like Elvis, and his "people" encircled him like Elvis's Memphis Mafia. Mr. Volpe was always in Luciano's dressing room, too—to make sure he made it onstage.

You never knew nightly whether he'd be feeling up to performing or not. He was getting older and it was difficult for him to move around. Every night, until he got onstage, the management was nervous. When Luciano sang, the house sold out. It was in everyone's interest to do whatever it took to get him out there: it proved to be a big group effort.

I remember when he would leave his dressing room to walk to the stage he'd walk behind his dresser, Bill Malloy (now head of costumes at the Met), and rest one hand on Bill's shoulder for support. En route, Luciano had a little superstitious ritual he liked to observe. As he walked, he always looked for a bent nail on the floor left by stagehands, and he'd keep them as good luck charms. If he spotted one, he'd stop, slowly bend down and pick it up, then hand it to Bill with a big smile on his face.

I'd already experienced Luciano's disappearing act when we worked together a few years back, in *Ballo*. I kept in mind this time that when you worked with him, the usual staging rules didn't apply. For instance, he always wanted to stand behind me, no matter what the scene, even if it called for him—*needed* for him—to be in front. I think it was his way of trying to hide his size a bit, thinking it made him look smaller. I could relate, of course. I would have liked to have done the same thing! But Luciano got first dibs on that move, and every night he'd rearrange the blocking to suit him.

He did this with others, too, and I know it annoyed some singers. In his final years, though, how he positioned himself became more about simply supporting himself. If you were singing a scene with him, he'd hold on to you a bit as you moved across the stage together, making you his human walker. I didn't mind at all. And the audience was so delirious to hear him sing, they didn't care how he managed to stay on his feet, or if he acted well or not—they just wanted him to open his mouth and sing, live and in the flesh. There were moments, though, when I panicked and was sincerely worried for him.

We were doing a Saturday-afternoon radio broadcast, and at the end of the opera, our characters, Aida and Radames, end up entombed so they can suffocate and die together. Romantic, I know. Luciano and I were singing the final duet when suddenly Luciano clutches his chest and starts making choking sounds.

Oh my God, he's having a heart attack!

And then I nearly laughed out loud because my second thought— just for a split second, mind you—was imagining the future trivia "question" on *Jeopardy!*: "The soprano in whose arms Luciano Pavarotti died onstage at the Metropolitan Opera." How sick am I? I know, pretty twisted. My third thought, a better one, was to inch toward him in the tomb and whisper:

"Luciano, are you okay? *Luciano?*"

He opens one eye, and he's dripping with sweat.

"*Sì, sì,* baby. I'm acting, baby. I'm acting!"

He's acting, he says. Now, he hadn't really flexed his acting muscles in any performance thus far—not that it mattered. But here he was, giving his all—*for the radio broadcast?* You had to love him.

At another performance it really was a near tragedy. One of the big technical marvels of the Met stage is how it can function as an elevator, rising up or sinking down to reveal or hide an entirely different stage and set underneath. In one scene, the stage was rigged to descend and give the illusion of our being buried alive. On this night, Luciano was sitting on a prop rock with his legs dangling across the gap between the moveable part of the stage and the part that stays stationary. At any moment the stage section where he was sitting would start to move downward, I knew. But his legs and feet, draped across the non-moving part of the stage, would not.

His legs are going to go up and he's going to fall backward and smash his head on the tombstone! Doesn't he see what's happening? Doesn't anyone see this?

"Luciano! Luciano!" I whispered to him. "Luciano"—I was standing behind him—"pull in your feet!" He didn't hear me. I tried again, this time louder, as the floor began to move. It was like one of those scenes in *Batman* where someone's about to be crushed in some sort of device, and at the very last minute . . .

I reached over and quickly pulled Luciano's legs around just before he would have lost balance.

That scared me. When he realized what almost happened, I think it scared him, too.

When you sang with a star like him, you never knew what big celebrity might show up backstage to say hello. A week after he was out of office, President Bill Clinton attended a performance and came backstage after Act II. He was with Chelsea and her boyfriend at the time, who wanted to be an opera singer. We all stood in an informal receiving line to meet the former president; I was at one end and Luciano was at the other. On Luciano's side, the area lit up with camera flashes and hummed with motor drives, courtesy of the press, who were snapping President Clinton and Luciano posing together. When it looked as if the president's Secret Service guys were going to pull him away before reaching me, I had to do something.

He's my *president, after all! And the name of the opera is* Aida, *and I'm* Aida! I jumped out of line and rushed toward Mr. Clinton like a wide receiver making for the end zone, zigzagging through the throng of Secret Service guys and intercepting him before he exited stage right.

"Mr. President, would you pose in a photo with me, too?"

He gave me one of his eye-crinkling megawatt smiles. "Why of course, Miss Voigt!"

My hair was in cornrows, I was in blackface because I was playing an Ethiopian princess, and I was wearing a muumuu that made me look humungous . . . not my first choice for a photo shoot with the most recent Leader of the Free World. That didn't bother the president. As I'd heard, he liked women with a little meat on them. And I swear to God, the entire time we posed, and as the cameras snapped away, the president was rubbing his hand up and down along my hips, my waist . . . and under his breath, he's saying:

"Miss Voigt, you sang beautifully tonight"—*rub, rub, rub.*

"Thank you, Mr. President."

"You were really *on*. And that muumuu is fabulously flattering on you"—*rub, rub, ruuuub.*

"Thank you, Mr. President. I *so* appreciate it."

It was almost as good as kissing Plácido.

TOSCA THAT SPRING came with plenty of drama. By this time, Mitch's behavior had worsened, though I suppose I'd gotten used to it. My new assistant, Jesslyn, however, was shocked and furious at the way he treated me. Jesslyn Cleary was a feisty, whippet-smart New Englander who didn't suffer fools gladly. She was an opera lover with years of experience working for conductors at the Opera Company of Boston and at the Santa Fe Opera, and working as a personal assistant to a long string of "demanding Park Avenue ma- trons and trophy wives," as she described them. Hers was the per- fect pedigree for me.

Which is not to say that anything in her background had pre- pared her for Mr. Mitch. She'd spent months on the phone with him trying to sort out the administrative mess he'd made of my paperwork when he'd served, briefly, as my assistant. During those calls, Mitch acted the prima donna, evading her questions and being unhelpful. That spring, Jesslyn came to Miami with me for my first stab at *Tosca* at the Florida Grand Opera, and I figured it wouldn't hurt if she met Mitch, who lived north, just up the coast from Miami.

I had bought a condo in Fort Pierce, near where Mitch lived, and the plan was for us to have a nice introductory dinner with Mitch, and then Jesslyn and I would say our good nights to him and go back to my condo to watch the television broadcast of *Tristan und Isolde*, star- ring a colleague I was fond of, Jane Eaglen. I had just signed to sing my first Isolde with the Vienna State Opera in 2003, and I wanted to watch this Metropolitan Opera broadcast to see Jane in the role. I didn't even consider inviting Mitch to join us since he loathed opera.

When we arrived at the restaurant a little late, Mitch was already on his way to being sloshed. As soon as we sat down, he began to grill Jesslyn on opera. Ha! He barely knew enough to ask a proper question. Jesslyn answered him politely, but the more he drank, the nastier he got. After I mentioned that we were going to watch *Tristan* together later—a big mistake—Mitch picked up the bread basket and hurled it across the table at us, barely missing Jesslyn's head and hitting me with a flying croissant. Well, the bread was softer than his boot.

"That's *it*," Jesslyn said, slamming her fork down onto the table and standing up. "I'm outta here."

That night, we watched *Tristan* in silence, and before she left to go back to her hotel, she asked: "Why do you stay with him? Why do you put up with this?"

I didn't have an answer for her. All I could hear in my mind was the sound of my own voice twenty years earlier, like a tape recorder on a loop, playing over and over the words I wanted to ask my mother when she went back to my father.

Why are you putting up with this? How many times are you going to go through this?

HAVING JESSLYN WITH me during my first Tosca was a blessing, because even apart from the Mitch toxicity, I was having difficulty. Everything started out great—Tosca is a dream role for a soprano because she's so fiery and diva-esque. And I was being directed by Renata Scotto, herself a very famous Tosca in her day before giving up the stage to teach and direct. Like Leonie Rysanek, when I played Chrysothemis, Renata didn't try to impress her portrayal of Tosca on me but encouraged me to find my own.

"If I had had the voice you have," she said to me, on our first day of rehearsal, "my God, what I could have done with this role." It was one of the most sublime compliments I ever received.

Still, I grew miserable because my weight had zoomed up and I was bigger than ever. It was difficult to be onstage playing a beautiful diva in love with a handsome, romantic painter who adores her madly when my real life was so the opposite. Would the audience believe someone my size in this role? It was a seemingly impossible acting challenge, even Meryl Streep might have hung up Tosca's signature tiara if she were me.

Behind the scenes, the makeup artist James Geyer was trying his best to make me look thinner with makeup tricks. In an attempt to give my round, chubby face some contour and give me the illusion of a chin, James painted slashes of dark triangles underneath my cheeks where my jawline would be. The slashes were so dark, I looked like I was wearing a beard. To top it off, I was sweating like a sumo wrestler in a sauna onstage, and so the black makeup started melting and trickling down my neck.

At the end of the opera, Tosca has her big, spectacular moment and one of opera's most dramatic finales when (spoiler alert!) she jumps from the parapet of the Castel Sant'Angelo to her death. It's a brilliant scene. You say this tremendous line—*Avanti a Dio!* ("In front of God!")—and then you jump and go to Him. There have been past Toscas so brave that they literally fall backwards in this scene, to make it as dramatic as possible.

I was supposed to leap from a height of four feet onto a big, soft mattress, and I was terrified. On the first day of "jump rehearsal" Renata gave me clear instructions:

"Okay now, Debbie. Run up the stage, run up the stairs, and then step onto the parapet, and then turn around and . . . jump!"

I did as she said—almost. It was so hot, but I ran up the stairs, stepped onto the parapet, took one look down at the mattress and . . . started to cry. I was overwhelmed by the thought of doing this little jump. After all, at 320 pounds, this "little jump" amounted to a lot of woman plummeting to the earth. Legendary actress Sarah Bernhardt injured her knee so badly doing the jump, she eventually had to have her leg amputated. And the idea of "leaping to my death" was disturbing me, too. It felt so art-imitates-life, and too prophetic. To Renata, I blamed the set.

"I think what's making me nervous," I explained to her, in tears, "is that I run up the stairs to the landing, then have to step up onto this tiny little box before I jump. The box feels so unstable. Can't I just jump from the landing?"

A bunch of stagehands showed up at the snap of Renata's fingers and—*saw, saw, saw, hammer, hammer, hammer*—soon enough, they took away the little parapet, so now it's time for me to try again. I

run up the stairs—say the line, *Avanti a Dio!*, turn around, and . . .
again burst into tears.

"I can't do it!"

Next thing I knew, Renata was bounding up the stairs herself.
She was about sixty years old, petite but sturdy.

"Darrrrrrling," she says, standing on the edge of the platform,
"you wanted to sing Tosca? You have to jump!" And with that, she
took flight—and shamed me into it.

At the first dress rehearsal, they'd added a thick foam pad to the
mattress at my landing spot. I was sweating bullets because of the
heat, and because I was so nervous. I ran, I reached the platform,
and without hesitation I made an absolute swan dive and landed on
my stomach, my face smashed deep into the soft foam. The cast and
crew gave me a round of applause. The next day, when I arrived
at my dressing room, the crew presented me with a little memento
of my leap. They'd cut out a big square from the foam where my
darkly contoured, sweaty face had landed, leaving an indelible imprint. You could even see the shape of my lips (formed in an "O,"
like in Edvard Munch's *Scream*) and the lash marks from my eye-
lashes.

"We call it 'The Shroud of Tosca,' " said James. We all laughed
about it. But, honestly, every night I dreaded that jump.

I HATED THOSE jumps because they reminded me of endings, of
giving up, of pain so great that you can't stand being yourself one
minute longer.

My ending with Mitch coincided with the entrance into my life
of a new male who would prove to be unconditionally loyal, loving, and sweet to me always—my Yorkshire terrier puppy, Steinway. In June of 2002, I went to a breeder and picked him out of a
litter of three newborn pups. He was still too young to take home,
and I had to go to Europe, anyway; so that would give him time
to be with his mother and grow a bit. But I was excited that I

would have his sweetness to come home to, sensing the ugliness ahead.

Mitch and I had been spending a lot of time together in Florida at his place when, after five alcohol-drenched, abusive years together, he suddenly dumped me for someone else—a mortgage broker who collected Coca-Cola memorabilia. Once he'd realized that I wasn't going to be his sugar mommy and bankroll his bad, expensive habits anymore, he went elsewhere to find someone who would. I wish I could say that I was the one who did the breaking up. I also wish I could forget the last bit of stinging dialogue he spat out as I begged him in his house one day, as if in a scene from a daytime TV drama: "Please don't do this, please don't leave me. You can't do this!"

"Look at that bed"—Mitch pointed toward the bedroom, where I'd had the edgiest sex of my life thus far. "Look at that bed and get it through your head that you and I will never be in that bed together—*ever again*." Now he pointed to the ceiling. "Do you hear those men working on the roof? I've got roofers who are better-looking than you."

Right about then is when I morphed into the Glenn Close character in *Fatal Attraction*. After he told me he didn't want me anymore, I grabbed a very valuable porcelain Lladró off a nearby shelf—it was a figurine of a wedding couple that had topped John's and my wedding cake years earlier. Mitch had seen me throwing it out once, recognized it as a Lladró, and wanted to keep it himself.

I grabbed it, ran to the bathroom and smashed it into a zillion tiny little smithereen pieces on the floor. Then I stormed out of the apartment and sat in my car out front and called Mitch's cell a dozen times in a row, like a madwoman. My key was in my hand but I couldn't make myself put it in the ignition and drive away. I was paralyzed. And I was in hysterics. Both! I dialed my therapist's number.

"Where are you?" she asked.

"Mitch's driveway."

Mitch had come out and was now standing a few feet from my

car, yelling at me and threatening to call the cops because I wasn't leaving, because I was breaking things, because I was acting like a crazy lady. I bet his ego loved it. I bet he loved that this woman who had taken him around the world and to whom he owed $20,000 was now in hysterics because he'd dumped her.

"You have to leave," said the therapist.

"I can't move."

She talked me through it, step by step, like I was a baby. First she told me to take a deep breath. Then she took me through the mechanics of leaving.

"Put the key into the ignition. Okay, it's in? Okay, good. Now put your foot on the gas. Is it on the gas? Good. Put the car in reverse." She stayed on the phone with me until I arrived safely at my own condo.

I was out of my mind with grief, sorrow, and regret that night. Lying awake, I thought about Tosca's despair, and I thought about hurling myself off my tenth-floor balcony. This time, maybe I wouldn't be afraid to leap. I often wondered if killing oneself was an act of courage or cowardice, and I'm still not certain what I think. But I do believe that God ultimately determines when it's our time, and that in His wisdom that even includes suicides.

I called back the therapist—she was earning every penny I paid her.

"I'm on the balcony," I said. "The pain is too much." I was weeping and starting to hyperventilate.

"Debbie, I want you to put the phone down and go get a glass of water."

"No! No!"

"Debbie, put the phone down and go get a glass of water. What lights do you have on in the room? What color is the couch?" She was trying to talk me back into myself, trying to reattach me to the concrete world around me by asking me questions and making me answer them. Slowly, patiently, she calmed me down enough that I stepped away from the balcony. But for weeks afterward, the pain of his rejection was so unbearable that I was still in *Fatal Attraction* mode. I checked his voice mail on the hour because I knew his password. I'd call dozens of times a day and if I heard a voice mail from a woman—*beeeeep!*—I erased it. I kept on doing this until a friend finally stood next to me at a pay phone, made me dial his number, and made me change his passcode without looking at the numbers so that I wouldn't know it. Mitch wouldn't either, but, hell—that was a bonus.

THAT SUMMER OF 2002, which Jesslyn refers to as "Debbie's summer of catatonia," I rented a magnificent villa for two months in Salzburg to prepare for my debut as Danae in Strauss's *Die Liebe der Danae*. It was a new production for the fiftieth anniversary of the Salzburg Festival, to be directed by famed opera director Günter Krämer. It was a very big deal and had created a buzz in the opera world months in advance.

I arrived a mess, and in need of a drink, or five.

Jesslyn came with me, and the first night we arrived we immediately got to work making martinis—badly needed after the long flight—but found no ice in the freezer. "Oh, God, no ice?!!" we yelled in unison.

But God always hears our prayers, it is said, especially when you least expect it. Maybe He doesn't answer the big ones, like, "Oh, please, don't let him leave me," but who are we to pick and choose which ones should be answered? A few minutes after Jesslyn and I moaned aloud about our tragic ice situation, the clouds grew dark and it began to hail—giant chunks of ice fell from the sky. Laughing, we ran out into the backyard with buckets and collected the ice, then rinsed them off for our drinks.

The next few weeks were decidedly unmiraculous. The new role didn't suit me well vocally, I felt, and it didn't help that I'd arrived unprepared. We bought an icemaker, and I sat on my bedroom balcony overlooking a sunflower field every morning and prayed that the pain would go away.

Soon, in a miracle of sorts, I was laughing and twirling in that very same sunflower field—literally.

A few weeks after we got there, a *Vanity Fair* photographer and reporter arrived to interview me and shoot a two-page spread. Because we were in Salzburg, I had a great idea for the shoot—why not dress me up as Maria von Trapp in *The Sound of Music*? I could never get enough of that singing nun. This time, I was imagining myself in a pretty, gauzy dress, reenacting the romantic scene in the gazebo, where the Captain kisses Maria. But no, the editors had another visual in mind. They wanted me to dress up like Maria in that very first scene, when she wears that unglamorous pinafore nundress, and spin around and around like Julie Andrews does with the Alps behind her. It was the iconic shot, after all, so I agreed. We spent an entire day with me twirling around, huffing and puffing, and getting dizzy. It takes a lot of work to spin 300-plus pounds around like a top. By the time we were done and they got the shot, I could barely stand upright.

I wasn't about to deny myself my gazebo moment, though. As soon as I'd recovered my equilibrium the following week, I went with my mother—who came to visit—on the Official Sound of Music Bus Tour. Mom, Jesslyn, and I had made a unanimous decision that I needed lots of merriment and happy musicals that summer to cheer me up. What could be peppier than a sardine-packed busload of Aussie tourists singing "The Lonely Goatherd" for six hours?

"Sing, Debbie, sing!" Mom kept elbowing me whenever I stopped. I couldn't help it. I'd never heard such bad singing in my life and I had to stop and listen, I told her. We burst out laughing, and soon I was singing "Climb Ev'ry Mountain" with the rest of the sweaty, obsessed fans. The bus made stops at the movie locations, including the church where the Captain and Maria got married and the lake where the kids fall out of their rowboat. The last, and my favorite, was the gazebo, where the Captain and Maria sing their love duet, "Something Good." Mom and I got out and walked inside it, debating whether Christopher Plummer was a good kisser or not (yes, we decided) and wondering where we could find a man like that for me. The summer had begun in the depths of despair but ended on bright notes. I stood in Maria's gazebo, singing the hopeful lyrics to one of my childhood classics—*somewhere in my youth or childhood, I must have done something good*. And while I may have been easy to forget in Mitch's mind, *New York Times* chief music critic Anthony Tommasini thought otherwise. He wrote in his August review of *Die Liebe der Danae*:

> As rain (water poured from above) trickles down, Danae, the great Strauss soprano Deborah Voigt, covers her head with her cloak and walks slowly away. It's an unforgettable image.

AFTER WE GOT home from Salzburg, I went to pick up little Steinway at the breeder's kennel. He was the littlest thing I'd ever held, and on the car ride home he threw up all over me. But just like it's good luck when a bird poops on you, I considered Steinway's barfing in my lap an omen that the upcoming year would bring good fortune.

And it did. Remarkably, my career stayed on the upswing despite the downward spiral of my love life. In April of 2003 I took Jesslyn and little Steinway to Vienna for a new production of *Tristan und Isolde*—my first completely staged performance of it—and we arrived six weeks before opening night for an unusually long stretch of rehearsal time.

As a side note, people often wonder how much opera singers are paid. I'm not going to get into numbers, but I will say that singers' fees are standard for each specific opera house and all of the top-tier singers are paid the same. But in Vienna, an exception is made if you sing *Isolde*. It's the only role and the only opera company as far as

I know where this is true, but for *Isolde* you get more money than the usual rate. Why? Because it's a "long song." So considering the salary bump, I wasn't about to complain about the insufferable heat, not really.

We arrived during a stiflingly hot spring (when it came to the weather in Vienna, I was truly cursed), and the Vienna State Opera house didn't have air conditioning. Thomas Moser was set to sing Tristan, and Günter Krämer was again my director. We had a great group, but the heat was making us all nuts.

For one big scene we had to wear heavy rain jackets over our already bulky costumes for a scene on a ship, and I had to lie on the floor at the edge of the stage with my head hanging over the orchestra pit. Every time I did it, one of the string bass players inches away from me would dart his eyes up at my dripping face, shooting me a look that said, *Hey, lady—don't you dare sweat all over my instrument!*

My costume was tight; I was bone-corseted to within an inch of my life because they were trying to make me look smaller. *Sigh.* How do you make a woman over three hundred pounds look smaller? My dress had a fifteen-foot-long train made of black tulle. When you wear a dress like that, you have to choreograph precisely how you're going to work in it, how you're going to move, because it's so easy for you to walk one way and the dress to go another. So the costumers made a replica for me to wear during rehearsals so that I could coordinate my movements and staging with the dress, which upped my body temperature at least a few degrees.

It was so steamy that as soon as we got a three-day break, Jesslyn and I drove south to Baden and stayed at the Grand Hotel Sauerhof, built in the twelfth century and once a haven for such guests as Beethoven and Antonio Salieri.

There, we took midnight dips in the hotel pool to cool off. Steinway was such a mama's boy that he followed me right into the water the first night, stepping off the concrete edge with a little yelp. It was a sink-or-swim moment for my little guy, and I'm glad to say he learned to doggie paddle quickly. His mama, on the other hand, impressed Jesslyn with the number of laps I could do and how long I could hold my breath underwater. She'd pull out her watch and time me:

". . . three minutes . . . *four minutes* . . . do all Wagnerian sopranos have this kind of lung capacity? Four minutes and thirty seconds. Debbie? *Debbie!*"

In the mornings, I'd let Steinway out on a little patch of lawn outside my first-floor hotel room to do his business, and I'd invariably end up chasing after him in my short nightie with my bare ass in the air.

During breakfast one day as we ate on the outdoor patio, Jesslyn was giving me a detailed history lesson on the hotel when I shushed her.

"Did you hear that bird?"

We held our breath and heard a song coming from the leafy sequoia tree nearby. If we both hadn't heard it, I'd never have believed it; the bird was whistling the unmistakable first five notes of Wagner's "Ride of the Valkyries," I kid you not.

BACK IN VIENNA, opening night arrived and I was scared out of my wits, and rightly so. I was an American singing Isolde—and in Vienna! I woke up that morning with the same mixed feelings I often have when making a role debut—thrilled and totally confident, alternating with a self-doubt so debilitating I'm paralyzed. To keep my feelings under control, I go on autopilot: wake up, coffee, pray, breakfast, a little walk, pray, lunch, pray, look at the music, pray, nap, a light dinner, go to theater, pray, *pray*, *PRAY* . . . makeup, costume, a last-minute prayer during the overture, and then—GO!

Once I'm onstage, I let myself feel something besides the fear I woke up with. I let the character inside of me. Playing Isolde that night my staging began with a loud emotional outburst as I knocked the armor of Morold, slain by Tristan, to the ground. It was a great way to channel my nervous energy built up during the day. Then, I put one note in front of the other and took it scene by scene. I can't go into these marathon Wagnerian evenings with my thoughts on the final note, or focused on what I have to do over the next few hours; that would be too overwhelming. I imagine it's how a mountain climber feels standing at the foot of Everest. If they look up too high, they'd probably think, *How the heck will I ever get all the way up there?* Instead, it's one step at a time.

Opening night was a huge success: a twenty-three-minute standing ovation reported on CNN live in a ticker-tape newsflash. Then came the second performance. I got laced up into my bone-corseted dress like a plus-size Scarlett O'Hara, walked onstage, began to sing, and . . . found I couldn't move properly. What was going on? Something wasn't right, but I couldn't figure out what. I looked down at my dress and saw that six feet of my train had been hacked off and no one had bothered to tell the leading lady wearing it. I spent the second half of Act I fuming. As soon as I got offstage, I confronted the costumers and asked in my not-so-great German: "*Vas* the *fück* happened to my dress?!"

Herr Holender, they told me, had decided he didn't like the length and had ordered them to cut it off.

Opera House Manager Herr Ioan Holender, a.k.a., "the Shark." That was his nickname in opera circles because of his perpetual tan, snow-white hair, and oversized, sharp, bleached teeth. I wanted to rip the nuts off Herr Holender, and I wasn't (and still am not) the only one in the world to feel that way.

"I want it back on my dress for the next show!" I told the costumers, and they nodded. Sure enough, it was back on the next day. The Shark took note of this.

"I see you've got your train back." He flashed his big teeth.

"Yes, my train, which should never have been taken away in the first place without my being told." I felt diva-ish responding like that because it was so not me, but the truth was my reaction was absolutely justified. It was unprofessional and detrimental to the entire production not to inform a performer of such a major costume change.

I didn't hear another word from the Shark after that, and especially after I got a glowing review in the *New York Times* a few days later. Anthony Tommasini, who attended that second, trainless, performance, and whom I was beginning to love from afar, wrote:

> Amid intense expectation . . . an intriguingly updated modern staging by Günter Krämer opened here last week. Ms. Voigt, in her prime at 42 and singing her first complete staged Isolde, is the first major American soprano to undertake the role in more than 20 years and the first American soprano ever to have a new production of the work mounted for her by this prestigious company, a bastion of Germanic culture.
>
> At the second performance, on Thursday night, which I attended, Ms. Voigt sang with such confidence and vocal ease you would have thought the role had long been in her repertory. In this intimate 1,700-seat house (with room for 500 standees) her sound sliced through Wagner's thick orchestration. Yet she preserved the lyrical beauty and sumptuous colorings that have made her such a cherished artist in the Strauss and Verdi repertory.

My cup runneth over that week. The opening-night standing ovation was another turning point in my career, albeit a bittersweet one. A few weeks before opening night, my stepsister Melinda— Lynn's daughter—had mysteriously fallen into a coma while in remission from mesothelioma cancer. The whole family had been set to come to Vienna to see me in this important role, but Dad and Lynn, of course, stayed behind to be with her. A few days before opening night, I got a call from Lynn and Dad from Melinda's bed-side at the hospital.

"Debbie, we just turned off Melinda's respirator and she only has a few minutes left," Lynn said. "Would you sing to her?"

She held the phone to Melinda's ear and I told her goodbye, that I loved her, and I sang the first melody that came to my lips:

> *Amazing grace, how sweet the sound*
> *That saved a wretch like me.*
> *I once was lost, but now I'm found.*
> *Was blind, but now I see.*

I sang to her again on opening night. I had managed to set my grief over Melinda's death aside for most of the evening, until I got to the transcendent "Liebestod"—that intense aria of "love and death"—in the final act. In the scene, Isolde is saying goodbye to Tristan as she sings, and I couldn't help but tear up about Melinda. But the special beauty of this aria is that it is filled with as much joy as sadness. It's about beginnings as well as endings, and about life going on beyond this place.

That's probably why I felt "Amazing Grace" welling up inside of me the moment Melinda passed.

Because, despite the anguish and pain we all endure in our lives, I believe that blessings, grace, and beauty are possible. Both in this world and in the next—for Melinda for sure, and maybe even for a wretch like me.

14

Little Black Dress
and Sexy Salome

THE HURRICANE WINDS that would wreak havoc around my Florida condo in the fall of 2004 began swirling around me earlier that spring. The infamous "Little Black Dress" episode that brought me to the attention of the non-opera-going public, and which, in a very profound way, changed my life, crept up on me unexpectedly.

I had been scheduled to sing *Ariadne*, which had by now become a signature role for me, in a revival production at Covent Garden when my manager, Andrea Anson, got word that the director had a casting change of heart. He wanted to take a more "modern" approach to the opera, they said, and in his new vision he decided that Ariadne should wear what fashion observers know as "the little black dress." My childhood idol, the petite Audrey Hepburn, made hers iconic in *Breakfast at Tiffany's*. Now tipping the scales at 330 pounds, I did not fit the director's idea of this new, svelte Ariadne who wore a size "little" of anything. To put it bluntly: I didn't fit the dress.

To put it even more bluntly, the Covent Garden people told Andrea that I was too fat for the role. It's really amazing that in this day and age someone can get away with saying those words. Telling a woman she's too fat for a job may be the last prejudicial statement, the last ugly judgment, that people think it's okay to make. Unlike the areas of gender, ethnicity, age, and religion—it's still open season on overweight women.

It wasn't the first time I'd been told by a director that I was too hefty for a part, of course; it's happened several times. It's even happened when how I looked shouldn't matter. About ten years earlier, I auditioned for legendary conductor Sir Georg Solti for a recording he was planning to do of Tristan. At eighty-plus years of age, he was still handsome, lean, and fit—the kind of man who never gained a pound. When I think of him, I always remember a rumor I'd heard that he'd have great, torrid romances with opera singers and when he was done, he'd give each one a white grand piano as a parting gift.

I auditioned for Maestro Solti in a big rehearsal room in London, and when I'd finished I knew I'd sung very well, and so did he.

"That was beautiful," he said, with a smile—"you'd be a great Isolde."

Then he got up from behind his desk and walked over to me. "Why are you so fat?" he asked matter-of-factly. "Is it the food?"

I was stunned. He was being rude, I felt, but at the same time he was genuinely puzzled and curious.

"Well, Maestro, it is the food, yes," I answered. (What did he think, I was OD-ing on water and broccoli?) "But it's other issues as well."

He still looked confused, not understanding why someone would be this large on purpose. I was scheduled to see him again several months later for some concerts. "If you lose weight by the time I see you for Beethoven's Ninth," he said, "you can have the job."

And this was for a recording, I must point out—I didn't even have to appear on stage! No one was even going to see me! Still, the legendary conductor didn't want to be associated with a fat broad, even if you only saw my photo on the CD cover.

(P.S., I lost weight and got the job, but he passed away soon after so we never did the recording).

If a director for a stage production complains about my weight, usually the opera house boldly steps in and supports me, overriding the director's decision, and the quality of my singing trumps the readout on my scale. Since I was currently considered the Ariadne of choice in the opera world, you'd think in this instance my voice would be more important than my dress size.

Plus, they knew me well at the Royal Opera House. I'd sung there twice before—once with Pavarotti (when he did his disappearing act during our duet in *Ballo* in '95) and the second time in *Die Frau ohne Schatten* in 2001. It was no secret to anyone what I looked like when I signed on for the role; it's not like the director hired a new singer from a headshot. Covent Garden's artistic administrator, Peter Katona, could have easily, and should have, told the director to alter the dress and get on with it. But that didn't happen. Even though I had a signed and fully executed contract, they wanted to recast the role.

"Fine," Andrea told them.

Andrea wasn't the brash, in-your-face Herbert Breslin type. He came from an aristocratic British family on his father's side—his brother was in Princess Diana's wedding party, for heaven's sake! And his gorgeous Italian mother came from a well-to-do family in Rome where they still had an enormous family estate that he visited regularly in the off-season. Andrea embodied elegance, efficiency, and a Zenlike confidence and spirituality.

"What role," he calmly asked the Covent Garden people, "do you intend to give Debbie to sing instead?"

Common protocol dictated that if an opera house removed a vocalist with a fully executed contract from a part, they were required to offer another role of equal "value" or pay out the contract in full.

"We don't have anything," they told him.

There was a pause on Andrea's end. Some back-and-forth ensued—the details of which he never disclosed to me because he's a gentleman—before Andrea swiftly insisted upon arrangements for my payout. I was hurt about the situation, for sure, but I had no intention of making a fuss over it. Andrea handled the legal particulars and the case was closed.

Until a few months later, when I gave an interview to a reporter from a major London daily to publicize an upcoming recital. I went to dinner with my new publicist, Albert Imperato, at Ruth's Chris Steakhouse in New York, and the reporter was meeting me there after dinner. Albert has the swarthy good looks of an Italian male model coupled with the bright eyes, energy, and enthusiasm of a rambunctious kid. He was excited about the interview, and after dinner he made the introductions and waited at the bar while I chatted with the reporter. Had he stayed at the table, who knows what might have turned out differently—the interview, my weight, my life! As it was, I was alone with the reporter and I was in a truth-telling mood. All was going swimmingly until the reporter asked:

"So when will you come back to sing at the Royal Opera House?"

I hemmed and hawwed. I hadn't spoken about the incident to the media, and I wasn't sure if I should. Because my contract to sing Ariadne was for a future season that hadn't been announced yet, no one knew of my casting of and subsequent *un*-casting from the role. What happened wasn't hushed up, per se . . . but I'm sure the Royal Opera House never thought I'd speak of it, and neither did I for that matter. We all thought it would just go away.

But he asked, and now he was waiting. *Hummanahummanahummana*. I didn't know what to say. They say the truth shall set you free, so I leaned in that direction.

"Well, I don't think I'm coming back," I answered.

The reporter's eyes widened. "Why not?"

"Well . . . I was supposed to be back to sing Ariadne, and . . ."

"What happened?"

"They decided I wouldn't 'work' in their production."

The reporter leaned in.

"You wouldn't *work*? What does *that* mean?"

He knew he was on to something. He knew I was one of the leading Ariadnes in the world and that what I was saying made no sense. As I sat there, trying to explain, I was getting pissed off thinking about it—maybe I was having a delayed reaction. What should I say to this guy? That Covent Garden didn't think I was talented enough? That they couldn't find anything else for me to sing? Or should I say I didn't want to sing there? Should I lie? *Why should I protect them?* The only thing left to say, the only thing I could say, was the truth. I didn't think about the fallout.

"They said I was too fat," I told him. "I'm too fat for their concept."

And that was it. The minute I said it, the beans came spilling out. I didn't think they would fall further than the local London papers. I didn't imagine the interview would go around the world, reaching Dubai, Thailand, . . .

I went over to the bar after the interview and told Albert what had happened. I saw a fraction of a second of worry on his handsome face, then he brushed it aside. "I'm sure everything will be fine," he said, in his *molto* positive way.

Two weeks later, while I was performing in Switzerland, Albert rang me up.

"Um, Deb. That interview you gave? It's taken on a life of its own. I just wanted to warn you that you might be getting some calls from the ladies and gentlemen of the press."

Then the media hurricane hit, and hit hard.

After I hung up with Albert, my phone rang nonstop. I got interview requests from every major news publication in the world and landed on the couch of *Good Morning America* to discuss the new hot topic: Has Opera Gone Too Hollywood? A lot of people, especially Covent Garden's music director, Tony Pappano, believed I'd released the story to get publicity because I had a CD, *Obsessions*, coming out around that time. I only *wish* I was that smart!

My firing was making such big news because it baffled people. We lived in the world where "it ain't over till the fat lady sings," and people expected their opera singers to be big. I wasn't an actress expected to starve for a TV role on *Ally McBeal*. So to hear that an opera singer, of all people, would be fired for being too fat—not to mention an internationally famous singer in a role she was internationally famous for singing—was ludicrous, even to non-opera lovers.

And while we're on the topic, why is it okay for the male opera stars to be big and not the women? The double standard is alive and well in the opera world when it comes to men's and women's bodies. When I was singing Wagner's *Lohengrin* at the Met a few years earlier with plus-sized tenor Ben Heppner, I got my foot caught in my dress as I was getting up off the floor of the stage. It was embarrassing, to be sure, but it's the kind of thing that happens, to big girls and little girls alike. The review in one newspaper the next day reported that "Voigt's performance was impeded by her girth," while "Ben Heppner had the shoulders of a linebacker." I can't tell you how many times I've read articles that praise the huggable, teddy-bear roundness of Pavarotti.

Yet today, in retrospect, I can understand why Covent Garden didn't want me in the role. When I look back at pictures of myself that year, I look like a poster child for obesity. True, there are actual physical reasons why opera singers are traditionally big in stature—having a bigger chest cavity is often what gives a vocalist the depth, range, and strength to sing those powerful arias. But if a person is grossly obese, it becomes distracting. If you walk out onstage at 400 pounds, it's like seeing a drunk alcoholic or a stoned drug addict in front of you—you see the problem, the addiction, not the performance.

Did the firing influence me to do something about my weight?

No. I had been trying since I was seventeen to lose weight in every way imaginable. And at the time when I lost that role I'd already consulted with a doctor about gastric bypass surgery. The irony is that the fee Covent Garden paid me for not singing gave me the money and the time to do the surgery.

But first, one has to poke a little fun at the whole craziness, no?

A month after the media exploded with the story, I made my Carnegie Hall recital debut. What better arena in which to make a statement?

When I walked out onstage to thunderous applause, you could feel the question hanging in the air: Is she going to say something about it or not? You betcha. I waited until the end of the evening, until my encore, when I sang a parody song called "Wagner Roles." It was written by Ben Moore, who's penned several songs I've recorded (two years later, Ben would also write the parody, "We're Very Concerned," which I sang at Joe Volpe's retirement tribute gala). In the lyrics for "Wagner Roles," I lament about how I'm only offered Wagner roles and why can't I sing something light and fun? Like Rossini? Or Johann Strauss, instead of the darker, more brooding Richard?

Then I sing the line:

"And this business we're in, well, it's really a mess; *not to mention the deal with the little black dress . . .*"

The hall went nuts. The audience cheered and yelled so loudly, I had to stop singing because I couldn't hear anything. It was great fun, and my way to provide a little humor to the situation and say: Let's get past this now and put on a show.

THE NIGHT BEFORE I went under the knife for gastric bypass surgery—it was July 2004—I had a "last meal" the same way a convict on death row does before execution. I ate a thick medium-rare steak and baked potato, downed a few cocktails, and scarfed down a gigantic dessert smothered with whipped cream. It felt like saying goodbye to best friends who'd been there for me in my times of need, but now I was moving on, to another life, and might never see them again.

From the moment I woke up, the weight, as they say, fell off me. The first week I was eating half a jar of baby food for each meal—pureed chicken, beef, vegetables—and I lost ten pounds. It was the easiest "diet" I'd ever been on, because the most shocking thing happened. I'd take a few spoonfuls of the baby food and *feel full*. I don't know if I'd ever really felt full before in my life. If anything, I had a new problem: how to eat enough to get the calories I needed to stay healthy. That was a new one.

Every day when I looked at my reflection in the mirror, I saw myself disappearing. Or maybe it was simply that the real Debbie was emerging from underneath layers and years of pain eating. The Germans have a brilliant word for the fat gained when you eat from sadness: *Kummerspeck*, which translates literally as "grief fat"—or, "grief bacon," or even "sad pig lard." Ouch. Way back, when that voice teacher at Chapman College would force me to look in the mirror as I sang and I'd burst into tears, that's exactly what I was seeing when I looked at myself—grief fat.

But even more amazing than the weight coming off so easily was that I stopped *thinking* about food all the time. I marveled at that and wondered if the doctor hadn't cut out a part of my brain.

That first year, I lost over a hundred pounds, and followed that with various skin-tightening surgeries to adapt to the quick weight loss. My self-image, however, was slower to adapt—there should have been a surgery for that, too. Although my eyes could see me getting smaller when I looked in the mirror, my subconscious lagged behind and still thought of me as a fat girl. I kept dressing in the same old baggy pants and tentlike muumuus, until my new part-time assistant and stylist, Jaime, insisted on going shopping with me. I had hired Jaime to fill in when Jesslyn was out of town. She was young, fun, and voluptuously beautiful—she, too, struggled with weight, so she understood my mentality.

I'd emerge from fitting rooms at Bloomingdale's, saying, "Look, aren't these pants great?" and she'd say:

"No! They're not! Debbie, these are two sizes too big for you, can't you see that?" She'd pull at the extra fabric like it was my old, stretched-out skin—my old sausage casing.

"Are you sure?"

"Debbie, it's okay if the clothes touch your body. That means they fit."

I had no idea.

Life as a nonobese person took some getting used to those first few years. Moments other people take for granted were for me red-letter days. Like the first time I was able to fit into an economy seat on an airplane without having to raise the armrest, and—imagine this—able to fit into the tiny airplane bathroom! I traveled so much for my work and always had to be careful about what I ate and drank before getting on a transatlantic flight because it was so difficult for me to get into the darn bathroom. Let me tell ya, 333 pounds, my all-time high before my surgery, does not fit onto that tiny plastic seat. Same goes for movie theaters, which I used to avoid because my body would overflow from my seat onto the seats and strangers next to me.

I WAS SOON to learn that for as many postsurgery triumphs as I experienced, I also had difficulties. For every twenty or twenty-five pounds lost, I had to make major adjustments in order to feel comfortable singing. Suddenly I felt like I wasn't connected to my body, as if my voice had lost its home, its base. When we sing, we engage certain muscles to support the sound, like having a girdle press on the abdominal muscles. When you're over three hundred pounds and you take a breath, all that fat sitting on you automatically does extra girdle duty for you; the weight presses down and helps engage the musculature. You don't really have to think about it, it happens automatically. But now, I didn't have the extra weight for support and compression. I felt physically shaky, ungrounded. It wasn't an easy transition—much more difficult than I expected, or had been warned.

The critics attending my early, postsurgery performances were quick to point out the change in my voice.

"She used to sound more golden, now she sounds more shrill"— I've seen that in print a few times since my surgery. Those reviews were difficult to read, especially because my presurgery reviews were often so admiring. Not that I put much weight—forgive the pun—on reviews. I don't read them anymore because they can be upsetting if you are having an off night. You can't become an international opera star if you don't consistently give good performances; but everyone has an off night once in a while. And when you do, it's not the audience or critics who judge you the harshest—the audience, in fact, is especially forgiving. It's the administration, the ones who do the hiring and firing, who don't always understand the organic and mercurial ups and downs of a voice. In my early days onstage, James Levine, whom I called Jimmy, taught me to accept the ebb and flow of my instrument.

During a performance one night at the Met, I had screwed up a note in an aria. Jimmy called my dressing room during a break—in those days, I was his dramatic soprano darling and he'd call me in between every act to touch base. I hadn't messed up the note too badly—I've never gone onstage and cracked a note like a strangled dog. But that night, the note didn't sit right and I knew it. I was berating myself in my dressing room when he called.

"Jimmy, I'm so sorry that note didn't go well."

"Oh, baby," he said, in that resonant, deep voice he has. His grandfather was a cantor, and Jimmy's voice had a sort of Old Testament resonance to it. "We're human beings, not machines."

I've never forgotten his words. The whole beauty of live performance is that anything can, and will, happen, good and bad. If you have a great conductor like Jimmy Levine, he can help you through a rough spot. During rehearsals once for *Ariadne*, I was having technical difficulties. At one point the score called for me to drop into a low part of my voice from a high G to a very low G in the aria "Es gibt ein Reich" when I sang the word *Totenreich*—meaning, "the realm of the dead" or "the netherworld."

I couldn't settle into the note, my voice didn't want to go there. Jimmy was probably one of the few conductors able understand instinctively what I needed to do—he knows more about singing and vocal repertoire than anyone on the planet. I had to take more time, I had to give the note a proper setup. I wasn't breathing correctly, I was too fearful of the scary note, he told me.

As we approached the dreaded *Totenreich* low G during our first performance, I looked at Jimmy and he looked at me. He gave me a reassuring look and he took a breath with me. With that breath, he gave me the freedom and the belief that I could do it. We connected in that moment, two artists together inside the music, and everything aligned perfectly. I knew exactly what he meant for me to do, and I did it, and it worked—my note was perfect. It was like being inside each other's minds, it was so intimate. It was like Spock's Vulcan mind-meld in *Star Trek*. In the same way that Jane was a musician-whisperer, Jimmy was a voice-whisperer. After our mind-meld, I never had a problem with that note again.

BUT BACK TO my weight loss—I don't believe it changed my voice for the worse, I just had to think more about how I moved, and how to support the air. It took me a lot longer than I thought it would to feel my voice was back to normal, to where it was before the surgery. Voices change and evolve for many reasons—menopause, age, overuse, and just life. A voice is naturally bound to change over a ten-year period in the same way one's body changes. Also, if I have a different sound today, it may be due to my transition in repertoire. I've gone from singing the arias of a spinto soprano in roles like Aida and Tosca, to heavy hitters like Brünnhilde, which is a totally different vocal category.

Sometimes a role doesn't work for you because of bad timing.

My experience with Strauss's Marschallin in *Der Rosenkavalier* was hit and miss. I was first contracted to sing the role for a run in Vancouver in the fall of 2004, a few months after my surgery. At the time I was living full time in my Florida condo, the exact spot where two devastating hurricanes were about to hit within three weeks of each other.

I had reached beautiful Vancouver, Canada—literally, at the other side of the continent from my home—days before the first hurricane hit, and when I saw the devastation on the news after rehearsal that day I panicked. I had no idea what, if any, damage had been done to my home and couldn't concentrate during the rest of the rehearsals. Furthermore, hurricane number two was in the works and ready to hit. All I could think about was getting back home to batten down the hatches, as they say. The management knew I was distracted and I knew I couldn't do the part justice because of it. Since we were all in agreement I called Andrea and told him, "I want out." It was one of the few times I had ever done that.

I made it to my condo before the second hurricane hit. The first one hadn't done any real damage, so I decided I'd bravely stay and ride out the second one until it was over. Everyone else in the condo had pulled down their aluminum, impact-resistant, hurricane-proof windows and doors and abandoned ship; everyone except me and one couple in the whole twelve-storey building had evacuated. That should have given me a clue. The night before the second hurricane was to hit, I heard a crash on the roof. The wind had blown part of the roof loose and it was slamming against the building like a wrecking ball.

I'm outta here. I called every inland hotel, but they were all booked—even overbooked, with people sleeping in cots in the ballrooms. Then I remembered my friend Holly, who lived nearby in a flood zone, and called her. She was freaking out, too, and we decided to escape together to our friend Mary's—she was on higher, safer ground. Holly grabbed her cats, I grabbed Steinway, and we drove in my car as fast as we could.

Mary worked at a pet store, and all the animals had been divvied up among the employees to take home during the hurricane—Mary, just our luck, was given the aviary and her entire dining room was wall-to-wall cages of birds. Someone at the pet shop got to take home the cute little puppies and kittens . . . but not Mary. So there we were—me, Holly, Mary, Holly's two cats, Steinway, Mary's two dogs and five fish tanks, and about forty birds flying all over the place like in a Hitchcock movie. The birds were flying in slow motion and shitting all over poor Mary's shag carpet. Okay, maybe that last part of my memory comes courtesy of the Xanax we were taking to calm our nerves. But that's my recollection, and I'm sticking to it.

Had I been one of Hitchcock's icy-cool blondes, maybe I could have turned the situation into a suspenseful, romantic drama instead of what it was—bedlam. I just prayed we wouldn't have a flood and drift off like a little Noah's Ark.

We all slept lined up on the floor, listening to the wind howl and the house rattle and the birds squawk. As for food, I had grabbed a pre-cooked, honey-baked ham from the freezer before I left, and it turned out to be all we had to eat. We spent the next day sitting on the front porch, hacking off chunks of thawing ham with knives, popping Xanax, and watching the electrical converters blow up around us on nearby streets like fireworks.

I couldn't help but believe that the chaos around me was symbolic of the year I was having.

I FINALLY SANG the Marschallin a few months later, in Berlin, in January 2005.

It was at a Strauss festival—though one of the big newspapers there called it a "Deborah Voigt Festival" because I also sang the Kaiserin and *Vier letzte Lieder*, Strauss's beautiful "Four Last Songs," at the festival.

Christian Thielemann, the chief conductor of the Staatskapelle Dresden, was conducting, and under the direction of Götz Friedrich we created a very playful production of *Der Rosenkavalier* because he saw the role of the Marschallin as much younger than how she's usually played—the character is meant to be in her thirties but is often played older. Friedrich's youthful vision is what I think made the production such a success.

But as I was saying, there are many variables that come into play that affect one's voice and performance. Sometimes it has to do with the specific director, the production, or even the opera house. A few months after Berlin, I sang the Marschallin again at the Vienna State Opera and although I mainly got good reviews, it wasn't as successful. Why? The production is much loved by the Viennese public but it's old and dusty. And, unlike in Berlin, the director wanted me to play the character very stodgy and staid, and it didn't suit me. Plus, there was a long and established history between that piece, the opera house, and the women who've sung her there. The very fine soprano Felicity Lott had been their most recent Marschallin, and she had delivered exactly what they wanted and were used to. So to have some American come in and not fall in line with tradition . . . I didn't have a prayer. Which was unfortunate, because I generally had great luck in Vienna, though not with this one.

So there are a lot of things that can go right or wrong when it comes to a performance. A lot of people felt I took too big a risk having the surgery, but I look at it this way: there are roles I play now that I could never have played at 330 pounds. There is no way the Metropolitan Opera would have made me Brünnhilde as they did years later had I still been obese—it just wouldn't have happened. Besides, being able to move better and look more the part at my slimmer size, I feel I can do these roles more justice acting-wise, because my face, my expressions, are not lost in an indistinguishable blob. A single gesture with my arm reads so much more clearly to the audience because I don't have forty pounds of fat hanging from it.

But the most important factor in deciding to do the surgery was my health, and that trumps all the challenges that came with it. And I'm not the only opera star to think this way.

Late one night about two years after my surgery, my landline rang at an ungodly hour and when I picked it up, all I heard was static, and then:

"*Buon giorno*. Is this Debbbbeeee Voigt?"

"Yes, it is. . ."

"Please hold the line for Luciano Pavarotti."

Crackle, crackle, crackle. A minute later:

"Hey, Debbeeeee! It's Luciano! *Ciao, bella!*"

"Oh, hey, Luciano, how are you?" I was half-asleep, not sure if I was dreaming or if this was a crank call or if it was really . . . *him*. "Um, what's up?"

"Well, Debbbeeeee. I am wanting to talk to you about something."

"Sure. Anything, Luciano. What do you want to talk about?"

"Well, I know you had this surgery, Debbbeee. You had this bypass thing. Tell me about it."

I lay back in bed and explained the technicalities of it to him, about what the surgeons do with the stomach and the intestine so that you only ate small portions of food and lost a lot of weight.

"Why are you asking, Luciano?"

"Well, you know Debbbeeee, I keep gaining the weight and is not good for me and my knees and my back, and I'm thinking, maybe, I have this surgery like you."

"Well, I would never tell you or anyone else that they should do it, but, you know, Luciano, we want to have you with us and also onstage as long as we possibly can."

He was full of questions: he wanted to know how long it took me to lose the weight and if it was painful. He wanted to know how to find a good doctor.

"You're Luciano Pavarotti, I'm sure you can get the best doctor in the world to do this if you want to do it."

"You don't overeat now? You never overeat?"

"Never. I don't. But, Luciano, you have to understand that the surgery is just a tool, not a cure. If you don't follow the rules, if you don't eat what and how much they tell you to eat, your stomach will stretch and you'll gain it back."

"Ohhh . . . okay, okay. Well, I really appreciate it, Debbbeee. You take care, good night. *Buona notte, bella*. . . ."

"Goodbye, Lucian—"

Click. In all the times I'd worked with him over the years, I'd barely had a one-on-one conversation with this legend, and now we were talking provolone, internal organs, and life and death. I hung up the phone and thought how sweet and vulnerable it was for him to call me up and ask me those questions. He had a very young daughter with his new wife, Nicoletta, and he wanted to be healthy for both of them. But sadly, Luciano was diagnosed with pancreatic cancer just a few weeks after our late-night phone chat.

When I heard he had died a year later, I said a prayer for him. He had the most identifiable opera voice I'd ever heard; one note, and you knew it was Luciano. Not only was it beautiful, expressive, and with a wide range of colors . . . no matter what age he was, his sound was fresh and youthful. It was a voice that could coax *Ballo*'s Amelia to declare her love on the gallows at midnight and soothe Aida as she took her last breath.

Luciano was larger than life, and his voice will live forever.

IN THE FALL of 2006, just over two years after my surgery, I strutted onstage practically naked in front of thousands of strangers and showed off my new body. Singing in my first fully staged production of Strauss's *Salome*, at the Lyric Opera of Chicago, I had to dance the sexy Dance of the Seven Veils as the biblically inspired and sexually charged Salome, who demands the head of John the Baptist. This role is a perfect example of a part I never would have been able to play in my former body, and she is one of my favorites.

For the first and only time in my life, I worked out like a fiend to prepare for a role—I knew it would be a challenge, both muscially and physically, and I wanted to look fantastic. For four months, I got my ass into the gym every day to sweat on the elliptical and pump iron. I was down to 180 pounds, my pretty and curvaceous high school weight. The next challenge was to find a man who could pick me up—literally.

During rehearsals, we auditioned all sorts of men for the part of the Executioner—a mixed bag of theater extras, muscle men dug up at the gym, and brawny character actor–types. It was a role without any lines; instead of acting-singing ability, it called mainly for brute force, because his essential job was to throw me around. The director, Francesca Zambello, lined up ten potential Samsons to test their strength.

"Okay, now, guys," she instructed, "I want you each to walk over to Debbie, throw her over your shoulder, walk to the other end of the stage with her, and toss her down onto that pile of pillows."

I was terrified. In my mind, I still saw myself as 330 pounds. *There is no way any of these guys will be able to do it!* I was wearing knee- and elbow pads just in case one of them dropped me. Even little Steinway, whom I'd brought to rehearsal that day (Francesca dubbed him "the Dustbuster") was shaking in trepidation.

The first guy who walked onto the stage looked ninety-five pounds soaking wet. Francesca whispered something in his ear and he left. The second guy picked me up but only made it five feet across the stage before he had to put me down. One by one, they each tried and faltered, until it was Number Five's turn. He came charging at me, ripped the prop head of John the Baptist out of my hand, threw it across the stage, lifted me up like a sack of potatoes over his shoulder, and charged across the stage, ready to throw me onto the pillows. I was shrieking. Or, to be more precise, I was squealing like a teenager.

"Okay! Okay, okay . . . *okay!*" Francesca yelled. "You've got the job. Now please put Debbie down—*gently.*"

Everybody laughed, and I was in shock, not to mention exhilarated, that any man could pick me up like that. Our rehearsals after that consisted of us wrapping our bodies around each other and Number Five manhandling me like a brute—I loved it. Offstage, he took me for motorcycle rides in the freezing Chicago evenings without a helmet. I wore jeans, black leather boots, and a black leather jacket. It felt good to be wild girl Rizzo on the back of a Harley instead of goody-two-shoes Sandy.

And while I was at it, I couldn't resist giving my new figure a whirl, too. During rehearsals for *Salome*, my old standby boyfriend Dane came to visit. I'd met Dane ten years earlier on one of those Big Girl dating websites during my wild fen-phen days—he was the poet/Harvard law student/former heroin addict who made love tenderly—*that* Dane. We'd kept in touch over the years, seeing each other in between our other relationships. I truly cared for Dane—I loved him, in fact—but since he was married for much of those ten years, having a real relationship with him was problematic. During my Mitch years, he'd been out of the picture, off somewhere having kids. But now that Mitch was old news, Dane had returned for a cameo.

Because he was a former addict who'd been going regularly to Narcotics Anonymous meetings for twenty years, he was the first person I confided in after my Mitch nightmare about a worry I had.

"I think I have a problem with alcohol," I told him one night, during his visit to Chicago. I had learned to drink heavily with Mitch, and in the last year it had escalated on my own. I was hoping I could talk to him about it, that he'd understand and give me some twelve-step advice.

"You? Nah, you couldn't," he said, very sure of himself. "If you were an alcoholic you'd be drinking around me, and you never do."

I tried to explain that I didn't drink around him out of respect for his own addiction, and that when our dates were over and he went home, I'd go to the bar and drink until closing time. But he'd have none of that talk. He was the kind of addict I'd meet and recognize later on—the kind who had to be the "star" addict, who had to have the most dramatic story, who had to upstage everyone around him as the more serious addict, the worst addict in the room. Was that something to be proud of?

I remember meeting Dane's mother once when she attended a concert of mine in San Francisco. She was a lovely woman, and after the concert we talked a bit.

"You're one of the best things to ever happen to my son," she said, and I smiled. Apparently I had approval from the mother, which was major.

"But if I were you," she added, "I'd turn around and *run*."

I never got the chance to take his mother's advice, because Dane always ran first. He visited me in Chicago and then went home to the wife, or some other girlfriend, as usual. But at least I had a gorgeous man that I adored see me up close and in the buff while I was in the best shape of my life. Who knew how long I'd be able to maintain those workouts?

For my big nude scene in *Salome*, I had to belly dance across the stage behind a gauzy scrim, then climb up a chain-link fence like a cat and swing my butt back and forth. I wasn't going to be *completely* naked. I'd be wearing a skin-tone body stocking painted with nipples and pubic hair and with a built-in bra for extra va-va-voom lift. But

I'd look naked. I figured I better warn my parents about it ahead of time since the last time they'd seen me show skin on stage was back in my high school Daisy Duke days, so I did.

About two weeks before opening night, I got a call from Mom.

"Debbie, I've been thinking about you playing this Salome character, and I don't think this is something a nice Christian girl would do."

I had to smile. I had to smile thinking about all the things that she and I had both done that a nice Christian girl wouldn't do.

"Don't worry, Mom. I won't do anything too inappropriate," I promised. "But this is an acting part, and I have to play it properly. I hope you understand."

I didn't dare tell my mother about the final scene, in which Salome clutches the severed head of John the Baptist to her chest and rolls around with it on the floor, making out with it as she sings.

Some things you have to let moms discover all by themselves.

15

Princes, Rogues, Blackouts, and Bottoms

IF I WAS going to be a good Christian girl like my mother wanted and find a good, honest, Christian man like John the Baptist, what better place to look than in church? Seek and you shall find, says the Lord. And one Sunday morning in early 2007, I sought and found the handsome face of Peter in the same pew as me at a church on Manhattan's Upper West Side.

I was getting my life together and trying to make healthier choices. After seeing Dane the year before and accompanying him to his NA meetings, I started going to AA meetings on my own and had gotten ninety days sober under my belt by the time I met Peter. I was also starting to go to church more often to allow God back into my life. A churchgoing man would complete the picture.

Peter was a divorced father who worked in real estate, he told me. At first, just like with Mitch, spending time with him was thrilling. We traveled to Hawaii and went paragliding off a cliff—something I never would have done when I was heavy. It felt so freeing to sail through the air like that.

I loved that Peter loved God as much as I did. Perhaps even more. For the first five months of our romance we had what I called "Christian sex"; as many a Catholic schoolgirl will tell you, that means we did everything *but*. I didn't know about Peter's commitment to chastity until a few weeks into dating when we were making out and he stopped abruptly.

"I can't do that."

"What do you mean you *can't*?" I asked. (Uh-oh. Did that mean he *couldn't*?)

"Well, I'm Christian and I believe that you should wait until you're married."

Obviously, Peter didn't understand "Christian sex" the same way I did. Unmarried sex was sinful, sure, but you did it anyway then felt guilty about it and/or paid a big price for it afterward. Sheesh. But . . . *no* sex? Well, every relationship I'd had so far had been based on sex, so I thought, okay, let's give this a chance. He's got potential.

I appreciated his dedication to his faith, of course. But the problem with this no-sex thing was that it began to feel like the same dynamic I always felt with men—that they were aloof, holding back, unreachable . . . unavailable. And if I sensed that, I'd end up begging and pleading for the attention I needed. And if I didn't get it, I learned in therapy, I'd overeat, overdrink, or fill the empty hole inside me some other way—this was my pattern.

Our Christian sex continued for five months—two divorced adults in their forties saving it for the wedding night—until month six, when I couldn't take it any longer and boldly took the initiative one night. The next morning, he got up to leave and didn't say a word about it. I couldn't gauge his mood—was he in shock? Was he angry? After two days without acknowledgment of our long-awaited consummation, I brought it up. It was such an intimate step in our relationship, I felt it was important to talk about.

"Peter, I think something happened between us the other night."

"Yes," he said, deadpan. "It did."

It was all he said before changing the subject. He obviously didn't want to talk about it, so we didn't. But he didn't say he wanted to stop doing it, either, so we didn't (stop, that is). But it's not like the romantic floodgates burst open after that. Once again, I was in the begging role.

On one vacation in the Dominican Republic we were staying at a friend's gorgeous summer home and I'd been trying to lure Peter to the bedroom. I'd just bought a sexy bathing suit especially for him—black, and cut all the way down to my navel—and I walked into the room where he was watching television and modeled it for him, sashaying across the floor like it was a catwalk. He didn't look up.

"Notice anything?"

He looked up. "Oh, new suit? That's really great." He looked back at the TV screen.

I went out and lay by the pool, in a huff. The sun was setting, and the ocean waves were splashing nearby—it was the ultimate setup for romance. When Peter came outside, I got my hopes up—but all he did was pick up the hose and start watering the plants around the pool.

"Peter! I don't get it!" I blew up. "We come down here to this beautiful, romantic place, and I feel like you don't want me. Any man, I don't care what I look like, would be all over me in this situation!"

Secretly, I was beginning to wonder if he was gay and he didn't want to admit it. Either way, I took it as rejection, and that feeling led me . . . to take a drink. Once I took that first one, the dam was busted. As they say in AA, you think you've licked the disease, but really it's out in the parking lot doing push-ups, getting stronger. If you start up again after being sober for a while, the alcohol hits you twice as hard.

FOR THE FIRST time ever, the drinking affected my work—something I had never let it do before. I was in Barcelona in the fall of 2007 to sing a new role at the Gran Teatre del Liceu—Maddalena, in Giordano's *Andrea Chénier*, and I was frustrated with the role before performances even began. Maddalena's an aristocrat during the French Revolution who discovers love with poet Chénier, and in the end she goes to the guillotine with him. Unlike most of the roles I'd played, I couldn't find a way to identify with her. Her story was dramatic enough but there wasn't much complexity to her personality or arc to her character. You couldn't compare her to Isolde, for example, whose love affair and arias were so much richer. It would be like comparing a plain sorbet to rocky road ice cream. Plus, it's really a tenor's opera. Maddalena has one great aria and her other two substantial pieces are duets. Which suited our tenor in the title role, José Cura, just fine. Cura is a very good-looking Spanish-Argentinian tenor, and with an ego so large it sucked the air out of a room.

I had arrived in Barcelona a week before rehearsals began in order to work with a private coach, but once I got there I discovered we'd gotten our details crossed and she was on vacation. I could have easily found another coach, of course, but that's not how the alcoholic mind works. The alcoholic mind will find any excuse possible to say, *Oh, fuck it! It's not working out, so I'll drink today!* Today turned into two days, then three, four, five days. I was alone and, as always, was looking to get away from myself—I didn't want to be in my own skin. Apparently it didn't matter if I was fat or slim, I still didn't want to be there. So I partied the week away by myself in my hotel suite, and the next thing I knew I had to be in rehearsal bright and early the next morning and I didn't know the part. I called in sick. Then I called in sick on day two, day three, day four . . .

The opera house called up Andrea in New York: "She's not showing up for rehearsals, what should we do?"

There was nothing they could do. If they had come to my hotel room to see how "sick" I was, they'd have found me dousing myself with champagne, red wine, white wine, and vodka until I passed out.

To protect themselves, the management hired a cover. In Europe, one didn't automatically have a cover like you did in the

United States. The countries are so close together that if a lead woke up one morning feeling sick, you could fly in a cover from an opera house in the country next door in an hour. Knowing that, I canceled opening night to protect myself. I didn't feel ready to face the critics and convinced myself that all would be better with a few days of rehearsal. My ploy to skip opening-night reviews didn't work. When the critics found out I wasn't singing, they all returned for when I was.

Barcelona was the only time in my career that I've ever been penalized at work—they docked my pay ten percent because they had to hire the cover. It was also the closest I'd come to feeling as though my inner demons were taking over: my disease was raging.

What was happening, I realized later, was something I had vaguely heard about—cross addiction. Before gastric bypass surgery, patients are supposed to undergo counseling about the psychological aftermath of the procedure and the possible dangers that lie ahead. For many patients, once the ability to overeat is taken away, they substitute a new addiction, and it's usually alcohol. I skipped much of the counseling part because as soon as I had those few weeks free from the Covent Garden schedule, I jumped at the first opportunity to have the surgery while there was a free block of time in my busy schedule. It didn't occur to me that anything could go wrong after the surgery; I was certain, in fact, that it was going to solve all my problems.

Thanks to Mitch, I had grown to love drinking. But before the surgery I'd never had the feeling that I *had* to drink. I'd had that feeling about food and men, for sure, but not alcohol. Now those feelings had transferred to drinking. And with my added postsurgery anxieties—like relearning how to breathe and sing properly, and adapting to the rapid weight loss—I had more reasons to try to calm myself down with booze.

When our run was over in Barcelona, I went to the company manager's office to apologize. I told him that I knew I'd been unreliable and explained it was because of personal problems, promising it would never happen again. The manager sighed a breath of relief.

"We thought you just didn't like your time here in Barcelona," he said, "and that you were coming in today to cancel your upcoming contract for *Tristan and Isolde*!"

It was the last reaction I expected. (I did indeed go back a few years later to sing a very successful run of *Isolde*.) They had no idea what bad shape I'd been in. I was doing a good job of living a dual life, and even those closest to me—my friends and family—didn't know how much trouble I was in. Jesslyn and Jaime worked closely with me and sometimes traveled with me and they were smart, observant women and still, they didn't see it; I was a better actress than the music critics thought. If we were eating dinner in my hotel room and having wine, no one noticed that every time I went to the bathroom and casually took my glass with me, I'd refill it from the wine bottle hidden under the sink.

The blackouts began in early 2008; the first one happened when I was in L.A. for a concert. I spent a night alone in my hotel room—or so I thought—drinking, and when I woke up the next morning my body was covered in bruises. I was black and blue down one arm, on my forehead, on my back, and—here's the scariest part—I had a purple handprint on one of my arms.

What the . . . ?

I stared and stared at it, trying to figure it out. I tried to fit my hand on it and saw there was no way it was mine. To this day, I have no idea what happened that night. Best case scenario? I ordered room service and took a fall and somebody grabbed me and helped me up. Worst case? I went downstairs to the bar and . . . I'm afraid to imagine the rest. After that night, I got in the habit of reaching for my BlackBerry as soon as I awoke in the morning, to check texts for clues as to what kind of mess I might have made the night before.

* * *

I TRIED TO keep a sense of humor about the minor onstage mishaps in the following weeks even though at the time, they were not so funny. In February of that year, I was singing Sieglinde at the Met, when, in the middle of a long passage of music . . . I forgot the next line. I stood onstage, dumbfounded. I had sung that part so many times—at least every two years for a decade—the words were as familiar to me as "Happy Birthday." But a quick, frantic search of my memory brought no words to my lips. Any opera singer will tell you that it happens to the best of us, but I never, ever expected it to happen with a role I could sing in my sleep.

I wasn't too worried. After my initial shock, I looked downstage toward the prompter box. I had become an expert at using a prompter, I knew every trick in the book on how to read their lips, translate their eyewinks, and decipher their nose wriggles and ear pulling. Each prompter in every country, in every opera house, had their own personal "sign language" they used to give you your next line if you forgot it, and I had made it my mission to learn all their dialects. They, in turn, are trained to recognize the universal "deer in the headlights" look an opera singer gets onstage during a memory lapse and jump to attention. If they are really astute, they learn the subtle signs each performer gives as their personal SOS. When I need help, I turn my head slightly at a certain angle and make eye contact with the prompter. I've noticed Russian soprano Anna Netrebko does the exact same angle as me.

"If I have to lie on the floor for a scene," Anna once told me, "I make sure my head is facing toward the prompt box."

Being a prompter is an art unto itself. The best ones don't wait until you're in trouble, they feed you cues along the way, whether you need them or not.

Except on this night, when I was in trouble. I wandered across the stage with my eye on the prompter box, telepathically screaming at the top of my lungs: LOOK AT ME! LOOK AT ME! TELL ME

MY NEXT LINE!!! I could see the light reflecting off the top of my prompter's balding head as he looked down at the music. I still had a few bars of music before my next line, so he was unaware of my crisis. He had been my prompter for this role many times before and knew how well I knew it.

A few bars later—it felt like hours—the window of opportunity closed and I had to move on, my line was up. What did I do? I made up some nonsensical German-sounding gibberish and hoped no one in the audience that night knew German. Out of the corner of my eye, I could see Maestro Levine look up at me from the pit, thinking: *What did you just say?*

THE NEXT MONTH I was in a production plagued by illness, and it got so ridiculous, it was more like a British farce than a German opera. Tenor Ben Heppner and I were paired up to sing *Tristan und Isolde* at the Met for five performances. But when opening night arrived, Ben fell sick with the flu and called in his cover—to simplify the story, I'll call him Tristan #2.

Opening night went fine with Tristan #2, but a few days later, for our second performance, #2 got sick too, and we had to call in Tristan #3. But I barely got to sing with #3 that night, because then it was my turn. That morning, I felt the unmistakable rumblings in my stomach of whatever flu was going around, and by the time I reached the theater that night, I had a fever and called for my cover.

Because we were singing Wagner, which was "through composed," I knew I had to bow out immediately rather than try to go on and wing it. "Through composed" means that each act of the opera is filled with an uninterrupted stream of music, without any pauses for clapping—or running off the stage to puke one's guts out, if need be. Verdi, by contrast, always has plenty of natural moments during his acts where a girl can tiptoe daintily into the wings—in character, of course—and barf into a prop bucket. But Wagner was not so generous. If I started Act I and felt even worse—and I was feeling worse by the minute—there would be no break to make a graceful exit.

"Ah, c'mon, Deb. You can walk offstage if you feel sick," the on-duty administrator told me. "You'll be fine."

It was their job to get me onstage, and they did. I don't know how I got through the first act without gagging, it was pure luck. By Act II, though, I knew my luck had run out and asked for the cover again.

"But Debbie, you already did Act I, and you were great! You'll be fine for Act II!"

Convinced again, I went out onstage. As soon as I started the beautiful love duet, one of the longest and most opulent love duets in the history of opera, I got dizzy and felt the bile bubbling up inside of me. Poor Tristan #3. As he sang his heart out, I pulled a Luciano on him and ran offstage, wild-eyed, in the middle of our duet. In the wings, a stage manager had a trash can ready. I grabbed it and tossed my cookies so violently I bet they heard me in the last row of the balcony. (To this day, my brother Kevin, who was in the audience with Peter, does a hilarious impression of T-3 standing forlornly onstage, as I did when Luciano abandoned me in *Ballo*, still singing and wondering: *Is she coming back, or what?*)

But it gets worse—or rather, funnier, depending on your sense of humor. The curtain closed mid-duet and mid-cookie-toss, and I was crying and hysterical. Juliet Velri, my wig lady and confidante of many years (you know how it is in the hair biz, they put their hands in your hair and you spill all your secrets), rushed over and put her arm around me to console me.

"Deb, Deb . . . it's going to be okay, Deb," she said soothingly, steering me purposefully toward my dressing room. For one tough broad, Juliet was being incredibly sweet to me. In fact, she was being unusually, *scarily* sweet for Juliet. As soon as we got inside my dressing room she closed the door, swiveled around, and held her hands and arms up in front of her like a Greco-Roman wrestler, ready to pounce.

"All right, honey. *Gimme that wig!*"

In a mad rush, she started pulling the long, blond, Pre-Raphaelite curls off my head as one of the dressers popped his head into the room.

"Debbie, you know we love you, you *know* we love you . . . but we need your costume—*now! Give me that dress!*" My cover, Janice Baird, was in the next room, about to be pushed onto the stage to finish Act II, and she was waiting for hair and costume. Juliet and the dresser fled the room just as my brother and Peter arrived. After I'd run off the stage, Maestro Levine had put his baton down and someone came out and announced I was sick. They came back to see if I was okay, and found me hairless, dress-less, and sobbing onto my piano keys.

The next day, it was all over the opera chat rooms online: "Debbie Voigt barfed in the wings at the Metropolitan Opera last night!"

Ah, the glamorous life of an opera diva. If you check the Met archives online, it lists my performance that night as "Acts I, II . . . *partial.*"

For our third performance, I was healthy and Tristan #3 was healthy and we both performed; it was a stage catastrophe that nearly did our Tristan in this time.

I was in my dressing room, waiting to go on in the middle of Act III to sing the love-death "Liebestod" when I heard, over the intercom speaker backstage, the audience gasping, then applauding vigorously when they shouldn't have been. *Huh?* What happened, I found out soon enough, was that during the scene in which Tristan has been stabbed and is lying on a makeshift mattress, dying (but singing a perilously difficult and anguished aria, nevertheless), the mattress came loose from its moorings and Tristan and his bed slid downstage like a runaway train toward the prompter box. The prompter on duty let out a piercing scream—the bed was moving toward her so fast, she feared it was about to decapitate her, like a Brian De Palma production of *The Phantom of the Opera.* The performance stopped, and once Tristan, the prompter, and the bed were all inspected and deemed intact, the show went on and the audience applauded.

But with the next performance came another new Tristan. Number 3 took sick and Tristan #4 took over. At this point, we were all scared to even breathe on each other. Someone in the press dubbed the run "the revolving door of Tristans."

Finally—finally—for the fifth and final performance, Ben and I were onstage together. According to the *New York Times*, it was "well worth the wait."

> . . . these acclaimed Wagnerians seemed to feed on each other's intensity and determination. . . .
>
> Mr. Heppner again gave an impassioned, courageous and vocally thrilling performance. . . . And Ms. Voigt sounded liberated.
>
> With a Tristan who could match her in sheer power and vocal charisma, she, too, took risks as she sent gleaming phrases soaring over the orchestra. But what may especially linger in the memory were the moments of tender lyricism and the aching exchanges of desire during their Act II love duet. . . .

After such a challenging spring, I had a triumph in June. Four years after my Little Black Dress saga, I returned to London's Royal Opera House to sing Ariadne, the role I had been removed from. Life is funny that way, isn't it? I would have loved to take Steinway with me but wasn't allowed because the U.K. had a six-month quarantine for cats and dogs at that time to prevent the spread of rabies. Elizabeth Taylor and Richard Burton once rented a 200-foot floating kennel (read: yacht) to house their four pooches for two months while Burton was filming near London, to get around the regulation.

I took Peter with me instead, and this time, 125 pounds lighter, you can be sure I fit the dress. To promote the run, Albert and I made a hilarious, tongue-in-cheek video that we sent out to the press and posted on YouTube. In the video, the infamous black dress shows up at my Manhattan apartment like a film noir–ish character (ringing a doorbell that chimes like the "Ride of the Valkyries") and asks me, in a British accent, for another chance, like a lover begging for forgiveness. We called it "The Return of the Little Black Dress."

When I got to London for rehearsals, it took the artistic administrator, Peter Katona, a few days before he popped into my dressing room to say hello. Unlike the dress he didn't come groveling, but he was contrite.

"I have a file in my desk drawer several inches thick, full of letters," he told me. "They're from patrons and opera fans, angry about what happened. I framed one and put it up on my office wall."

It was as close to an apology as I was going to get, so it would have to do.

While in London, I also sang at a charity event at St. James's Palace hosted by the Prince of Wales. He was late in arriving because it was Royal Ascot time and he'd been to the horse races that day, so we delayed the performance until he and Camilla, Duchess of Cornwall, could get there. I wore a gorgeous aqua gown and sang "Dich, teure Halle," Elisabeth's aria from *Tannhäuser* in which she greets a magnificent hall where a singing contest is about to take place. So appropriate for St. James's Palace, I thought. And then I threw in a few of my favorite show tunes and saw the prince tap his foot in the front row. Behind him sat a star-studded group: Liam Neeson, Natasha Richardson, Vanessa Redgrave, and Joan Rivers, to name a few. After the performance, Prince Charles came up onstage to shake my hand and pose for photos, which thrilled Peter to no end. He was much handsomer in person and very charming, but my eyes couldn't help but drift from his face to the throat of his wife and the spectacular, blinding, necklace she was wearing.

I was out of my league when it came to riches and baubles. At the black-tie dinner later that evening, I sat next to a very tanned

Greek yacht designer who was designing a boat for director Steven Spielberg. He looked like Ari Onassis, and his wife who was sitting across from me, upstaged even Camilla with the biggest, most sparkling canary diamond necklace I'd ever seen.

"That's a beautiful necklace on your wife," I said. I pushed away flashbacks of Mitch, ripping my own humble diamond from my neck.

"Yes," the tanned, Greek yacht designer said, nodding emphatically. "It's so difficult to find good jewelry these days, don't you agree?"

"Oh, yes . . . yes," I said, clutching the modest Macy's knock-off I wore at my own throat.

The flowers and table settings were gorgeous—each place card calligraphically handwritten. And leave it to the British tradition of service to have succeeded in serving two hundred guests an appetizer that included a perfectly poached egg. How in the world do you time that?

After dinner, I mingled a bit and talked to Natasha Richardson, who was beautiful and warm. (Nine months later, I'd be stunned to hear the news of her death following a tumble during a skiing lesson.) All of a sudden, the room went silent and everyone stood up and began leaving the room in waves.

"Time for us to go," Natasha whispered, grabbing her purse and signaling Liam. Sure enough, two palace pages were making their way from one end of the room to the other, telling people to leave. The prince was leaving, and that meant we had to as well.

As Peter and I went down the stairs to leave, we bumped into Joan Rivers. I was a big fan of hers and told her so.

"And we have something in common," I added. "I have a Yorkie, too. Isn't it a shame we couldn't bring them to London because of the quarantine?"

"Thank you for reminding me . . . *you bitch*!" she said, very loudly. I stood on the staircase with my mouth open. I guess even

St. James's Palace wasn't too sacred a place for Joan's jabs. I hope the angels have a sense of humor.

Despite being sworn at by a big star, it was a dazzling, sparkling night, and *Ariadne* had been a success. So I should have been happy, right? But I wasn't. The newspapers praised my comeback performance and my pretty face and figure. But when I looked in the bathroom mirror after we returned to our hotel suite that night, all I saw was the sad, bloated face of another addiction that had replaced the old one.

That night, I woke up at four a.m. in a panic. Peter was sleeping peacefully, and I shook him awake.

"I'm so afraid, Peter." I clung to him.

"Of what?"

"I don't know, I can't define it. Aren't you ever afraid?"

"No," he said, with a yawn. "I don't have anything to be afraid of. My Lord tells me not to be fearful."

That kind of blind faith makes life so much easier, and I wish to God I had it.

BACK HOME IN New York, everyone at the Met was getting ready for Plácido's fortieth anniversary with the company. General Manager Peter Gelb, who took over for Joe Volpe two years earlier, was planning a black-tie soirée to happen right on the Met's stage. Mr. Gelb also had a funny, sexy idea to kick-start the evening, and it involved me.

His plan was for José Carreras, the other third of the Three Tenors, to begin the night with an adoring speech about Plácido and our late friend, Luciano Pavarotti. But, as Carreras told the guests with a wink, perhaps it was time to pass the baton over to new talent and new tenors.

That was the cue for the black curtain on the stage to part, and as the orchestra played the opening bars of Puccini's "Nessun dorma" from *Turandot*, my fellow powerhouse singers Susan Graham, Pat

Racette, and I appeared dressed up as the Tenors in tuxedos and tails. The party guests went wild. Our tuxedos had strings in back that were intricately rigged so that our costumes would "break away" with a tug. As the aria rose to a crescendo, someone above us pulled a few strings and yanked the suits off our bodies to reveal us wearing sparkly, skintight *Dreamgirls* gowns—me in turquoise, Susan in red, and Pat in blue. Everyone cheered!

Plácido sat a few feet from us, clapping and laughing . . . as we then went into our rendition of the Gilbert & Sullivan hit from *The Mikado*:

> *Three little maids from school are we*
> *Pert as a school-girl well can be*
> *Filled to the brim with girlish glee*
> *Three little maids from school . . .*

All three of us were natural hambones and we played it to the hilt. Then we each took turns singing excerpts from the operas we'd done with Plácido, ending our show with a reprise of "Nessun dorma"— and this time the three of us belted it out—that had Plácido in tears. At the after-party up onstage, Plácido hugged me tightly:

"Debbie! It was so funny, you were the Three Tenors and then suddenly these Dreamgirls!"

We'd come a long way from our "first kiss" twelve years earlier, Plácido and I had. And I was proud not only to call him my illustrious colleague, but now, also, my friend.

IT WAS YET another spectacular night of special nights, and I've had many of them over the years. But the higher we fly, the harder we fall. And after that night, I went down. It was like falling off a balcony in slow motion.

My alcohol intake reached an all-time high in the second half of 2008. When I wasn't working, I was drinking. On days off I started the moment I woke up with vodka and orange juice and just kept going until I passed out. On performance days, I didn't touch a drop until the work was over. But as soon as I arrived home I'd rush straight to the kitchen without taking my coat off and pour a big glass of wine and chug it as quickly as possible. I wasn't drinking for pleasure at all anymore; I was drinking to get as drunk as possible as fast as possible. I had three different liquor stores on speed dial and I'd rotate them when I called for delivery so they wouldn't think I was ordering so much. Sometimes when I called, I pretended I was ordering for a party.

I was so miserable, I must have been miserable to be around. I have a dim, heartbreaking, regretful memory of playing with Steinway one drunken morning and pulling on his whiskers too hard. He yelped in pain and to remember it brings me to tears. My Steiny must have been wondering, *What is happening to Mama?*

By November, my slow-motion free fall was gaining momentum.

I was in Vienna to sing *Salome* at the Wiener Staatsoper and Peter was supposed to meet me there. I'd bought him a plane ticket and got us a plush, expensive hotel suite so we could have a romantic time. I was waiting for him to call from the airport to let me know he was boarding, but I didn't hear from him. A few frantic hours later, as his flight was over the Atlantic I called his cell again and he picked up. He was still in New York. He'd never even gotten on the plane and hadn't bothered to tell me.

What mature person—and a so-called Christian to boot—does that to someone they supposedly love? His actions should have answered that question for me, but I didn't want to face that reality.

On a dreary, cold Sunday, Jesslyn and I slipped into the gothic St. Stephen's Cathedral and went to mass. We were shivering cold in a back pew, and the mass was in German so we barely understood a word, but I didn't care. The church bells tolled, and they tolled for me—I needed God, so badly

By Christmas, I'd forgiven Peter again and we visited his family

in Florida for the holidays. I was determined to be on my best behavior—I didn't touch a drop of drink for the three-day visit even
though it put me in severe withdrawal. I wanted to make a good
impression on his family because I still, stupidly, hoped for a future
with Peter. He had told me when we met that he never dated a
woman he wouldn't consider marrying, and that thought kept me
on a string. We had a nice Christmas Eve dinner with his parents at
their home, and I was feeling pretty good until I noticed an elabo-
rately framed photo of Peter with Prince Charles displayed proudly
in the living room—the one and only photo taken that evening that
didn't include *yours truly* in the frame.

Peter and I got into an argument in the car on the way back to the
hotel. He was only dropping me off, by the way, he wasn't staying
with me—he was still in denial that we even had sex (which we did)
and he knew his parents wouldn't think it proper if he stayed with me.

As we drove, Peter was boasting about how he intended to buy
houses for his parents and his sister and take care of all his loved
ones.

When he stopped in front of my hotel, I was ready to burst into
tears.

"Peter, I don't understand what's going on here. You tell me
you're open to marriage or a permanent relationship, and yet you're
constantly talking about buying homes for your parents, your
brother, your sister . . . but what about you and me? Where do I fit
in? I want a partner. I feel like we're not on the same page. If you're
not serious about me, you need to let me go."

He remained silent, and I got out of the car and slammed the
door. We had plans to meet in New York for New Year's after he
visited a friend outside of Nashville, but I couldn't get hold of him
in the days following Christmas. I called, left messages, and filled
up his voice mail. Frantic to reach him, I found the number for the
friend he was visiting.

"Hi, I'm so sorry to bother you, but I'm trying to find Peter. . . ."

I'd reached the friend's mother. Funnily enough (though I wasn't laughing), the mother had the same name as an iconic Wagnerian heroine.

"Oh, he's not here, dear," she said. "They all got in the car and drove to Nashville for New Year's Eve."

And still I forgave him. To make it up to me, he promised to visit me on Valentine's Day 2009 in Chicago, where I'd be singing about love potions and poisons in *Tristan und Isolde*. I made romantic plans for us once again—reservations at the best restaurant, tickets to a sold-out performance of the hottest play in town, and a sexy new negligee. I even got Valentine's Day treats for Steinway, whom I'd brought to keep me company during the run. Poor Steiny. Who knows how many times during those years he bore the brunt of my unhinging world—and sometimes the blame. One morning after a night of heavy drinking and debauchery in Chicago, I woke up in my rented apartment to find it looking like a rock band had trashed the place—spilled booze, smashed wineglasses, food smeared into the carpet, furniture upside down. Okay, maybe it wasn't that bad, but you get the picture.

"Steinway!" I scolded him, "*what did you do?!*"

Only an alcoholic could blame a six-pound dog for such mass destruction.

Two days before Valentine's Day, Peter telephoned.

"I don't think I can come. I haven't got my paycheck yet and I don't have the money for the plane ticket." Was this the same man who was buying houses for his entire family?

"Peter, I'm not going to let a cheap airplane ticket get in the way of our lovely Valentine's Day plans. I'll buy your ticket. You can pay me back, or consider it a Valentine's gift."

He was silent. "Debbie. I don't think it's a good idea." He continued to say that we were indeed "not in the same place," as I had said in the car at Christmas, and that he wasn't coming to be with me and that it was over between us.

I hung up the phone, aghast. I had told him to tell me if he wasn't serious about me and had urged him to let me go if he wasn't. And now that he had, I couldn't handle it. The reality was too painful. I needed to do whatever it took not to feel the black hopelessness that began gripping me like a tight fist. I went downstairs to the grocery store and bought six bottles of cheap white wine, went back up to my apartment, and drank until I passed out.

At some point after my Valentine's Day heart massacre, I made a few drunken phone calls. One was to Jesslyn.

"I have a bottle of Xanax and a bottle of Ambien," I told her, sobbing. "I'm going to swallow them and jump off the balcony. Please, please," I begged her, "come and get Steinway after I'm gone and give him a good home."

16

Fathers, Love, and the Ride
of the Valkyries

UNLIKE TOSCA, BUT very much like Debbie, I didn't take the leap.

After calling Jesslyn, I passed out before taking even one pill. But my suicidal phone call set off a chain of events that had my family jumping in cars and boarding planes to get to me. Jesslyn called my brothers, who called a family relative who lived nearby. I don't know how many minutes later it was that Cousin Tony showed up at my apartment. In that time I had woken from my stupor, gone downstairs to buy more booze, and returned to find him banging on the door.

"Tony? What are you doing here?"

"Hi, Deb," he said, eyeing the paper bag still in my arms. "I came by to see how you were doing." He slowly reached toward my bag, careful not to make any quick movements.

"Here, let me take that for you. How are you feeling?" He talked soothingly as he got me inside.

"To tell you the truth, Tony, I'm not feeling so good."

Once inside, I passed out again. I have a vague, discombobulated memory of hearing voices. First there was Tony, saying to someone on the phone, maybe it was 911, "Yeah, I've got the pills. There's all different kinds here. . . . She says she didn't take any. . . . Yeah, I'll get rid of the booze. . . ." I remember waking up some time later and seeing my sister-in-law, Angie, Rob's wife—they lived in

Atlanta—sitting next to my bed, watching me anxiously. I remember hearing Kevin's voice talking on the phone, saying, "It would be best if you didn't call Debbie anymore, Peter. Leave her alone."

My mother and Don arrived the next day, and Mom was devastated. She hugged me and cried and kept saying, "I can't believe my little girl would want to kill herself." I tried to explain to her that I didn't—not really, and that I was so drunk I didn't know what I was doing. I thought to ask her about when I was sixteen and she herself had phoned my father late at night crying, with a bottle of sleeping pills next to her. Had she wanted to harm herself? Mom didn't take the leap then, either. Like mother like daughter, as Dad would say. But I didn't have the energy to go there, and I didn't want to upset her by bringing it up.

Amazingly, I managed to pull myself together and sing the next night, and sing well. Actually, it wasn't that difficult. I had a good, reliable technique, and I focused on that instead of how I was feeling physically or emotionally—which I always tried to keep separate from my performances. That's how I usually worked, and it pulled me through just about anything. Maybe this time I let a little bit of heartache seep through during the final act. Because there's nothing like using a little real life-and-death drama of one's own to add extra oomph to that "Liebestod" when Isolde surrenders to death.

Despite my drinking and heartache (or maybe because of it?) the critics gave me good reviews. From the *Chicago Tribune*:

LYRIC OPERA'S "TRISTAN" A TRIUMPH FOR THE SHINING ISOLDE OF DEBORAH VOIGT

. . . Voigt threw herself into a vocally fearless, dramatically incisive portrayal of the proud Irish princess who engages in a passionate affair with the knight Tristan that eventually consumes both of them.

She made the "Liebestod" a gripping song of transcendence; as the orchestra surged, Isolde surrendered to death,

standing transfixed under a single spotlight, surrounded by
a darkened stage. Voigt and [tenor Clifton] Forbis were at
their best in the long, ecstatic love duet (here slightly cut)
in which Tristan and Isolde poured out their longing for the
bliss of eternal night.

Mom and Don stayed with me for two weeks, during which
Mom cooked comfort food from my childhood. On my days off,
we went to movies and out to dinner. I couldn't stop crying. I felt
like I'd hurt everyone so much, let alone what I'd done to myself.
I was ashamed that I was not what they all thought I was—that I
was not the strong, sunny, happy Debbie they expected and wanted.
People, even my family, often look at my life and think, "Oh wow,
how fabulous, how fantastic," and don't think there can be a sad side
to it. My old publicist, Herbert Breslin, who had urged me to present
a darker, more complicated image to the public instead of being so
"sunny," would have eaten this stuff up. He would have been sending
out press releases.

"What you need, kid," he used to say, "is a good scandal."

I found a therapist to speak to in Chicago, and she laid out the
situation clearly:

"You can go to rehab or you can go to AA or," she said, "you can
slowly kill yourself. Or, you can quickly kill yourself. What are you
going to do?"

I didn't have time to go to rehab, and I wasn't even sure I believed
in it. So I took the AA route, determined to take my commitment
seriously. The meetings had helped in the past—I had several sober
months under my belt when I met Peter. But with all my traveling I
had begun to skip them, and then stopped all together, which was
not good.

"You forget you have a disease," said the chairperson of a meeting I went to in Chicago. "You start to think you don't need the
meetings. It's a disease that doesn't want you to believe you have

a disease. It's a disease that wants you dead. Don't forget, 'meeting makers make it.' "

I admitted (again) to myself that I was powerless over alcohol and that my life had become unmanageable. I began counting days (again), this time counting hours, since whole days without drinking seemed unimaginable. *I've got twenty-four hours sober. Now I've got forty-eight hours sober. Now I have a week.* During my first few meetings, all I could do was weep. The only words I could whisper were, "Hi, I'm Debbie, I'm—"

Once I stopped crying long enough to speak, I was afraid to share with the others, as they call it. When I finally forced myself to talk, that's what I spoke about: fear. I told strangers that I'd always been afraid ever since I was a little girl. I was afraid of my father's elbows pounding the dinner table in a pocket of silence. I was afraid the laundry wouldn't be there when we got back, and of my mother crying. I was afraid of that steel-toe boot smashing against my face.

I said the Serenity Prayer over and over and over again:

God, grant me the serenity to accept the things I cannot change,
The courage to change the things I can,
And wisdom to know the difference.

ONE SOBER YEAR and a half later, I floated up, up, up into the clouds in a hot-air balloon in Aspen, feeling weightless. I was performing at the Aspen Music Festival in the summer of 2010 and as a birthday present to myself, I took a balloon ride to see the world from my new perspective. As the balloon rose in the sky I felt free—free of 150 pounds of weight off my body (I had lost another 15 pounds from not drinking); free from the Mitches and Peters in my life; and finally, free from the disease and poison that was killing me, alcohol—I hadn't had a drink in eighteen months (roughly 540 days, or 12,960 hours, and counting . . .) and I felt healthy and transformed, like I was soaring. I remembered that card a stage director gave me once, of an angel tethered to the ground. Now, twenty-two years later, I had cut the rope and freed myself.

I was also in love again, and this time it was going to be different.

Jason was in the chorus at the Met, and he was singing in Wagner's *Der fliegende Holländer* ("The Flying Dutchman") earlier that spring as I sang the role of Senta. We'd noticed each other before but had never spoken until I ran into him on the street during *Dutchman*. We recognized each other from work and chatted as we stood on a busy Manhattan sidewalk. I was immediately attracted to him—he was my type in looks: tall, slim, dark, and with a sexy beard.

"Maybe we should have a coffee," I ventured. "After all, we've been making eyes at each other for years now."

He suggested dinner, and a week later we had a surprisingly relaxed and chatty meal in a cozy eatery on the Upper West Side, not far from the Met. During our date I confirmed some essential facts: one, he didn't drink; two, he was divorced and was a doting father to his teenaged daughter; three, he wasn't a religious freak; four, he wasn't looking for a woman to pay his bills; and, five, he was dating a woman who also sang in the Met's chorus.

"Well, you're not married," I pointed out, "and you don't live with her." We both laughed.

He told me all about his daughter, and I admired how he was so attentive to her, taking her out for dinners and movies and hanging out together, talking and having fun—the sort of moments my father and I never had together. I don't remember doing anything alone with my father growing up, not even a stroll around the block.

Jason and I talked for hours; I felt completely at ease with him. Spending time with him was so unlike what it was with Mitch or Peter—I felt more comfortable with him than I had with any other man I'd ever known.

In fact, being with him was the only time I ever felt completely comfortable with myself, in my own skin. After dinner, Jason hailed a cab for me and before I got in he pulled me in to him and planted one hell of a kiss on my lips, loaded with chemistry and heat.

The next night, as I got ready for the show, I pumped a costumer friend of mine who knew Jason for tidbits about him.

"Oh, no, don't go there, Debbie," he warned me, mysteriously, "he's not for you. Don't do it."

He obviously didn't know that was the wrong thing to say to keep me away from a man. Besides, he didn't understand how perfectly we clicked together and that we both felt it. Soon Jason and I were texting constantly ("Hi sexy!") and making out for hours like teenagers on my living room couch and in my dressing room.

In *Dutchman* I was singing the role of a young woman in a sailing village who becomes obsessed with a portrait of the legendary Flying Dutchman, cursed to sail the seas until he finds a wife who will be true to him. Senta wants to save him from his horrible fate and can only think about being with him and wanting him to be in love with her. Every time I gazed at the handsome portrait onstage, while singing my love-drenched arias, Jason would be standing ten feet away offstage, behind the portrait, looking at me, irresistible in his fisherman's hat and wool sweater. We'd lock eyes and share a secret smile. His outfit in *Dutchman* was rivaled only by his turn as a cowboy packing a big rifle when we did *La fanciulla del West* together at the Met at the end of that year.

At first, Jason was hesitant to have a romance with me because, as he put it, "you're an international star that I've watched from afar for years." But we got rid of that nonsense. And in due course, he got rid of the girlfriend. And somewhere between my first *La fanciulla* Minnie—a feisty, Bible-reading saloon owner and feminist before her time—in San Francisco in the fall of 2010, and my second Minnie, at the Met that winter, our romance was official and out in the open.

A FEW MONTHS later, I embarked on the role of my career.

I had sung Sieglinde a dozen times all over the world, but to take on the more mature Brünnhilde in Wagner's epic Ring Cycle of four operas—*Das Rheingold, Die Walküre, Siegfried, Götterdämmerung*—is a monumental challenge and turning point for any dramatic soprano and a demanding role that must be earned. One has to wait until her voice matures, you can't sound like a young little bell. You don't come out of a conservatory singing Brünnhilde, it's a gradual journey that leads to her. You have to sing a few Toscas, Minnies, Ariadnes, and Chrysothemises first and, if you're lucky, those roles take you to that great and fearless Valkyrie shieldmaiden.

My voice was ripe for it, and my leaner body was the right size. (Though, ironically, the famous expression "It ain't over till the fat lady sings" is supposedly a reference to Brünnhilde's famous sacrificial fire scene at the end of *Götterdämmerung*.)

The new production was to be helmed by Canadian film and stage director Robert Lepage, and his vision and concept for the set was controversial. It had over two dozen removable planks that were set up like a line of seesaws in a concrete jungle. I and the rest of the cast called it, unaffectionately, "the Machine." I always referred to the set as female in gender, and always capitalized her pronoun, because She was the biggest diva in the entire production. *She* was the one who was the most temperamental, the most prone to mishaps, very particular about her lighting, and She was the heaviest—the stage floor had to be reinforced to bear Her weight. And She was definitely overpaid—She was more expensive than the combined fees of the entire Ring Cycle cast.

I started studying the libretto six months ahead of time, which would still be considered last-minute cramming for most sopranos, who'd begin studying Brünnhilde years before their first performance. I pored over the thick binder of text for hours on end and worked especially hard on my technique. The role has a lot of "middle voice," and as a soprano my voice likes to live a little higher, so I had to spend a lot of time "anchoring" my middle register—the very opposite of what I had to work on when I first walked into Jane

Paul's studio decades earlier. But each opera in the cycle has its own specific challenges. For *Die Walküre*, it was very important for me to be hooked into the middle voice, whereas for *Siegfried*, I had to send high C's into the balcony. *Götterdämmerung* is more an exercise in pacing and is very dramatic vocally. It's as if each one was written for an entirely different type of soprano. I worked especially hard with my voice teacher, David Jones, whom I'd been with for a few years at that point. I also flew to Cardiff, Wales, to spend a week working with conductor and opera coach Anthony Negus, who is known as a "Wagner specialist."

I also concentrated even more on my acting. I was surprised to discover that one of the biggest challenges to playing this role was acting the part when I had nothing to sing. I remember reading an interview with Meryl Streep in which she was asked what the most important quality a good actor needed to have, and she said that "acting is listening" to the other characters. As Brünnhilde, I had a lot of listening to do. The foundation of the opera's story is the complex relationship between Brünnhilde and her father, Wotan, which I studied carefully. When we first meet her, she's a young woman who is teenager-like, both vulnerable and willful. Her wrathful father, Wotan, who is the Chief of the Gods, passes harsh judgment on her for disobeying him by siding with her nephew in a battle. He strips her of her Valkyrie status and banishes her to an eternal magic sleep on the mountain, where she is prey to any man who happens by. (Hmmm. It all felt so familiar to me, but I just couldn't put my finger on it . . .) For much of the opera, Brünnhilde must endure and listen to all of her father's angry monologues, and it takes a lot of energy to absorb and react to all of that.

With all its physical and emotional challenges, the part is also a daunting one to play because it is such an iconic Wagnerian role, any soprano who sings it is automatically compared to the great performers who came before her, like Birgit Nilsson and Hildegard Behrens. Even Bugs Bunny played "Bwunhilde" and donned the helmet! And in that same "What's Opera, Doc?" cartoon, Elmer Fudd hums the leitmotif to the Act III "Ride of the Valkyries" tune when he sings his famous "Kill the Wabbit" aria. Now that's a hard act to follow, folks.

Jason popped into my dressing room all through rehearsals to give me encouragement and kisses and was my date for opening night of the season at the Met in the spring of 2011. We were so crazy about each other that during the entire performance that night (it was the first of the Ring operas, *Das Rheingold*, the only one of the four in which my character does not appear) he kept rubbing his leg against mine in our seats in the audience. At the dinner party afterward, while I was seated next to director Lepage and having an in-depth conversation with him, I felt a foot crawling up my leg— Jason, from across the table, trying to distract me. We exchanged knowing smiles. I was so, so happy. I was in love, I had beat drinking, and I felt healthier than I had in my entire adult life—physically, emotionally, and mentally.

My family arrived for the premiere of *Die Walküre* a few weeks later and were amazed to see the gargantuan banners with my face, a hundred feet high and just as wide, hanging majestically from the rooftop of Lincoln Center. My mother and my brothers stood outside the Met and looked up at my face and their jaws dropped. I think they were proud of me. They didn't say it in words, but I think they finally "got" how big a deal it was, and how famous and successful their sister and daughter had become.

Even I was impressed. One afternoon I hopped into a cab after rehearsal, and as I looked up at the banner and gasped, I did something totally out of character for myself.

"Hey," I said to the cabdriver, tapping on the plastic partition to get his attention and pointing. "You see that face up there on that building? That woman with the long, red hair? That's me!"

"Nah, get outta here! That's you? Nahhh!"

I smiled. "Uh-huh."

"Wow. That's sumthin' else. That's really sumthin' else. Good for you, lady."

OF COURSE, ANY bravado this diva might have been feeling was completely demolished on opening night, when I made my entrance onto *Her*. All I had to do was step from the apron of the stage onto the high-tech, mechanical, She-machine and walk up her. I was excited—it was my big moment, my first Brünnhilde! But I guess She decided the Met stage wasn't big enough for the two of us, that one of us divas had to go, and the bitch took me down.

I stepped on my dress and slid—down, down, down—along the steeply inclined planks, landing with a thud downstage. I could almost hear Her yell out Brünnhilde's "Ho jo to ho" cry.

The *New York Times*:

As Ms. Voigt started to climb the planks that evoke the hillside, she lost her footing and slid to the floor. Fortunately Mr. Lepage and the cast had correctly decided to play this scene for its humor. . . . Ms. Voigt rescued the moment by laughing at herself. She stayed put on the row of flat, fixed beams at the front of the stage and tossed off Brünnhilde's "Hojotoho" cries.

The problem here was not just that in this crucial dramatic moment, with Ms. Voigt about to sing the first line of her first Brünnhilde, Mr. Lepage saddled her with a precarious stage maneuver. The problem was that for the rest of the scene, whenever Wotan or Brünnhilde walked atop the set, the beams wobbled and creaked.

If you'd had a tape recorder inside my head at that moment, what you would have heard on playback was a rather more X-rated *fuckfuckfuckfuckfuckfuckfuck*. At least by now I'd learned my lesson and didn't say it out loud.

The *New York Times*:

Among the cast Ms. Voigt had the most at stake. A decade ago, when she owned the role of Sieglinde at the Met, she seemed destined to be a major Brünnhilde. . . . The bright colorings and even the sometimes hard-edged sound of her voice today suits Brünnhilde's music. I have seldom heard the role sung with such rhythmic accuracy and verbal clarity. From the start, with those go-for-broke cries of "Hojotoho," she sang every note honestly. She invested energy, feeling and character in every phrase.

Playing such an intense role and hearing Jason talk about his relationship with his own daughter made me think a lot about my own sometimes tumultuous journey with my dad over the years. We'd both done some growing up and maturing since the days when he was my food and date marshal. We'd reached a better, stronger, place finally and I knew he loved me and I loved him, even though we didn't say those exact words to each other and didn't always know the best way to show it. I thought of my father when I was onstage and related to Brünnhilde's struggles with Wotan. Every night at the end of each performance, I'd be drained. I wondered if the night Dad and Lynn sat in the audience he, too, might be moved by the story and the relationship between Wotan and Brünnhilde. A few weeks after he and Lynn saw the show, I received a letter in the mail from him.

June, 2011

Dear Debbie,

I'm writing you this letter because for a long time I've wanted to assure you of something very important. From the beginning of our courtship, your mother and I were very much in love. Our parents thought we were too young and moving too fast and wanted us to take a break, but we wanted to be together. We decided that if we had a baby, our parents would let us get married. From the moment we knew you were coming, we were so happy. I wanted to make sure you knew that we planned to have you and we always, always wanted you. . . .

I was shocked and I immediately phoned up my mother to confirm this new bit of family history Dad had revealed. "I don't know what your father is talking about," she told me. "We didn't get pregnant on purpose. Why would he say such a thing?"

Of course, no parent wants their kid to think that she was a mistake or was unwanted, and perhaps he was trying to ease my pain in that area. Maybe he connected my suicide threat three years earlier to me not feeling sufficiently loved. If so, I had to give him credit for thinking about it and writing to me about it; trying to unravel the past was a big step for him, for both of us. Except for that brief moment in San Francisco when my father sort of apologized for contributing to my weight problem, we'd never talked about anything personal from our past—not the moment at the piano or the spankings and soap in the mouth or the food regulating or his breakup with Mom. With this letter, whether he was right or wrong in his facts, it was at least an attempt to reach out and help me, and I appreciated that.

In therapy, I had begun to see that choosing unavailable men in my life could be linked to growing up with a distant and strict father. Mitch was unavailable emotionally, the married Dane was unavailable technically, and Peter was unavailable sexually. Not to mention the strangers I dangerously picked up on the Internet. My therapist pointed out that those one-night stands were a way for me to get temporary fixes of the intimacy, attention, and love I craved, but with men who couldn't possibly sustain it. They were more extreme examples of what I was doing in my relationships—falling in love with men who were unable to give true intimacy and commitment. And then, when I tried to force them closer to me, they'd only distance themselves further.

With Jason, for the first time in my life, I felt I had found a man whom I connected with and could be close to.

AND RIGHT ON cue, Jason pulled away.

The same month my father sent me the letter, I invited Jason to join me at the Glimmerglass Festival in Cooperstown, New York, where I was singing *Annie Get Your Gun*. I rented a beautiful house in a wooded area and transformed it into a romantic getaway, filling it with beautiful flowers and all the foods and games Jason loved. We had a sweet, sexy, and easy time together doing jigsaw puzzles and swinging in the backyard loveseat and dipping our feet in the pond and laughing. After we got back to Manhattan, I reminded him he was my date for the openings of the New York Philharmonic (where I'd be singing arias from *Tannhäuser* and *Salome* live on TV, with Alec Baldwin hosting the event) and the Met—both of them black-tie galas and only a few weeks away.

He shuffled his feet. Keeping the dates will be difficult, he admitted, because he was seeing his ex-girlfriend again. He wasn't breaking up with me, to be clear. He cared for me (like my father, Jason had difficulty saying the L-word). But he couldn't bring himself to give up the chorus woman, either.

"And does your 'girlfriend' know of this new arrangement?" I asked.

He shook his head.

I went home and cried and analyzed the situation. It was easy to do intellectually: he told me that he could not and would not be available to me in the way I wanted him to be. This was my cue, I had learned in therapy, to break my unhealthy pattern and stop seeing him. It was the only logical step a rational woman with a shred of self-esteem would take. Problem was, I wasn't so logical, rational, or self-esteemed. So instead of breaking up with Jason, I spent the next seven months on one end of a tug-of-war, pulling at him, while the girlfriend pulled from the other end. I suppose my pride was hurt, never mind my heart. But I didn't want to stop seeing him. So I endured months of broken and forgotten dates and vague texts, dotted with days of focused attention and intense intimacy that I gorged on like a feeding frenzy.

I once read about a psychological study in which a bunch of mice had to tap on a lever with their nose to get a dose of sugar water. Some were given the sugar every time they tapped; others were given the sugar only some of the time, and they never knew when they were going to get it. The second group went a little crazy, hitting the lever day and night, never certain if they'd get their sugar fix or if it was gone forever. "Inoperant conditioning," I think it was called. I felt like one of those mice, furiously hitting the lever. Something had to give.

Jason usually walked me to the side of the stage before I went on to give me a kiss on the lips for luck, then he'd slip back to the dressing rooms. It was always dark in the wings, and we figured no one would see us. But on this one occasion, when he kissed me and disappeared, a fellow chorus member stepped out from the shadows. She was a friend of Jason's other girlfriend, who was now his official out-in-the-open girlfriend.

"Wow. What was that kiss all about?"

I suppose I could have told her it was nothing, or that in the dark she must be mistaken about what she saw. Instead, I smiled mischievously.

"Well, what did it *look* like?"

The news got back to the girlfriend three days later, on Valentine's Day 2012, to be exact. I didn't hear a word from Jason. Several weeks later, I was standing backstage, chatting with the very famous Russian baritone, Dmitri Hvorostovsky, when the chorus exited from the stage after a rehearsal. Jason walked by and I said hello brightly. He kept walking . . . right over to the girlfriend, who was waiting at the other end of the hall.

"Well, that was rude," Dmitri said, watching Jason go by. "What's the matter with him?"

Onstage that night I lost myself in the character of Brünnhilde. In the scene, the shieldmaiden's world has just fallen to pieces. She's been stripped of her Valkyrie status and punished and banished by her father.

They tell us in AA that relapses don't happen in the moment you take a drink; the emotional relapse begins months earlier. The heart goes first and then the hand follows. About two months later, my hand followed my heartbreak, and I dialed a liquor store on my block.

My thirst was unquenchable.

17

Fear and Loathing in Liège

ANOTHER YEAR LATER, another Valentine's Day.

For two weeks in Liège, Belgium, the sky had been a somber gray, just like my mood, and today I waited for Jason to send me a Valentine's Day text.

It had not been a good year. Since I "went out" and "picked up," as we call it in AA, taking that first drink ten months earlier, I hadn't been able to fully stop. My on-and-off drinking mirrored my on-and-off romance with Jason. He had temporarily banished his Brünnhilde after my pre–Valentine's Day transgression a year earlier, but we started back up again soon after in the same pseudorelationship we were in before. And here it was, Valentine's Day 2013.

I checked my iPhone for the twentieth time to see if he'd sent me a few words. He hadn't yet, so I typed:

Hi Sexy. Did you get my Valentine's card?

No answer. He must be with her and she's watching his every move.

I'D ARRIVED IN Belgium a week earlier to start rehearsals for *La fanciulla*—my third time singing Minnie, the Bible-thumping, gun-toting heroine—this time at the Opéra de Royal Wallonie. I usually love to play her, she's a great gal to act. She's tough, smart, and ahead of her time. And she reads the Bible to the miners and the tough cowboys, not unlike my childhood self. The more I play her, the more I realize she's a lot like me. On the surface, she's a strong and independent career woman who bosses the guys around her saloon. But underneath the bold exterior, she's got classic, insecure man trouble: she's in love with a bad boy, the bandit Dick Johnson, whom she suspects frequents the town prostitute.

So often when I sing these great female heroines onstage— Brünnhilde, Amelia, Ariadne, Tosca, Isolde—I temporarily take on their strengths, like putting on a costume. But I know I must have some of their resolve, or I wouldn't be able to sing them with any authenticity. I also know that women of all ages, eras, and cultures can relate to the universal, timeless joys and struggles of these women—to their stories of love, betrayal, insecurity, jealousy, faith, hope, and despair. Women often ask me about these heroines, as if portraying them also affords me the secret to happiness, or the recipe to avoid a tragic end. As if Puccini or Wagner embedded those secrets in the pages of the librettos I memorize. But when I take off the costume and the makeup at the end of the day with a slab of cold cream and look in the mirror, I only see Debbie. And I ask myself the same questions other women ask their own reflections:

Why am I doing this to myself? Why am I with this man? Why do I wake up every morning with a pit in my stomach? Why am I never happy? Why am I so scared? I don't know my lines, I'm going to fuck up, I'm not ready, I don't want to go to rehearsal today....

I'd been reading Joyce Meyer's *Battlefield of the Mind*, about how to reroute and retrain our thoughts to be more positive, like exchanging bad habits for healthy ones. In Liège, I tried to put her suggestions into practice.

Even though I'd sung Minnie before, I was struggling to remember the libretto and was nervous because the opera house was having difficulty finding a prompter. The role is known among sopranos as

"Minnie the Voice Wrecker," and it's the most technically difficult role I've ever done.

First of all, the orchestra is enormous and lush—very fortissimo—producing a lot more sound for the singer to project over than, say, a Mozart opera. Second, the range you need to sing it is wide and varied. In Act II, during a scene when Minnie describes what she loves about living in the mountains, Puccini suddenly includes passages that are "coloratura"—dainty little notes when you'd just been singing in a big, dramatic voice—and a high C that's very difficult to reach. Minnie is like Brünnhilde, in the same way that you need many different voices to sing her—except with Minnie it's all in one evening's work. Lastly, the character is so emotional and raw at times that I have to be careful not to get too high in voice when she's crying and pleading for Dick's life or I will strain it.

Plus, she's got so many props to handle, it's difficult to keep track—guns, poker cards, Bibles, glasses, and even a horse that I have to hoist myself onto and trot around on. There's always a horse wrangler on set, but that doesn't mean the horse doesn't stop to do his business right in the middle of an act if that's when nature calls—I've seen it happen. A pile of fresh, steaming horse manure is not the easiest thing to ignore as you sing about finding love at last.

I had a growing list of other worries adding to my anxiety as well: my knees were aching from recent bilateral knee replacement surgery and were shooting pain each time I kneeled for one scene; and the tenor singing opposite me, with whom I'd have to share a kiss, had a worrisome cough. I'd also had an upsetting appointment with a Belgian vet whom I took Steinway to see. As soon as we arrived in Liège, Steiny seemed weary and not quite right. In his half-English, the vet told me Steiny had a heart murmur and something wrong with his lungs. I burst into tears and went back to my apartment and gave Steiny all the doggie treats he wanted, then played with him until he fell asleep. The thought of losing Steinway was too much for me to even contemplate. Steinway was the only one who'd sent me a Valentine's Day card that year, care of Jesslyn. It had a picture of a Yorkie on the front, and inside Jesslyn had written in broken, doggy-English: "Deer Momee, I luv you . . . yer boy, Stine-eeeee."

After Steiny fell asleep, I turned on some mindless reality show to numb my feelings and had too many drinks until I fell asleep, too.

THAT NIGHT, THE night before Valentine's Day, I had the same recurring two nightmares I've had since I was a teenager. In the first one, my mother and I are arguing loudly—more aggressively than we ever have in real life—and she's ordering me to move out of the house. The dream ends with me in limbo: homeless, and not knowing where I will be living the next day. In the second nightmare I'm sitting in a classroom and I haven't done my homework. I've been skipping class, and all my teachers are angry and yelling at me. I sit there, not moving, as they yell, because I don't know what to do or where to go. I can't go home because then my parents will know how bad I've been. So I keep skipping classes, not doing homework, knowing it's going to end really, really badly.

In the morning I woke up gripped in fear—like that time with Peter in London—so I said a prayer:

Dear God. Please help me have a more peaceful life and lift this fear from me. Please let me have some confidence in myself and in what I've created in my life.
Please help me to not belittle it.

Later in the day, I pushed myself out the door and went across the street to the opera house for rehearsal. We were set to do Minnie's signature aria at the end of Act I, in which she tells Dick she's not good enough for him—"I'm only a poor girl," she sings, "there is nothing important about me. I'm a nobody, good for nothing. . . ."

It being Valentine's Day, I was feeling Minnie's pain more than usual. As I sat on a barrel, singing her woes, I was fighting back tears. After I finished, director Lorenzo Mariani called a break and approached me. Lorenzo had directed me in *La fanciulla* in San Francisco two years earlier, in my happy Jason days, so he'd heard me sing the aria many times before. He's one of those empathic directors who keys into his actors' emotions like a tuning fork. He also has a kinetic energy that ricochets off the floors and walls of a set. But now he stood very still, watching me.

"Debbie. When you sang just now, it was very real and deep. You were gone somewhere. I'm not sure where you were or what you were thinking, but . . . it was very moving."

After rehearsal, I walked down the street to a nearby cathedral to light a candle for Jesslyn and her father. After a long illness, he had passed away days before our scheduled trip and she'd stayed home to tend to his funeral arrangements. I had heard the church bells chiming six p.m. from my dressing room window, so I simply followed the sound. It was a Thursday evening and the church was empty. I sat in a front pew and looked around at the timeless beauty of the church and up at the crucifix. I wondered about the faith of those who built this church, stone by stone, with their bare hands. How many of those workers, I wondered, didn't even live to see it finished? I thought about how much faith that took, to build something and not know its future, but to keep faith anyway that all would end well no matter what.

And what kind of faith did I have?

I had wished at one time to have the same blind faith that Peter had, one in which I was certain God would take care of everything and I wouldn't have to worry about a thing. But Peter slept peacefully, like a baby, no matter what he did or how badly he treated the people who loved him. Then there was the kind of faith that I grew up surrounded by, the judgmental and finger-pointing kind that sent you to hell even if you were a good person. Maybe it was that kind of thinking that planted the pit of fear I wake up with every morning and the voice in my head that tells me I'm not good enough. Neither of these faiths felt right to me, and I knew I was missing something.

What I needed didn't involve someone else saving me or approving of me; it had to do with looking inside myself. It had to do with having faith in my own strengths and choices. It was the kind of faith that carried big blocks of stone and knew that I could build something strong and lasting. Jane had urged me to have faith in myself that day when I left for my apprenticeship in San Francisco. Now, two decades later, it was a kind of faith that still eluded me.

BACK IN NEW York, in May, I was onstage performing my final show as Brünnhilde in the Ring Cycle at the Met. In the last scene in Act III of *Götterdämmerung* ("The Twilight of the Gods"), Brünnhilde emerges from banishment and rightfully claims the ring of her husband, Siegfried. Then she sings a tearful farewell as the blazing funeral pyre is lit—the fire is meant to cleanse the ring of its curse—and she boldly rides her horse into the flames. It's an emotional, heartbreaking, brave and triumphant finale that leaves my nerves raw at the end of the night.

I walked onstage for my last bow and the audience jumped to their feet, applauding and cheering, sending a much-needed tsunami of love washing over me. I felt . . . everything. I was relieved that after two years I'd reached the end of Brünnhilde's ride, and proud that I'd completed two Ring Cycles despite the part of me that could have sabotaged it. I was afraid because I wasn't sure what my future held at that moment. I looked at the cheering audience sitting beneath the glittering Lobmeyr crystal chandeliers and wondered if this would be my final curtain call—as Brünnhilde, at the Met, or ever.

And, finally, I was sad because I also wondered if it would be the last time I'd be onstage with Jason, who was in the *Götterdämmerung* chorus. That night during Act II, there was a scene where the captured Brünnhilde is brought to the castle and the Chief Minister tells the men how to treat her. Unbelievably, Jason was singled out from the chorus to receive special instruction from the Minister.

"Brünnhilde comes near," he said to Jason. "Love your lady, faithfully help her; if she be wronged, swift be your vengeance!"

In the final act, Brünnhilde's end and her lover's death, felt like a funeral pyre for Jason and me as well. Onstage, all those emotions bubbled up in me and I burst into tears. Then, I went home and drank—not knowing how to deal with the feelings, or what to do with this overpowering sense of ending.

The next month, June, I was in Beijing to perform a Broadway musical concert, and I arrived a few days early to acclimate, rehearse, and see the sights. As every alcoholic will tell you, I woke up every morning with the best of intentions. My hotel was around the corner from Tiananmen Square, and every morning I'd say to myself: *Okay, I'm going to have lunch out today and see the historical square, I'll go to the gym, I'll do a little sightseeing and shopping . . .*

But by ten a.m. I'd have already ordered champagne with breakfast, and the day would continue with more drinking and end with me passing out, never leaving my room.

After a few days, my memories of China became a blurry, dramatic repeat of Chicago, but worse: empty bottles strewn across the floor . . . a frantic phone call to my father and Lynn . . . strangers knocking loudly at my hotel room door . . . doctors saying my name to me in an emergency room . . . I'm in hysterics, sobbing . . . nurses sedating me . . . "put her on suicide watch," says a disembodied, stern voice. . . .

A little Chinese lady sat in a chair and watched me all night and into the morning, until I left the hospital early the next day. I went to my hotel, took a shower, and was onstage rehearsing by ten a.m. After a small break and a nap, I was onstage, performing "You Can't Get a Man with a Gun" from *Annie Get Your Gun*. How did I do it?

It's what I do. And an IV drip in my arm all night plus a pot of coffee didn't hurt.

Somehow, in my most insane moments I find an enormous amount of resilience. I wouldn't call it sheer will, because my will would have wanted to curl back into bed and stay drunk. But my resilience knows that no matter what, the show must go on.

A FEW WEEKS later, I was in Florida, sprawled in the backseat of Dad and Lynn's car, guzzling a four-pack of white Zinfandel screw-tops as they drove me to rehab. The day before was Father's Day and I'd arrived to spend it with Dad and have my last blowout before checking into a place Dad and Lynn had found for me. At our Father's Day dinner, I put back three martinis and two bottles of wine by myself. If my drinking had to stop, then I was going to drink every drop I could find until the last possible moment and arrive at the sterile promontory stinking drunk.

After China, I'd had a turning-point conversation with my assistant Jaime.

Both she and Jesslyn had done what they could to help keep me away from booze, and Jesslyn—my one-time Salzburg drinking buddy who'd caught ice balls falling from the sky for us—made it a point never to drink alcohol in front of me again. When I got back from China, Jaime hit me with this little gem of truth:

"Debbie," she said, "you can't continue living a double life like this. Deborah Voigt 'the opera star' onstage, and off-stage . . . an out-of-control drunk."

I knew she was right. That second Debbie had to make her exit.

The next day I cleared my schedule and signed up for four weeks and $33,000 worth of intense rehab in Florida, in the hope that the thing that needed to kick the bucket was my old pattern of thinking and feeling instead of me myself. There was some serious saving to do, all right, and I had to do it and not expect someone or something outside myself to do it for me.

Before I left New York for Florida, Jason had come over to my apartment to watch a movie, fool around, and say goodbye.

"You know, Jason . . . if I'm able to leave rehab with even an ounce more self-esteem than I have now," I told him, "this relationship will be over."

He was silent; he was never one to say much, especially if the talk was serious. He had his own codependent reasons why he needed me as much as I needed him, I learned in therapy, so I'm sure my breakup prediction scared him. And he had the same difficulty letting go of people as I did, which was one reason why he couldn't let go of that other relationship, he had told me.

But what few words he did say as he hugged me before leaving that night were, to his credit, very good ones—"I love you, Deb."

18

A Tree of Life

SO NOW MY father was driving his good little church girl to rehab. What would the people at church think?

As I lay in the backseat, I drunkenly thought of Wotan and Brünnhilde and couldn't shake that father-daughter story out of my brain. Wotan had a temper, and he had punished her, his favorite child, when she didn't deserve it. But in my haze I remembered something else. At Brünnhilde's final request, Wotan created a ring of magical fire to surround her and protect her, to keep away all but the bravest of heroes from his girl. It's what I always yearned for, growing up, for my father to watch out for me and be my protector instead of the one I was afraid of. In the same way that I yearned for a loving and forgiving God, not a judgmental, punishing one. My father was trying to help me now, I knew.

Once we got there Dad handled all the admitting, during which they removed any perfumes or hairsprays from my suitcase. I went into twenty-four-hour detox, which I don't remember at all, but a fellow "inmate" later told me I kept rubbing my legs, saying, "I'm going to jump out of my skin!" The next day, I woke up at 6:20 a.m. with a roommate sleeping ten feet away in a "dorm" room that consisted of two single beds, a sink, a mirror, two sets of drawers, and a tiny bathroom. Someone was banging on the door—my wake-up call. Once again, the glamorous life of an opera diva.

In rehab they want you awake and moving early to help break old patterns and start new ones. The first thing we did every morning was a group meditation (the size of the group varied each day between eight and thirty patients) and then we read aloud from the *Twenty-Four Hours a Day* book, a collection of daily thoughts, meditations, and prayers known as "the little black book." Then came a reading of the Serenity Prayer—I knew that one by heart—then a day full of private and group therapy appointments and exercises. Each day ended with an AA meeting and someone coming into your room with a flashlight, shining it in your face, making sure you were in the proper bed where you belonged—alone.

We were sorted in groups by sex and age—mine was the women's Boomer group, for thirty-five years and up—and no cross-fraternization between groups was allowed. To get to the swimming pool, the Boomers had to walk past the Young Men's unit (ages seventeen to thirty) and we were given strict instructions to cover up—no Daisy Dukes allowed. Apparently the only thing wilder than a pack of young men drinking was a pack of young men trying *not* to drink. As evidenced by the night they went skinny-dipping in the entranceway's ten-foot fountain and showed up at breakfast one morning with Mohawks. And they weren't even *drunk*.

AT THE START of every group meeting, we each had to say our name, our addiction, and a "feeling" word for how we felt at that moment. My word alternated among three: *afraid*, *sad*, and *pissed off*. ("Technically that's *two* words," someone yelled out. Which pissed me off even more.)

Hi, I'm Debbie. I'm addicted to food, alcohol, and men. I'm terrified.

Hiiiii, Debbieeeeee!

Over the next month, I would get to know these strangers better than I knew my own family or myself, as we shared secrets and played "trust" games together.

For one exercise, we partnered up and took turns blindfolding each other and leading the other around the hallways and the outside gardens of the facility using only voice commands. The goal was for the blindfolded one to trust that the speaker would keep her safe and not let her fall off a curb or walk into oncoming traffic—your life was in their hands.

My partner was Betty, a petite loner from Florida who had white-blond, pixie-short hair and a tan that never faded. She was there on a court mandate because "I took an Ambien one night and the car took a ride with me in it," she'd say. She always left out the part where she punched a cop and slugged a paramedic after smashing her car into something, going fast. In rehab, I was surprised to find a handful of inmates still in denial about being alcoholic—even after they'd wrapped their cars around telephone poles and were wait-listed for a liver transplant due to cirrhosis of the liver. Betty came from big money and was socially awkward, so I picked her to be my "lead-around" because I figured no one else would ask her. Also, I had a slight soft spot for her—she'd go to the meeting rooms early each day and play the piano.

"Okay, turn to your left, Debbie," Betty commanded for the exercise. "Now turn right—no stop, *stop*! Okay, follow my voice, I'm here, I'm here . . . follow my voice, follow my voice, follow my voice. . . . Okay, now reach up to feel the tree next to you . . . a little higher, a little higher . . ."

I wasn't one to trust easily, but that was the point of the exercise. With my eyes shut and Betty's voice beckoning, I had to surrender to her help.

Next it was Betty's turn to be blindfolded. This time, I had to lead her by touch and no talking. I pulled her by the hand, I put her hand on the railing by the stairs, I tapped her hand on surfaces so she'd know what they were. The interesting surprise to me about this exercise was how I went from feeling completely vulnerable and dependent when blindfolded to now feeling very protective of Betty. It was as if first I was her child, then she was mine.

After the exercise was over and all the blindfolds were off, I turned to smile warmly at Betty—the exercise had made me feel close to her. But she had already turned away and was sprinting for the common room to reserve her favorite spot on the couch. I was flabbergasted! I had allowed myself to trust and be vulnerable and care for her—and then she abandoned me! This was another learning experience that we discussed later in "group." For me, that was my typical pattern; to love someone who was not "there" for me. The overall lesson of the exercise was that you can't recover alone; you have to surround yourself with people you trust. And you have to trust yourself.

Connecting with others was an all-important ability I needed to learn. I realized in private therapy that I had difficulty making and keeping intimate friends—that was one reason why I depended on a man, any man, to fill that void. My initial instinct, even in rehab, was to stay holed up in my room, reading or studying the stacks of music I had brought with me (I was set to sing *Isolde* as soon as I got out, as the season-opener at the Washington National Opera).

"You need to put your singing down for a day and go hang out with the others and talk with them," said my counselor, Daniella. "It's what you're here for. You need to learn how to establish these relationships."

When I entered rehab, I learned about biological and genetic factors that made one prone to addiction. No one else in my immediate family was an alcoholic, but I had one cousin who was, and another cousin who struggled with drug addiction. I also underwent a psychological analysis that showed that I had an enormous problem with self-esteem and depression . . . and, at the same time, an egocentric personality. I had no idea the two dynamics could go together in one person! Unfortunately, the combination of both helped keep my addiction going. The low self-esteem made me want to drink to blot out the pain, and the fact that I could still perform despite it all, despite spending all night sloshed and under a suicide watch, halfway around the world, without anyone detecting it, fed my ego.

Both low self-esteem and ego also led to me cutting myself off from people, said Daniella, which led to isolation and loneliness and then . . . eating, drinking, sex. I had to stop isolating myself, she said, and I had to start stopping right now.

The others at rehab hung out after dinner on the "smoking patio"— where the cool kids of any age, anyplace, always hung out. I'd hear them talking outside my window while I was inside my little bunker, studying my German libretto and torturing myself with Isolde's tragic love life. I love these characters, but after so much pain, can't any of these brilliant male composers ever reward these tortured women with a happy ending? Minnie was the only one who came to mind who got her happy ending.

I did what my counselor suggested and forced myself to venture out onto the patio in my sweats, ponytail, no makeup, and glasses—a total nerd at the cool kids' table. And soon they were politely asking me the questions about myself that I'd been dodging since I got there. But there was no avoiding allowed in rehab. They all knew I was some sort of singer; that came out in one of our earlier group chats. Out of politeness, someone pursued it now:

"So, what else do you do besides sing? I mean, to support yourself."

"I sing."

"That's all you do? You don't wait tables or . . ."

"No. I sing. That's what I do."

"What kind of music do you sing?" someone else asked.

"Opera."

"What do you mean, you sing opera?" asked another. She was on to me. "Do you . . . do you sing it at the Metropolitan Opera?"

"Um, yes."

There was an energy surge among the group, and someone asked another, related question, which led to me saying, quietly, "Well, actually, yeah, I just won a Grammy Award for that."

"What?" asked another. "WHAT?! You won a Grammy? Why are you not saying that proudly, out loud, for all of us to hear you?"

I started to cry.

"This is one of my problems," I said to them. "I've been able to accomplish all that I have, but I feel like shit about myself."

They all nodded, and each could relate in their own way. I was beginning to see how this talking to people thing worked.

The next day, Daniella and I discussed my accomplishments, and she pointed out that drinking was a way for me to sabotage myself. I had great success in my career, but I didn't know how to embrace it, so I had to kill it. I'd let opportunities escape me as well, because I didn't think I deserved them and was afraid of being *too* successful. Any more success would lead to the dreaded pride the Bible talked about, and then that big fall I was warned about a thousand times.

Well, I fell anyway—so the joke was on me.

Daniella and I examined a few interviews I'd given that we found on the Internet, and she pointed to one answer I repeated again and again.

How did you become an opera singer? asked the journalist.

It was sheer luck. I took one step after another.

"Bullshit," I said out loud.

"Why is it bullshit, Debbie?"

"Because I worked my fucking ass off. You don't rise to this level without having an innately wonderful gift from a higher power, coupled with working your ass off."

But it was something I never gave myself credit for and instead belittled myself. We went on to talk about God, men, and my parents. The root of my pain that started me overeating, I would learn, probably had to do with my father's belittling of my mother, and the anger, fear, insecurity, abandonment, and control I felt in our house growing up.

Through a lot of tears, I realized I had to find forgiveness for my father and his past anger. It dawned on me that he had been asking for it for quite a few years—in the car that day in San Francisco, and with the letter he wrote to me during my first Brünnhilde. I also had to find forgiveness for my mother and her more passive, frail nature, which always made me feel like I had to protect her instead of the other way around. I now saw my parents as kids themselves—they were seventeen and eighteen when they had me!—trying to raise children and doing the best they could, however flawed, as all parents are.

Near the end of my stay at rehab, we had "family week." Mom, Dad, and Lynn came in and did two days of therapy with a counselor; they were also free to ask other patients questions about their alcoholism without me there.

"As is the case with all addiction," the counselors told them, "alcoholism affects the entire family. It's not only the addict who must deal with this problem." They also told my parents that whatever unresolved issues that were still lingering between them were still affecting me.

On the third day, they added me to the mix. I walked into a conference room to find the three of them and two counselors seated around a U-shaped table. Dad and Lynn were on one side with an empty chair next to them, Mom sat directly across from them with an empty chair next to her, and the counselors were at the bottom part of the "U".

To say it was awkward would be an understatement. I felt like I was in the middle of some sort of experimental, psychological, family dynamic test. *Where the hell should I sit? This could be a very political move.*

I looked over at my mother and she gave me one of her bright smiles, but tinged with worry. God, it was a comfort to see her face. In her late sixties now, Mom was still pretty and voluptuous, as always. She gave me one of those reassuring mom-smiles, the kind filled with unconditional love that spoke volumes. It said: *I know you like only a mother knows her child. You will get through this. I love you.*

Mom and I had been through a lot together over the years and, in a way, we grew up together. Whatever struggles we had separately or with each other, I always knew one fact for sure about my roller-coaster, erratic life: She was a constant and consistent force. We had a special, sister-like solidarity, a natural instinct to look out for and protect each other in the trenches of life's war zone.

I had no other choice. I went over and took the seat next to my mother.

They told me to start, so I told my parents what the counselors had already said—the unresolved tension between them was keeping me locked in the unhealthy emotional patterns I'd learned as a child in order to cope with it. Amazingly, my parents got to the heart of the matter in the first few minutes.

My father, who had been working very hard on learning to express himself, spoke first.

"I don't think you ever forgave me for marrying Lynn," he said to my mother. "I know I cheated on you and left you to be with her, but you have to forgive me for this, for everyone's sake. It's been long enough."

"What are you talking about?" Mom answered. "We had that meeting when Debbie sang at Carnegie Hall seven or eight years ago and we all went to see her together and you told me you were sorry, and I told you that I forgave you."

Dad looked surprised. He could tell Mom wasn't making it up. "Well," he said sadly, "I guess I didn't feel you really meant it, that you hadn't really forgiven me . . . because of the way you still treat Lynn and me."

Over the next thirty minutes, I couldn't believe my eyes and ears. My head swiveled back and forth like I was following the ball in a tennis match. My parents were communicating with each other—calmly—in a way I had never seen.

As they talked together and sorted it out with the counselors' help, I had a sense memory—my very first memory from childhood: me as a little girl, age three, watching them argue as Mom cried and packed a suitcase and Dad slumped against the bedroom door frame. The image had been frozen, stuck, deep in my memory, and now it began to rise and dissipate. The pain linked to the memory began to fade. As Mom and Dad talked in front of me and forgave each other and even smiled at each other, I felt a childhood burden lift from my shoulders.

AS FOR THE men in my life, I already knew I'd been picking men who resembled my (formerly) distant and temperamental father because it was familiar to me. They were men to whom I could never say what I thought or felt for fear there'd be some sort of repercussion—I'd either be punished, hurt, ignored, or abandoned. I also saw that I'd spent time with them no matter how horrible they were, just so I wouldn't be alone.

"What is it that Deborah Voigt doesn't like about Debbie?" asked Daniella during one of our last sessions together. "What makes you not want to spend an evening with yourself?"

I wasn't sure. Maybe I wasn't even sure who "Debbie" was. Over the last three decades—role by role, trait by trait—I had become Amelia, Ariadne, Minnie, Brünnhilde, Lady Macbeth, Salome, and Isolde. Where do these characters end and where do I begin?

"Here is your homework for tonight," she instructed. "I want you to write down on a piece of paper who you are offstage. I want you to give me five sentences."

I lay down in my little cot while my roommate was out on the cool kids' patio that night and thought about it. It took me a long time, but I came up with three.

I'm a sister.

I'm a daughter.

I'm an aunt.

One of the last exercises we did at rehab was to draw our lives. The counselors put on sappy music (think: "Wind Beneath My Wings" and "You Light Up My Life") and gave us each big sheets of paper and a box of crayons. We had to draw a "Tree of Life" that showed our past, including both good and bad, and a "Tree of Hope" that showed where we wanted to go for our future.

My Tree of Life had musical notes and God in the sky and little Steinway playing on the branches, and me as a little girl singing in church, and in the branches' shadows I drew the men who had broken my heart and bottles of liquor with a poison "X" over the top of each one. My Tree of Hope also had God, Steinway, and music . . . but it included an added feature: me in love, happy, and free.

That's why one morning, the day before leaving rehab, I was ready to do what had previously been impossible.

Jason and I had kept in touch a little by e-mail while I was away, and now I was ready to send him a last one—a final goodbye letter. Both my counselor and psychologist drilled it home to me that I had too many issues with attachment and abandonment that made our romance dangerous for me.

"If you go back into this relationship," the psychologist told me, "you will pick up a drink. You can't afford to wait until you don't want Jason anymore to break up with him. You have to change your behavior first," she said. "The emotions will change as a result."

My team decided I should do it while I was still in the controlled environment of rehab, in case I went into an emotional tailspin. They looked over my shoulder as I logged onto my e-mail at the computer in the common area and began typing:

Dear Jason,

I'm leaving rehab and I told you the last time I saw you that if I had even an ounce of self-esteem that this relationship would be over. That time has come. I can no longer continue on this path with you. I have loved the time we spent together.

Love,
Debbie

I logged off and closed down the computer.

The next day was Sunday and I'd promised my new friends I'd sing in church—there was a little chapel on site that held nondenominational services. At the end of the sermon, I went up front and sat at the piano. I started with the song, "This Heart That Flutters," based on a poem by James Joyce and composed by Ben Moore. Then I segued seamlessly into my favorite gospel hymn from my childhood church choir days, "His Eye Is on the Sparrow."

> *I sing because I'm happy,*
> *I sing because I'm free . . .*

It felt so comfortable and familiar up there, singing a hymn I loved for people who did not come to judge me but came to listen to a beautiful tune and root me on. I felt five years old again, singing in church, or in Grandma Voigt's living room.

My rehab-mates sat on the edges of their plastic chairs with their mouths open. Not one had ever been to an opera before, never mind felt the goose-bumping effect of a big-voiced dramatic soprano ten feet away from their eardrums, belting it out for God.

As I sang, I could feel that indelible, mystical connection between me, the song, and the audience—a bond I'd felt since childhood, an invisible force of sacred energy and light we shared together.

When I finished, there was a moment of silence. Then all thirty of them jumped to their feet, clapping and whistling.

There's a ritual audiences used to do in my early days of performing that I always loved. At the end of an excellent show, they'd stand up and rip their programs into ribbons and toss them into the air. Joe Volpe hated it because it meant so much cleaning up afterward—which is probably why no one does it anymore. But I loved it; it was like being showered with confetti and streamers like at a big birthday celebration.

That's how I felt when I saw my audience jump to their feet—like it was my birthday and the start of a new life. Even though they were somewhat captive, like my family in Grandma's living room, they were one of the best audiences I ever had.

As I stood there, I realized that no matter what happened in future days, months, or years, no one could ever take this away from me:

You are here to sing.

God told me so, and I was going to keep doing it—on the opera stage or on the rooftops of the world.

I stood up from the piano and smiled, giving my rehab-mates an overly dramatic bow with plenty of melodramatic flourish. I wanted them to receive the full diva effect, after all, and get their $33,000-per-seat money's worth.

The next morning I packed my Bible, libretto, and Trees of Life and Hope into my suitcase and left the facility, stepping into the sunlight.

I wasn't afraid. I had faith in myself.

And if Puccini and Verdi didn't see fit to compose happy endings for their tragic heroines, then this reluctant, down-to-earth diva was going to write one for herself.

Finale: Voigt Lessons

January 2014

IN THE SPRING of 2013, after I got home from Liège and as I was en route to my condo in Florida, I drove through a little town that looked like a forgotten corner of another world, lost in time. The streets were crowded with overgrown weeping willows heavy with hanging Spanish moss, giving them a spooky pallor, but for the tiny dots of light peeking out from the darkness. The run-down Victorian homes I passed were decorated with Christmas lights and burning candles on the front porches.

Where was I, the Twilight Zone? I passed a sign: *Cassadaga: The Psychic Capital of the World*. I'd heard of this town; it had been known for its "spiritualistic" camp a century earlier and was now declared a historic site, though most of its original characters were long gone and buried in the local cemetery, rumored to be haunted. The cemetery has a bench nicknamed "the Devil's Chair," where, legend has it, if you leave an unopened can of beer on it at night, you'll find it empty in the morning—but still sealed.

That's one desperate drinker, I thought. I'd never been to a psychic before—it's considered sinful in the Southern Baptist religion to do so. In our house, we weren't even allowed to have a deck of regular playing cards to play crazy eights as kids. It was drummed into my head that talking to a psychic was engaging with the devil himself.

But my thoughts on the devil and hell have evolved over the years since the fire-and-brimstone sermons of my childhood. I no longer believed hell was an actual physical place of eternal fire, tortures, and pitchforks. Or that people would automatically be doomed to go there if they hadn't been dunked in baptismal waters and saved. I came to believe that hell was a state of mind, a place we put ourselves in when we veered off the loving path.

I drove by a pink clapboard bookstore with a hand-painted sign out front: *Psychic Readings! All Welcome!* and found myself pulling over. *What the hell.* I don't believe anything is random or coincidental in this life.

Inside I met Shane, a tall and lanky twenty-two-year-old with tousled hair to his shoulders and puppy-dog eyes. He wore a faded, tie-dyed T-shirt and looked like a teen idol circa 1972. Just my luck, he was the psychic on duty that afternoon. Shane sat me down at a little table in the back where he'd lit candles and incense and began shuffling a pack of Tarot cards. Before we started, my Christian sensibility kicked in and I needed to clear the pot-scented air.

"Shane, where does God fit into something like this?"

He looked surprised. "What I do is all about God," he answered. "It's all about divinity. I get my messages from above. The longer I work on my own faith and 'let go and let God,' the stronger my connection with God is, and the clearer my messages become." Hmmm. I recognized his "let go" phrase from AA and felt an immediate kinship with young Shane.

That satisfied me, and so we began. I didn't say a word about myself; I wanted to see what, if anything, this kid would come up with. I wasn't taking any of this too seriously. Shane placed the cards in rows on the table and studied them. A slightly pained expression spread across his unlined face.

"You've been through a very difficult several months," he said, "both physically and emotionally. You beat yourself up too much. You have to let go of this defeatist attitude, stop banging your head against the wall. It's not going to get any better until you change your thinking. You're rubbing two rocks together with rough edges, hoping things will smooth out, but they won't unless you let go of some things."

"What things?"

"Old attitudes, old habits, old information and ways of thinking . . . places and relationships that don't serve you well anymore."

I didn't say a word. He flipped a few more cards and smiled.

"There's a lot of transition that's going to happen for you in the next six months—a *lot*. It's going to be a big year for you, a lot of good change—with career, with personal life, with your living situation. You are going to make your life smaller, get rid of excess . . . but that will make your life bigger. You tend to pick up the crumbs, especially in your romantic relationships. It's going to be a year of less picking up the crumbs so you can be ready for an entire pie."

I appreciated the kid's food imagery. I wondered if he was having a psychic vision of me from my old bingeing days. "It was vanilla-coconut cake," I wanted to correct him, "not pie." Young Shane kept talking for another twenty minutes about how my entire life was on the verge of a major overhaul, and I silently thought to myself, *I hope so . . . I hope so.*

"It will be a year of renewal," he said, with assurance, wrapping it up. "And now, I'm going to pick two cards from the bottom of the deck. These will be your two dominant cards for the next year."

He took out the cards and placed them on the table, face up.

"Happiness," he said, with a grin, "and . . . Peace. Two very good cards indeed."

I nodded and agreed. He'd said a lot of things that could be true for anyone, I suppose, but they definitely resonated with me in particular. And even if guys like Shane were what the Bible called "false prophets," I imagine his words could still be used to inspire a person to make positive changes.

I got up and thanked him, and as I turned to go, Shane asked me his first and only question of the entire thirty-minute session.

"Hey . . . do you sing?"

IT TURNS OUT that Shane, the teen idol psychic from the mysterious commune of Cassadaga, had been right on all counts.

A few months later I was in rehab, dumped the sometime boyfriend, sold my Florida condo, and broke the lease on my Manhattan apartment. In September, I found a cozy little house in Fort Lee, New Jersey—a fifteen-minute drive over the George Washington Bridge from Lincoln Center but worlds away from the life I'd led for decades. After making such sudden, major changes in my life over the summer in rehab, I wanted to plant myself somewhere solid where my new life could take root and where little Steinway could have a yard to run in. I wanted new scenery and new people to go with my new life choices. I took Steinway for walks and met the neighbors. When they asked me what I did for a living I told them, and I usually got the same amused reaction.

"I thought opera singers were, you know, bigger," both my plumber and the guy who delivered my new couch said.

"Yeah, well . . ." I smile, but I don't go into the whole story about my eating addiction and my 333 pounds and all that drama. I take their words as a compliment and move on. As per Shane, I'm letting past information and attitudes go.

Here on the other side of the bridge, I spend my days rehearsing at my piano and going to AA meetings, and my nights learning how to be comfortable by myself, in my own skin. I think of Daniella's question to me in rehab: "What is it that makes Debbie not want to spend an evening with herself?" I try to examine that as I busy myself reading, watching TV, and writing e-mails. And if a moment pops up when I want to anesthetize myself with drink, and

those moments do come, I remind myself of what they say in AA:
"There's no bad situation that can't get worse with a drink." Sobri-
ety is an ongoing process, I have learned—a building upon building
of new habits and rewiring of thoughts.

EVERY AGE HAS its transition, and today, in my early fifties, comes
another one as I enter a new phase in my life.

Like many artists who reach success in their field, I'm finding
great joy in giving back to young singers who are entering the opera scene. Amazingly, I'm now the age that Jane Paul was when I
showed up one day at her studio, a green kid with no direction. Several years ago, my dear friend Jane had a stroke and it's difficult for
her to speak now. But when I gave her the news during our most
recent visit together that I was going to sing Brünnhilde, Jane got
teary-eyed and mustered up the shieldmaiden's battle cry as we said
good-bye—*Ho jo to ho!*—as her way to say to her student, "I knew
you could do it. I'm proud of you." Had someone told me that day
I first met Jane that I would later accomplish what I have, I never
would have believed it. I don't think my family comprehends it,
either, even though in our hometown of Placentia there's a street
named after me: Deborah Voigt Avenue.

Years ago a reporter asked me what it felt like to be a "star," and I
couldn't answer her, because I didn't feel like one. Only now, today,
am I beginning to own that feeling, to accept that I've had success
and be proud of it without feeling guilty or bad about it. My success was based partly on my gifts, but I had to work hard to develop
those gifts. When I think back and recall the early days onstage and
the thousands of pages of memorizing and the fears I had to over-
come and the highs and lows and insecurities that go with an opera
career, I take a deep breath and shake my head at all of it.

Time passes quickly; I've passed the age of Beverly Sills when
I saw her in concert in my early twenties during her farewell tour,
in which she thanked the audience for joining her in her twenty-

five years in the business that gave her "as much joy and passion as this poor little heart can bear." She continued, saying, "I prefer to think the book isn't finished, it's only a chapter that's finished, and we're going on to another one . . . and maybe [I can] help someone else's dream come true as mine did. I can only hope that the best is yet to come."

I feel the same way. For the last few years I've been teaching master classes to young opera students and I try to teach them what I've learned. It's exciting to help them with their future, and I'm also excited with my own new beginnings.

On my piano stand—in front of my kitchen window overlooking the backyard bird feeders—I've got my *Wozzeck* libretto, which I study every morning. At the Met, in the spring of 2014, I was to play Alban Berg's Marie, a flirtatious and unfaithful yet kind-hearted, Bible-reading (again!) common-law wife who is tragically murdered by her husband. It's a great dramatic part full of fire and pain, like life, and it's a part I'd never played before, so I'm eager to immerse myself. Every morning I make myself a coffee, feed Steiny, and nudge myself over to the piano . . . slowly changing old habits of procrastination.

I do the best I can do, I try to be good to myself, I try not to judge myself harshly, because what I have learned is that we are all in this together and we are all afraid at some time or another, not just me. We all have our off nights or off weeks—or even off years—but we can pick ourselves back up.

And as my good friend Maria von Trapp used to say, "When God closes a door, somewhere He opens a window." (Or was that the Mother Superior?) One surprising new job at the Met that I first grumbled about but quickly grew to love is hosting the live HD performances. Instead of dressing up in costumes or glamorous gowns, I put on my serious Barbara Walters suits and become a journalist, interviewing my colleagues backstage. I've been told by producers and my Twitter and Facebook followers that I have a knack for it.

Perhaps it's because I feel compassion for and solidarity with my colleagues, not competition.

Opera singers are more fragile than an audience member would ever believe. We loom larger than life up there, and when people meet me in person, I think they expect me to be seven feet tall. To catch us as we're running offstage to change costume, or when we've flubbed a difficult aria or forgotten a line, puts us in a very vulnerable situation—never mind having cameras lingering on our every pore and nose hair at every turn.

I remember when the idea of doing the live HD broadcasts was first being discussed at the Met and the buzz backstage among performers was concern.

"I don't know, what do you think about this HD thing?" Ben Heppner asked me at the time, when we passed each other in the halls at the Met a year or two before our revolving-Tristan run.

"I think it's a great idea, I think it's wonderful."

"But what if we have a bad night, what if we crack a note?"

"Ben, we're human beings, and our audience is, too. If we are willing to admit that to them, and say, 'Wow, that really didn't go the way I wanted it to,' and talk about how that makes us feel . . . that's only going to endear us to them. The idea that we're these revered people on a pedestal who make no mistakes and have only confidence and only put out the best performances . . . it's not humanly possible."

That's me, the anti-diva. I'm all for making us human to the public, because the alternative is too difficult to live up to. I take great comfort in knowing my fellow colleagues get nervous, or make mistakes, like me.

I remember the first time I interviewed someone who had a "bad night." I was the HD host for *La traviata* and the role of Violetta was being sung by soprano Natalie Dessay. As every soprano who has sung the role knows, there's a perilously high E-flat at the end of Violetta's aria that's a killer. It's not written by Verdi that way, but somewhere along the way it became tradition, and not everyone can do it. The rest of the opera doesn't require that kind of vocal pyrotechnics, but that one note. So Natalie got out there and went for that high note, and it really wasn't bad, but it wasn't great. I knew it and she knew it.

When she came offstage she was shaking like a leaf.

"I blew it!"

I grabbed her hand and we started the interview.

"Ah, that was not such a good note," she said, embarrassed. I told her, on camera, that it was just one note, and what she brought to the role was so much more than that one note.

Even Plácido gets nervous when he's acting as HD host for the night. He was assigned the job during one of my Brünnhilde performances in *Die Walküre* and as I walked off the stage and we hugged like old friends, his glasses fell to the floor and we both fumbled around, trying to pick them up. Everybody was momentarily flustered, especially Plácido, and then . . . everything was fine.

None of us is perfect, we are only human, as Jimmy used to reassure me. And it's important that we bare and share our humanness with each other—it's the main reason I'm writing this book. And it's the main reason why I developed *Voigt Lessons* with playwright Terrence McNally and my Chicago *Salome* director, Francesca Zambello.

Voigt Lessons is a one-woman, ninety-minute autobiographical theater piece in which I talk about the ups and downs of my personal life and my career, much as I've done in this book, and sing the songs and arias important to me throughout my life. I also talk about the eight words that saved my life: "My name is Debbie, and I'm an alcoholic"—followed by a rendition of "Smile" (. . . *though your heart is aching*). After a year of writing and rehearsing, we showcased the piece in Boston in November of 2013 to see if an audience would be open to a truthful, honest Debbie. Deborah

Voigt, unplugged. I'm happy to report that they laughed and cried as much as I did.

It feels good not to live a dual life anymore. A friend helped change my life when she told me it was time to stop being one person onstage and another in private. Incorporating the two Debbies together means I have to accept my flaws; I hope others do the same. As Shane, my new "spiritual advisor" says, I've spent way too much time beating myself up and it's got to stop. Out of the mouths of babes, and it's good advice for all of us.

Last Christmas I went to visit my family in Wisconsin, and Mom and I went through boxes of old photos that we hadn't looked at in decades. We sat on the couch and the memories spilled out of the boxes. Here was the pic of Mom in her beautiful black dress on New Year's Eve (when Dad told her she needed to lose ten more pounds) . . . there was the pic of me as a curvaceous teenager, right around the time I met John . . . here was a pic of the family during "devotional time" . . . and so on, and so on. My mother and I both had simultaneous reactions as we held the photos up: "Look how slim and pretty I am!" And yet neither of us knew it *then*. Instead, we wasted precious time, torturing ourselves about our bodies.

MY NEW PERSPECTIVE—TO accept myself as I am and bare my flaws and mistakes to the world—feels like hang-gliding, something I did for the first time a few years ago emboldened by my earlier paragliding experience with Peter in Hawaii. I was in Zurich playing concert performances of *Salome* and driving into the city from the airport when I looked up and saw dozens of people flying through the sky. The next morning, at six a.m., I was driving up the side of a mountain to meet my hang-gliding instructor, the person to whom I'd be tethered for the ride. Here were his instructions:

"We're going to start running, and we're going to come to the end of the little hill, and whatever you do, don't stop running!"

So I did what he said, I kept running and running, and the next thing I knew we were in the air . . . flying. We flew over the hills in the middle of a fog and could hear cowbells ringing below us.

I laughed—it was heavenly and liberating. It was the kind of feeling I get when I sing.

Last year began so horribly, but ended so beautifully.

Before Christmas, I performed several concerts in Utah with the Mormon Tabernacle Choir. The staff treated me like a princess all week, sharing their spirit, soul, and faith with me, and after we finished our last show they presented me with a gift.

"Debbie, if you would please turn around and face the choir," said the choir leader. The smiling group of 360 looked at me and sang the hymn "God Be with You Till We Meet Again." It's a hymn you sing when someone is going away and will be missed.

> *God be with you till we meet again!*
> *When life's perils thick confound you,*
> *Put His arms unfailing round you.*
> *God be with you till we meet again!*

I felt so touched, appreciated, and loved, I burst into tears. It had been a difficult year—filled with "life's perils thick confound you"—and their Christmas gift gave my year a happy ending. A big part of my life began when I heard God's inspiring voice encouraging me onward, and now the most difficult year of my life had ended the same way—comforted by it.

On the night of December 31, back home in New Jersey, I sent out a video—taken with my iPhone—to friends and family of my faithful Steiny and me. In it, we lit candles by the fireplace and sat by the decorated Christmas tree, sipping hot chocolate (me) and eating doggie cookies (Steiny). I wore my flannel pajamas, and it was so cozy, the two of us.

I was able to be alone, yet I wasn't alone. I had loved ones who cared for me nearby, and I had myself. Finally, I had myself.

I thought of those little lights peeking out from the darkness down in Cassadaga and they reminded me of a children's gospel song I used to love as a child. I hummed it for Steiny as the clock turned to midnight and the fireworks went off in the east, over the Hudson River, signaling a New Year and a brand-new start.

This little light of mine . . . I'm gonna let it shine . . . let it shine, let it shine, let it shine . . .

My name is Debbie. I'm a daughter, a sister, and a friend. I sing for God and I sing for others. And now, more than ever, I sing for myself, too—and that makes me happy.

About the Author

A Chicago native raised in southern California, soprano Deborah Voigt is increasingly recognized as one of the world's most versatile singers and one of music's most endearing personalities. A leading dramatic soprano, internationally revered for her performances in the operas of Wagner and Richard Strauss, she has also portrayed some of the heroines of Italian opera to great acclaim. Voigt has an extensive discography, has given many enthusiastically received master classes, and is an active recitalist and performer of Broadway standards and popular songs. She is also co-creator of *Voigt Lessons*, a one-woman show she developed with award-winning playwright Terrence McNally and director Francesca Zambello.

Deborah Voigt appears regularly, as both performer and host, in the Met's *Live in HD* series, which is transmitted live to movie theaters across the U.S. and overseas. Among her appearances as a TV and radio host was a special five-night presentation of Wagner's complete "Ring" cycle on the PBS series *Great Performances from the Met*. Robert Lepage's visionary new staging, which starred Voigt as Brünnhilde, was also released as a Blu-Ray DVD set that won the Grammy Award for Best Opera Recording of 2013.

Audiences have seen Deborah Voigt in many important national media outlets, including a CBS *60 Minutes* profile, appearances on *Good Morning America*, *Charlie Rose*, and CNN, and features in *People* and *Vanity Fair*. Voigt is a Chevalier de l'Ordre des Arts et des Lettres and received an Honorary Doctorate from the University of South Carolina.

She has won many awards, including *Musical America*'s Vocalist of the Year and an *Opera News* Award for distinguished achievement. Known to Twitter fans as a "Dramatic soprano and down-to-earth Diva," Voigt was named by the *Los Angeles Times* as one of the top twenty-five cultural tweeters to follow.

www.deborahvoigt.com
www.facebook.com/DeborahVoigt
twitter.com/debvoigt